W. J. Amherst

The history of Catholic Emancipation

and the progress of the Catholic Church in the British Isles (chiefly in England) from

1771 to 1820 - Vol. II

W. J. Amherst

The history of Catholic Emancipation
and the progress of the Catholic Church in the British Isles (chiefly in England) from 1771 to 1820 - Vol. II

ISBN/EAN: 9783744671002

Printed in Europe, USA, Canada, Australia, Japan

Cover: Foto ©ninafisch / pixelio.de

More available books at **www.hansebooks.com**

THE HISTORY

OF

CATHOLIC EMANCIPATION

AND

*THE PROGRESS OF THE CATHOLIC CHURCH
IN THE BRITISH ISLES (CHIEFLY IN ENGLAND)*

FROM 1771 TO 1820

BY

W. J. AMHERST, S.J.

"The ways of Providence are incomprehensible, and we know not in what times, or by what methods, God will restore His Church in England, or what farther tryalls and afflictions we are yet to undergo. Onely this we know, that if a Religion be of God, it can never fail, but the acceptable time we must patiently expect, and endeavour by our lives not to undeserve."—*From* DRYDEN's *Dedication of the Life of St. Francis Xavier to the Queen.*

IN TWO VOLUMES
VOL. II.

LONDON
KEGAN PAUL, TRENCH & CO., 1, PATERNOSTER SQUARE
1886

CONTENTS OF VOL. II.

CHAPTER XIV.
CONTINUATION OF THE VETO QUESTION.

Meeting of the Irish bishops in 1808—Milner retracts his "Letter to a Parish Priest"—Resolutions of the Irish bishops—The Government idea of a veto—Justification of the Irish bishops—Butler and the Irish bishops—Lord Grenville and the Irish bishops—Lord Grenville and Milner—Lord Grenville and the Catholics—Duty of loyal Catholics—Lord Grenville and the veto 1

CHAPTER XV.
CONTINUATION OF THE VETO QUESTION.

Resolutions of the Irish bishops in 1799—The "Letter to a Parish Priest"—"*O felix culpa*"—The Church and a concordat—The veto in 1810—Lord Grenville's letter to Lord Fingall—The Catholic gentlemen and Lords Grey and Grenville—The "fifth resolution"—The Catholic Board—The dinner at Doran's Hotel—The meeting at St. Alban's Tavern—The bishops "jockeyed"—Objections to the fifth resolution—Grattan and Lord Donoughmore unsuccessful—Reflections on the state of the "Catholic Question"—The want of organization 18

CHAPTER XVI.
THE FIRST TEN YEARS OF THE CENTURY.

Attack on monastic institutions—The "King's speech" in 1802—Milner consecrated bishop—Pitt's second Ministry—Fox declines to move in the "Catholic Question" in 1806. In 1805, Lord Grenville presents a petition in the House of Lords and Mr. Fox in the House of Commons 50

CHAPTER XVII.

DISMISSAL OF LORD GRENVILLE'S ADMINISTRATION BY GEORGE III.

Army and Navy Bill—The "No-Popery" cry of 1807—Reflections on the dismissal of Lord Grenville's Ministry 60

CHAPTER XVIII.

CATHOLIC EMANCIPATION FROM 1811 TO 1812.

Grattan and Lord Donoughmore in 1811—Political parties—Lord Byron's vote—Letter of the Princess Charlotte—Canning's motion in the House of Commons—Lord Wellesley's motion in the House of Lords 69

CHAPTER XIX.

THE FIRST MEETING OF THE BISHOPS AT DURHAM IN 1812, AND THE BILL OF 1813.

The meeting of the bishops—The bill of 1813—Meeting of the Catholic Board—Unauthorized interference—The meeting at Lord Clifford's—Grattan's motion for a Committee of the whole House—Mr. Canning and Sir John Hippisley's motion—The Canning and Castlereagh clauses—The "Schismatical Bill" 78

CHAPTER XX.

MILNER AND THE BILL OF 1813.

The Committee on the bill—Milner and Dr. Poynter—Milner on the bill—Milner left alone to oppose the bill—The bill abandoned—The expulsion of Milner from the Select Committee of the Catholic Board 104

CHAPTER XXI.

THE GRAND ATTACK ON MILNER.

The second meeting of the bishops at Durham—Milner's character ... 123

CHAPTER XXII.

THE GRAND ATTACK ON MILNER (continued)—THE ATTEMPT TO DISCREDIT HIM IN ROME.

Monsignore Quarantotti—The Quarantotti rescript—Milner's journey to Rome—Milner in Rome—Address of the English Catholic Board to Pope Pius VII.—Pope Pius' answer to the address 141

CHAPTER XXIII.

"ROMA LOCUTA EST, CAUSA FINITA EST."

Cardinal Litta's letter to Dr. Poynter ... 160

Contents.

CHAPTER XXIV.
MILNER AND O'CONNELL.

Dr. Moylan's letter to Milner—Dr. Murray in Rome—Proceedings in Ireland—Resolutions of the Irish bishops—O'Connell's attack upon Milner—O'Connell apologizes—Rev. Mr. Hayes' letter—The two Irish bishops in Rome—Letter of Pope Pius VII. to the Irish bishops—End of the veto question—Sir Robert Peel on the veto—The victory   176

CHAPTER XXV.
PROGRESS OF AGITATION FOR RELIEF.

Proceedings in 1814—O'Connell and Grattan—Meetings in Ireland—Speech of O'Connell—Sir Henry Parnell presents the petitions—His motion defeated—Mr. Daly's speech—The debate in the Commons in 1815—The debate in the Lords in 1815   200

CHAPTER XXVI.
THE CATHOLIC CAUSE IN 1816.

Emancipation an open question in the Cabinet—Petitions of English Catholics—The "Seceders"—Petitions of Irish Catholics—State of the question in Ireland—State of parties in Ireland—State of Catholic parties in England—Proceedings in Parliament—Petitions from Ireland—Proceedings in the House of Lords—Lord Donoughmore's speech—The bugbear of "Popery"—Loyalty of Catholics—Attacks on Catholics—Proceedings in the House of Lords—Speech of the Bishop of Norwich 229

CHAPTER XXVII.
THE ACT OF 1817.

The Test Act—Declaration of indulgence—Pretended conspiracy—The Test Act—The Act of Indemnity—The dispensing power—Catholics under William and Mary—The Annual Act of Indemnity—A Catholic refused a commission—The case of Captain Whyte   250

CHAPTER XXVIII.
PROCEEDINGS IN IRELAND, AND DEBATES IN PARLIAMENT.

"Friends of reform in Parliament"—Catholic and Protestant co-operation—Principle of Catholic action—O'Connell and the Vetoists—The "Conciliating Committee"—Speech of O'Connell—Intrigues of the Irish Vetoists—Grand resolution of the Irish Catholics—Debates in the Houses of Parliament—Motion and division in the Commons—Motion and division in the Lords—Dr. Milner on the debates—The threat of a second Board—The Tralee dinner   270

CHAPTER XXIX.

THE CATHOLIC QUESTION IN 1818.

General Thornton's motion—Fox's dictum—Action of the English Catholic Board—Proceedings in Ireland—First remonstrance of the Irish Catholics to Pope Pius—Rev. Mr. Hayes' mission to Rome—Second remonstrance of the Irish Catholics—The Pope's reply to the second remonstrance—Mr. Hayes' remarks on the Pope's reply—Remarks of the affair of Mr. Hayes—Bishops Milner and Collingridge on the bill of 1813—Milner challenged to fight—Milner's portrait—Termination of the Blanchardist schism 287

CHAPTER XXX.

THE CATHOLIC QUESTION IN 1819.

English Catholic meetings and petitions—Meeting of Protestants in Dublin in favour of emancipation—Meetings in Ireland—Speech of O'Connell—Aggregate Catholic meeting—O'Connell's speech and letter—Proceedings in the House of Commons—Grattan's speech—Remarks on Grattan's speech—The debate in the Commons—The debate in the Lords—Lord Grey's bill—Butler's remarks on the state of the Catholic Question 308

CHAPTER XXXI.

THE YEAR 1820.

Death of George III.—King George III. and Catholics—George IV.—George IV. and Catholics—Address and petition to George IV.—The death of Grattan—Plunket—Milner receives a rebuke from Rome—Milner's conduct under censure—Reflections on Milner's writings in the *Orthodox Journal*—Proceedings in Ireland—No petition to Parliament this year 324

CHRONOLOGY OF EVENTS BEARING ON CATHOLIC EMANCIPATION ... 341

INDEX 347

THE HISTORY OF CATHOLIC EMANCIPATION.

CHAPTER XIV.

CONTINUATION OF THE VETO QUESTION.

Meeting of the Irish bishops in 1808—Milner retracts his "Letter to a Parish Priest"—Resolutions of the Irish bishops—The Government idea of a veto—Justification of the Irish bishops—Butler and the Irish bishops—Lord Grenville and the Irish bishops—Lord Grenville and Milner—Lord Grenville and the Catholics—Duty of loyal Catholics—Lord Grenville and the veto.

THE Irish bishops, as we have seen, reserved a public expression of their opinion on what had passed in Parliament until they could all meet together to consider the question. This meeting, which had no small share in securing the liberties of the Church in the United Kingdom, and to which every Catholic in the British Isles must look back with pride and gratitude, took place on the 14th of September, 1808, in the House of the Dominican Fathers in Dublin. The Irish bishops, as is their wont, acted nobly on this occasion. The state of mind into which they had been thrown by the speeches in Parliament prepared them to avoid half measures. It must be a most pleasing thing to all English readers to know that the first resolution which they passed was that

"Dr. Milner's account of his conduct as their agent is satisfactory." "Then," says Milner, in his "Supplementary Memoirs"—

"they passed those two ever-memorable resolutions, equally expressive of their pastoral watchfulness and their civil loyalty, as follows:—' Resolved, That it is the decided opinion of the Roman Catholic prelates of Ireland, here assembled, that it is inexpedient to introduce any alteration in the canonical mode, hitherto observed, in the nomination of Roman Catholic bishops, which mode, by long experience, has been proved to be unexceptionable, wise, and salutary.'

"' Resolved, That the Roman Catholic prelates pledge themselves to adhere to the rule by which they have been hitherto uniformly guided; namely, to recommend to his Holiness only such persons, as candidates for vacant bishoprics, as are of unimpeachable loyalty and peaceable conduct.'"

Milner also says, in his account of the meeting, that the prelates—

"universally regretted that the proposal of Government in 1799, with which the far greater part of them now became acquainted for the first time, had been acceded to."

The reader will now see that these resolutions were no half measure. I will reserve for a while any comment upon them, and merely notice that at this meeting the Irish bishops undid all that had been done in 1799, put themselves from a false position into a true position, and stood with their liberties as they were before Castlereagh, at the instigation of Pitt, offered them the new fetters in exchange for the old penal chains. Milner also behaved like a true Christian hero. He might, as he tells us, have explained his "Letter to a Parish Priest." But that course would not have been sufficiently thorough for such a man as Milner. In fact, it would have left matters, so far as he was concerned, pretty much as they were. People might have said to Milner, *qui s'excuse, s'accuse*. In order, therefore, to put himself in a right position, and to make it abundantly evident what his real opinion was, he proceeded upon the supposition that the letter had been, what in fact it was not, a serious advocacy of an objectionable veto, and he publicly retracted and condemned it.[1] In doing this, Milner showed himself truly great. Many, perhaps most, other men would have stood upon their defence, explained and justified the letter. If Milner had thus acted, his conduct would have led to a correspondence on the subject, and not unlikely to further negotiations, as far, at least, as the appointment of the English bishops was concerned. In this way the question of the veto, as it affected England, would have been separated from the question as it affected Ireland, the union amongst the bishops of the British Isles would have been destroyed, and very unfortunate consequences might have been the result. But, in acting as he did, Milner not only recovered an independent position, he also preserved in an important matter that union which should always exist between the British and Irish bishops; and he had a large share in the work of keeping the action of the Catholic Church in the British Isles unimpeded by Government interference. If Milner had been as ambitious and diplomatic as he was bold and straightforward, he might have been able to make terms with the parliamentary supporters of the Catholics, and with Charles Butler and those who acted with him; he might have stood at the head of the Catholics of England, and with a tempting compromise to offer, he might have made the English people at least more inclined to grant Catholics relief. And it must be remembered that, so far as the Catholics of Great Britain were concerned in these veto negotiations, Milner seems to have stood alone.

[1] " Supplementary Memoirs," p. 130.

What part the other Vicars Apostolic in England and Scotland may have taken in the affair may perhaps be recorded in private letters which have never seen the light; but certain it is that neither in Butler's "Memoirs," nor in Milner's "Supplementary Memoirs," is there, with the exception of Milner himself, any mention of the bishops in Britain, either collectively and individually, as taking any part, or expressing any opinion on the question of the veto in the year 1808. And it was not altogether impossible that Parliament should have legislated for England independently of Ireland. In the year 1791, when Ireland had a Parliament of her own, it was the deliberate policy of the Irish Government at that time, that in measures of relief the Irish Parliament should, in favour of the Irish Catholics, follow what the English Parliament should have done for the English Catholics. This is shown by a letter written from Ireland by Mr. Hobart to the Marquis of Buckingham. Mr. Hobart had been secretary to the Marquis in his last administration of Ireland, and was continued in that appointment by his successor, Lord Westmoreland. In this letter Hobart says, amongst other things—

"Notwithstanding a variety of objections, I cannot help thinking that the safest principle for the Parliament of Ireland to adopt is that of following England upon all questions relative to Roman Catholics; but it is of the utmost consequence that the Government of England should accede to no measure upon that subject without a due consideration of its effect in Ireland, and fairly weigh the benefits to be attained in the one country against the disadvantages that may arise in the other. The example of England, if adopted as a principle, may be extremely useful as a means of resisting inconvenient pressure urged here.[1] . . . The only permanent, practicable system that I can discover is, that there should at all times be a perfect understanding and concurrence between the Government of the two countries upon this subject;

[1] That is, in Dublin.

that no step affecting the Catholics should be taken in England without a minute attention to Ireland ; and that the people of that persuasion should be on the same footing in the two countries."[1]

The Duke of Buckingham speaks of this text as an authentic exposition of the policy of Lord Westmoreland, then Lord Lieutenant of Ireland. Although time and circumstances had somewhat changed between 1791 and 1808, it is quite a conceivable thing, if not a probable thing, that if the English Catholics could have been relieved on terms favourable to the Government in 1808, it might have been an inducement to ministers to grant relief, and so to have established a precedent for giving afterwards the same relief to Ireland, on the same terms. If Milner had been less staunch and more ambitious, he might have been strongly tempted to independent action. But he remained firm and true.

With regard to the resolutions of the Irish bishops in September, 1808, it may be useful to understand why they adopted so decided a measure. In the first place, as we have seen, their lordships assembled at the meeting in Dublin, when those resolutions were passed, universally regretted that the proposal of the Government in 1799 had been acceded to. They were therefore, no doubt, glad of an opportunity in which they had ample reason for withdrawing from the position which they had taken up in 1799. The imprudent and foolish language used by Mr. Ponsonby in the House of Commons, and the more guarded but strong words used by Lord Grenville in the House of Lords, would have been sufficient to justify the bishops in the course they took,[2] Ponsonby's announcement

[1] Duke of Buckingham's "Court and Cabinets of George the Third," vol. ii. pp. 185, 186, Letter from Mr. Hobart to Lord Buckingham.
[2] Lord Grenville said that the Catholics of Ireland declared themselves perfectly willing to accede to the proposal that the Crown should exercise an *effectual negative* in the appointment of bishops. Vide Butler's "Historical Memoirs," vol. ii. p. 178, edition of 1819.

that the Catholics were willing to make the King virtually the Head of the Church, was not mere nonsense; it was not merely words, "full of sound, . . . signifying nothing." Ponsonby meant what he said. Both Grenville and Ponsonby intended that if a veto could be obtained, it should be a much more effectual one than one confined only to the question of the loyalty of the person proposed for office. By the words, "Head of the Church," Ponsonby did not of course mean that Catholics were willing to sever themselves from Rome and acknowledge the King as their Head, in the same sense as the King is Head of the Church of England. But he meant that the control of the King over the election of our bishops would be so great, that his Majesty would be, in that respect, virtually the Head of the Church of Rome in England. Ponsonby, in fact, "showed his hand" too openly. And this Lord Grenville himself notices in a letter to his brother, the Marquis of Buckingham, when he says, "When he"—that is, Ponsonby—"said that this measure would make the King virtually the Head of the Catholics, he stated a conclusion neither in itself accurate, nor at all desirable to have brought under the view of the Catholics."[1]

From what has been said above, the reader will understand in what respect Lord Grenville thought Ponsonby's language inaccurate, and in what sense he agreed with him. A note from Milner's "Supplementary Memoirs" shows what Lord Grenville and those who supported the Catholic claims in 1808 really understood by an "effective veto." Milner's words will enable the reader to understand better the eagerness of the Irish prelates and Milner himself to revoke the resolution of 1799. He says:

"The personage whose opinion he considered to be of the

[1] "Memoirs of the Court and Cabinets of George the Third," by the Duke of Buckingham, vol. iv. p. 275.

greatest weight in this business [that is, the business of the veto in 1808], explained the effect of the veto so as to make it exactly correspond with the *congé d'élire*, by which Protestant bishops are appointed. 'I will suppose,' he said, 'myself to be his Majesty's Minister, to whom you present a list of three candidates, whom your prelates judge worthy of the vacant chair. Very likely I may say to you, Neither Mr. A, nor Mr. B, nor Mr. C, is approved of; but if you choose Mr. F, he will be accepted of.'"

This personage was, not unlikely, Lord Grenville himself, but Milner does not mention the name. Later on we shall see, in Lord Grenville's own words, what his hopes were as to the result of the working of the veto.

The Irish bishops had, therefore, ample reason for changing their position. Their action was, indeed, what is called in military affairs, a change of front in presence of the enemy, and which is said to be always a very hazardous movement. But the movement was made promptly and with decision, and it was crowned with success. Lord Grenville and his party looked upon the action of the bishops and of Milner as extraordinary and unfortunate; they said, the bishops have ruined the Catholic cause. But "the Catholic cause" meant a very different thing in the mind of Lord Grenville and in the mind of a Catholic bishop: the latter understood it as the cause of the Church, the former understood it as the cause of his own policy with regard to Ireland. That the action of the bishops was successful is abundantly proved by the fact that from that time (September, 1808) down to the present day, the position taken by the bishops has never either been abandoned or forced. No Catholic prelate has since that time, so far as I know, ever directly expressed an opinion in favour of any kind of veto; and in the matter of internal government, the Church in the British Isles is as free now as it was then. That we have the freedom which we now enjoy we owe to the men who have preceded us; we owe it, under God's good providence, to their wisdom in taking decided measures to avert the danger as soon as they perceived it; we owe it to their humility in braving human respect, under the charges of folly and ingratitude which were made against them, both by Protestant friends in and out of Parliament, and also by some Catholics; we owe it to the preference which they gave to the rights of the Holy See over the demands of political supporters; to the right and holy choice they made when they had to choose between the antagonistic claims of the Church and of the State, when they were asked to give to Cæsar what belonged to God. The Catholic Church in these islands has suffered nothing from what those who choose may call the obstinacy, but what we call the prudent firmness of the Episcopacy. Honesty, loyalty to the Holy See, has always been the best policy. Time-serving, political intrigues, jealous suspicions, underhand workings to promote partial interest at the expense of universal good, never has made, and never will make, even a step towards the end we all have in view, the spiritual regeneration of England.

Even if the Irish bishops and Milner had pursued a different course; if the bishops had stood by the resolution of 1799, and if Milner had seriously maintained the opinions expressed in his "Letter to a Parish Priest," it is not likely that any concessions would have been made to us during the administration of the Duke of Portland. His Grace's Ministry had come into power on the "No Popery" cry; and its determination to resist the Catholic claims was so strong and so notorious, that it was known at the time, and has been handed down in history, by the name of the "No-Popery Ministry." But a few years later on, a disposition on our part to make the sort of concessions which are usually included in a concordat, might have hastened on the time of our relief. It would, however, have been a relief too dearly purchased. Something better was in reserve for us. It was in this year, 1808, that O'Connell made his first reported speech on Catholic affairs; after twenty years of agitation he forced on emancipation, without paying the price for it which William Pitt would have asked and obtained, if George III. had not opposed his designs.

The action of the Irish bishops and of Milner was badly received by Charles Butler and his friends, and by Lord Grenville and his party. Butler writes as follows:—

"As soon as the actual rejection [of the veto by the Irish prelates] was known, it was evident that the mention of it in Parliament had, in consequence of this rejection, become the most unfortunate circumstance which had befallen the Catholics since they had been suitors for relief. It may be said, with the greatest truth, that it was a matter of triumph to all the enemies, and a matter of great concern to all the friends of Catholic emancipation. Unhappily, there were not wanting those who too successfully exerted themselves to keep alive the general irritation which this wayward event had produced."[1]

Who the persons were who kept alive the general irritation, and what they said or did to cause it, Butler does not mention. He may perhaps allude to what he had written a few pages before the last extract I have made, where he says:

"Towards the close of the following month of July *the attack upon the veto* commenced in the public prints. It was led by a writer who assumed the signature of *Sarsfield;* he was followed by *Laicus, Inimicus Veto,* and many other writers under assumed signatures: some others published their declamations against it under real names. By them all the true nature of the veto was much misrepresented, and, in consequence of their misrepresentation, much discontent at it prevailed."[2]

[1] "Historical Memoirs," vol. ii. p. 191. Edition of 1819. [2] Ibid., p. 183.

What Butler here calls misrepresentations were most probably sound and sensible deductions, drawn from the speeches in Parliament and other sources, as to the use the Government would have made of the veto, had they obtained it. The discontent at the veto, which Butler says prevailed in consequence of misrepresentations, was no doubt the cry against it when the language used in Parliament put the people on their guard. But I am inclined to believe that it was not to these writers that Butler alludes when he says there were not wanting those who exerted themselves to keep alive the general irritation. It is not unlikely that he referred to the subsequent action of Bishop Milner, when in 1810 he stood out manfully and successfully against the celebrated "fifth resolution" of the English Catholics. We shall have, in a subsequent chapter, to read the history of this famous resolution. It will suffice to say now that Butler and his friends thought it necessary that something should be done on the part of the Catholics of England, which, by at least hinting at the willingness of Catholics to give up what the Irish Bishops had refused to surrender, would help to allay the irritation. But the schemes of the English Catholic diplomatists were brought to naught. Butler's words, "too successfully," refer, I imagine, to Milner's detection of the snake in the grass, and to another victory gained by "one John Milner" over Charles Butler.

Lord Grenville was, as the reader will see, extremely annoyed at the conduct of the Irish bishops and Milner. I will first give his words, and then comment upon them. They occur in a letter to his brother, the Marquis of Buckingham. He writes :

"I cannot say I am much edified with Milner's letter; on the contrary, I am more than ever desirous of publishing the few short words he authorized me (in writing) to say on the subject, which contain none of those fine-spun distinctions, but simply express a readiness to consent to an effectual negative. . . . Lord Grey is still very anxious for some public declaration on our part that we will not bring the subject forward without satisfaction on this point; but I can give no such pledge. They have marred their own cause; but that of the country may be wrapped up in it, and if I could unite Ireland in heart and affection with England, I should not care one farthing (comparatively speaking) how such blockheads as Milner and his colleagues were or were not appointed. Influence, it is clear, they have hardly any now, and in that case they would have none. All this I know, that the good people of England will not feel the danger is at the door, and perhaps till all remedy is too late, and then they will run headlong the other way, as they did in 1782, and never stop or strain at such trifles as these."[1]

Lord Grenville must have been vexed, and very vexed indeed, when he called Milner a "blockhead," even in a private letter to his brother. But although that letter was written more than two months after the September resolution of the Irish bishops, when it might be thought that vexation had somewhat subsided, it is impossible to suppose that Lord Grenville could have deliberately judged Milner to be worthy of so rude an appellation. The author of "The History of Winchester," "The End of Controversy," and the "Letters to a Prebendary," was no blockhead: the man who in 1791 convinced Burke and Pitt and Fox that he was right and that everybody else was wrong, and who single-handed defeated a strong and organized party, was no blockhead. And it may be added that Milner's wise and manly conduct in retracting all that he had written in favour of a veto, and thereby sharing with the Irish bishops the honour of establishing a freedom which has existed to this day, proved that he was very far indeed

[1] "Memoirs of the Court and Cabinets of George the Third," by the Duke of Buckingham, vol. iv. p. 281.

from being one who could be called a blockhead. Then, why did Lord Grenville call him one? Lord Grenville was one of a family remarkable for steady, cool deliberation in what they said and did; and he himself was a good specimen of the family character. It is not difficult, however, to understand why he should have written of Milner as he did. Lord Grenville was an advocate of the "Catholic claims;" and he was a sincere advocate. There were politicians in those days, as there were down to 1829, who continually voted for emancipation because they were Whigs, and the Catholic Question was one of the bones of contention which had been thrown down for Whigs and Tories to fight about. Lord Grenville may indeed have shared with others this motive of party spirit. But we may believe of Lord Grenville that he had a higher motive than this for interesting himself in the Catholic cause. He was no doubt sincerely desirous, as he says in his letter to his brother, of uniting Ireland in heart and affection with England.

The first step towards this desirable state of things was the emancipation of the Catholics. But in those days emancipation could not have been obtained without some sacrifice on our part of the liberties of the Church. Lord Grenville, no doubt, thought that there was at least some probability of obtaining emancipation if Catholics were prepared to pay a sufficient price for it. He thought also that the Irish bishops and Milner had put that price into his hands that he might offer it to the Government, and continually press it upon them for their acceptance. When the guardians of the Catholic Church found that the price demanded was more than they could afford to pay; when they refused to pay it; when by refusal they spoiled his plans and thwarted his policy, as a matter of course they were, in his estimation, all blockheads. So, no doubt,

Henry II. thought St. Thomas of Canterbury a blockhead ; Henry VIII. thought Sir Thomas More a blockhead ; Napoleon thought Pope Pius VII. a blockhead. And without a great stretch of imagination we may suppose that in the year 1850 Lord John Russell both thought and called Pope Pius IX. and Cardinal Wiseman two great blockheads. The reader must not imagine that Lord Grenville is here compared in enmity to the Church with the two Henrys, or with Napoleon, or even with Lord John Russell. Lord Grenville was sincerely desirous as a statesman of conciliating Catholics, especially the Irish, by obtaining our emancipation, and his sincerity in this was independent of his desire to fight a party question. The idea of turning round upon the Catholics and raising a cry against us, because we had thwarted his policy, as Lord John did in 1850 because he thought he had been outwitted by Cardinal Wiseman, probably never entered his mind. Lord Grenville is indeed one of those men who is entitled to the gratitude of Catholics. He advocated our cause consistently, according to his lights, and he and the late Lord Grey, only the year before—that is, in 1807 —made in our interest, as we shall see later on, the greatest sacrifice which public men can be called upon to make.

From all this, a lesson is to be learned which Catholic men would do well to attend to. When a Catholic belonging to any one of the political sections of the day, has to sacrifice the interests of party to the interests of the Church, he is sure to be thought a blockhead. This, of course, will arise from the fact that those who will thus miscall him will put the interests of the party above the interests of the Church. With the opinions they hold, it is natural they should do so. We cannot expect an English Protestant politician, or an English politician of no religion, to attend first to the interests of the Catholic Church. An English Catholic must therefore make up his mind to the inevitable result of being a man of sound steady principle. He will sometimes be thought, and perhaps sometimes be called, a blockhead. He may have every quality which goes to make up a fine character, he may also have had a first-rate education, taken his degree at Oxford or Cambridge, or successfully stood a stiff examination for honours at the London University; in addition to all this, he may be a man admirably adapted to engage in public affairs, wise in council, clever in debate, sagacious and firm in administration; yet if he should ever sacrifice the interests of party to the interests of the Church, he will be thought and called a blockhead. But he must not be discouraged on that account. If he stands steady by his duty as a Catholic, his greatness will be greater still. If he should be weak enough to follow his party over the frontier line which separates the interests of the Church from the interests of his party, he will merely have the reputation of being a party man. But if he acts as a loyal Catholic should act, he will have honour from whom honour is of any worth, and his name will go down as a follower, even though it should be *non passibus æquis*, of those great Englishmen who threw the whole energy of the national character into the character of a Christian, some of whom had their heads cut off, some were imprisoned, others were ostracized from public life, and all were called blockheads.

In his letter to his brother, Lord Grenville alludes to a letter written by Milner. "I cannot say," he says, "I am much edified with Milner's letter." It does not appear to what letter Lord Grenville alluded.[1] Lord Grenville's

---

[1] I cannot find, either in Butler or Milner or Husenbeth, any letter to which Lord Grenville's words apply. It may have been a private letter never published.

words which immediately follow, are very puzzling. He says, " I am more than ever desirous of publishing the few short words which he " (Milner) " authorized me (in writing) to say on the subject, which contain none of these fine-spun distinctions, but simply express a readiness to consent to an effectual negative." It is difficult to reconcile these words with what Milner writes in the " Supplementary Memoirs." He there says :

" As to the historian's [that is, Butler's] assertion, that ' Lord Grenville made a proposal of the veto in the House of Lords, at the suggestion of Dr. Milner,' the latter is perfectly confident that his lordship will flatly deny it if it be advanced in his hearing. The only communication Dr. M. ever had with that nobleman, relating to the subject in question, was when he presented him with a copy of the protest, and all that then passed consisted in his lordship's objecting to the restriction on Government proposed in that paper, namely, that its negative power should be confined to avowed civil grounds." [1]

It is clear from this that, in his only conversation with Lord Grenville, Milner did make distinctions in the nature of a veto, and these distinctions must have been of precisely the same nature as "the fine-spun distinctions" which Lord Grenville alludes to in his letter to his brother. The "effectual negative" which Lord Grenville mentions in that letter, and which he says Milner expressed a readiness to consent to, must in Lord Grenville's mind have included those very distinctions which Milner says he made, which Lord Grenville objected to, but which Milner maintained. It is impossible now to reconcile these two accounts.

I have another remark to make upon Lord Grenville's letter. From it, it appears perfectly evident that he

[1] "Supplementary Memoirs," p. 127. The protest here alluded to was the one which Milner wrote against the misrepresentation of his words by Ponsonby.

thought one consequence of the veto would be that the influence of the bishops in Ireland over the people would be lessened. His object was "to unite," as he says, "Ireland in heart and affection with England." A most desirable object, no doubt. He therefore desired emancipation as the first and indispensable step towards that union. But there would have been at that time no chance whatever of obtaining emancipation, unless the Catholics were prepared to surrender some of the rights of the Church. He therefore wished for what he calls an effective veto in order to bring about, what he so much desired, a union of affection between Ireland and England: but a state of things in which the bishops would have no influence over their people. "Influence," he writes, "it is clear they have hardly any now, and in that case they would have none."

The Catholic young men of England would do well to study the history of the Catholic Church in England since the first Relief Act; and to study in it those many interesting volumes which of late years have been published of memoirs and correspondence of the men who have taken part in public affairs. During many years, "the Catholic Question," as it was called, was one of the principal questions, and for several years the principal question, before Parliament and the public. The study of the various motives which induced statesmen to advocate the Catholic claims is not only interesting, but most useful: it is, indeed, necessary for those who would take an active part in Catholic affairs. With regard to what Lord Grenville says of the Irish bishops, "influence it is clear they have hardly any now," the proposition is not quite so clear. Over the great mass of the people, the bishops certainly had complete influence. It may be that some of the Irish Catholics, eager for emancipation, and perhaps over-eager to be themselves in Parliament, had expressed opinions opposed to the bishops in the matter of the veto, and Lord Grenville's words may have been an exaggeration of their language. But Milner says that when he was in Ireland "he found the leading Catholics of Ireland jealous, not only of their religious discipline, but also of the independency of their prelacy as the only remaining monument, as they called it, of their national freedom."[1]

[1] "Supplementary Memoirs," p. 133.

CHAPTER XV.

CONTINUATION OF THE VETO QUESTION.

Resolutions of the Irish bishops in 1799—The "Letter to a Parish Priest"—"*O felix culpa*"—The Church and a concordat—The veto in 1810—Lord Grenville's letter to Lord Fingall—The Catholic gentlemen and Lords Grey and Grenville—The "fifth resolution"—The Catholic Board—The dinner at Doran's Hotel—The meeting at St. Alban's Tavern—The bishops "jockeyed"—Objections to the fifth resolution—Grattan and Lord Donoughmore unsuccessful—Reflections on the state of the "Catholic Question"—The want of organization.

As history is read to no profit, if from it a lesson is not learned for the present, it may be well to examine the acts of the Irish bishops, of Milner, and of the Government, and see what is to be gathered. In the first place, did the bishops do right in accepting the proposal of Pitt, through Lord Castlereagh, in 1799? This proposal contained a State provision for the Catholic clergy, and, on the part of the Government, a right of veto in the election of bishops. It must be remembered that the bishops accepted the overture of Pitt subject to the approval of the Holy Father, at that time the venerable confessor, Pope Pius VI. If the bishops did not do right, was their act culpable? If not culpable, was it a serious error of judgment, or only an excusable misconception of what, under the circumstances, was the best thing to be done. The circumstances must be recollected. The chief grievance under which Catholics lay at that time, was that they were not represented either in the Irish Parliament, which was then in existence, or in the Parliament of Great Britain. Neither was there to be any provision for the representation of Catholics in the Act of Union, the bill for which was to be laid before Parliament in the following year. William Pitt, then in the zenith of his power, engaged to bring in a separate bill to redress the chief grievance and admit Catholics to a share in the Legislature. But for this act of emancipation he demanded a price: and the price was contained in the proposals made in his name to the ten bishops by Lord Castlereagh. The determined opposition of George III., which induced him to part with Pitt rather than yield further concessions to the Catholics, was not at that time foreseen. So that the state of things was this: it was quite certain that if the bishops would not accept the proposals, Pitt would not even bring in a bill for our relief. The question for the bishops to decide, and a momentous question it was, appears to have been this: Will civil emancipation, with a surrender of our freedom from State interference in Church government, be a better state of things than continued exclusion from the Legislature, with the perfect freedom we now enjoy in the election of bishops? They thought it would. But the whole course of history down to the present day has proved that, to enjoy the freedom we now have, it was well worth while to wait even for thirty years more. The bishops were therefore mistaken in accepting the offer of Castlereagh. But under all the circumstances of the time, it is impossible to say that they were culpable in so doing. It is extremely difficult for us in these days to put ourselves in the place of those Catholics who lived at the beginning of tlfe century. Endeavouring, however, to do this, as far as possible, it would certainly seem, in the great question which the bishops had to decide, and at the time they had to decide it, that the balance was so evenly held that no serious error of judgment can be imputed to them in the choice they made, and that at most their decision was a consequence of an excusable misconception of what was the best thing to be done.

With regard to what Milner said to Ponsonby, it might perhaps have been more prudent if he had not said that he believed, on good grounds, that the Irish bishops were disposed to attribute *a negative power* to the King. In a matter of this importance it would have been better to have said nothing, than to have spoken without instructions from the bishops on the subject. It is true there was no time to communicate with the Irish prelates. Milner's interview with Ponsonby was on the 21st of May, and the debate was to come on on the 25th, only four days later. Under these circumstances it might have been better to speak in a much more guarded way, if he thought it necessary to say anything in answer to the very direct question put to him by Ponsonby. Still, Milner, as the agent of the bishops, would be anxious not to say or leave anything unsaid, which would unnecessarily lessen the chance which Lord Grenville and Ponsonby thought they might have of carrying a bill of emancipation.

There is a matter connected with what Milner said to Ponsonby which seems to require some explanation. If there are any documents in existence which would throw light on it, they would be read with interest by those who study the history of these times. Milner said to Ponsonby, "I believe, on good grounds, that they [the Irish prelates] are disposed to attribute *a negative power* to the King." What were these grounds? As he was speaking of the Irish prelates in answer to Ponsonby's question, which referred to all the bishops, Milner would not have been speaking from any knowledge he might have had of the resolutions of 1799, which he would have known were passed by only ten out of twenty-nine bishops. And, as a matter of fact, it would appear, from what Milner says in the "Supplementary Memoirs," that on the 26th of May, five days after the interview with Ponsonby, he was aware for the first time that anything had passed between Government and the ten bishops several years before, that is, in 1799. Had the Irish bishops unanimously expressed their opinion in favour of a limited veto, but without giving their agent, Milner, any instructions to act upon that opinion? For Milner says, " I believe on good grounds," etc., and then adds, " I have no instructions from them on the subject." Was Milner aware of any such expressed opinion? It is very difficult to suppose that the Irish bishops did unanimously express their opinion in favour of the veto. And it is still more difficult to imagine that they should have expressed such opinions, and "the far greater part of them" have remained in total ignorance of the resolutions of 1799. And Milner says that by far the greater part of them became acquainted with the proposal of Government in 1799 for the first time at their meeting in September, 1808 ; that is, more than three months after the interview with Ponsonby. And if they had expressed such an opinion, would they not have done so on purpose to instruct their agent? Milner had made his first tour in Ireland in 1807 During that visit, he said that, " being in company with eight or ten Catholic prelates, he warned them of the storm that was gathering over their heads on the subject of episcopal appointments, to which admonition one of them answered in the hearing of the rest, 'We cannot allow the Ministry to choose our bishops, but we will choose none whom they object to '—namely, on *civil grounds*, for so the writer understood the answer."[1] Milner may have supposed

[1] Husenbeth, in his "Life of Milner," giving an account of this tour in Ireland, makes no mention of his having spoken to any one Irish bishop on any subject whatever. Considering the importance of the subject on which Milner did speak to some of the bishops, surely this omission is an error.

this to be the general opinion among the bishops. In the absence of any information on the subject, this is the only way in which I can account for the words he used to Ponsonby.

With regard to Milner's "Letter to a Parish Priest," it was no doubt a mistake; but a great deal more was made of it against him than the letter justified. Milner was not made to be a diplomatist. He was a great deal too open and straightforward, and, it must be added, a great deal too unguarded in what he said, to play a part which requires so much secrecy, so much discreetness in words, and often so much talent for intrigue. When he had an antagonist as straightforward as himself, or one from whom he had torn the mask, but who was willing to fight, there was no man like Milner for a sharp encounter. But *finesse* was not his *forte*. When a sense of duty dictated to him that the letter must be retracted and condemned, then he appeared in his true character—brave, humble, conscientious. He himself tells us that he "heartily condemned his own folly."[1] It is easy indeed to forgive such a man as Milner. It is something grand to contemplate an act of folly repaired by a great act of wisdom. And his conduct when he discovered the wiles of his enemies, was the truest wisdom. He took up a position on such firm ground that he maintained it to the last day of his life; he held it against repeated attacks, and from it he more than once drove in confusion the enemies who would have dislodged him from the post.

Nothing further of any public nature occurred with respect to the veto until the year 1810. We may, therefore, pause in the history for a moment and make a few reflections which are forced upon us. It is impossible not to discern the overruling hand of God in all that has been

---

[1] "Supplementary Memoirs," p. 132.

related on this important question. The mistakes that were made by Catholics, the opposition of Protestants, all tended to bring about the result which we now enjoy—the freedom of the Church from State interference. If George III. had not been advised that he could not sign our emancipation without a violation of his coronation oath, and if he had not obstinately followed that advice, we should to this day have been living under a concordat.[1] For Pitt could not have made the arrangement he desired without a concordat, or some agreement in the nature of a concordat. And so in 1808, even the mildest form of a negative veto would have required a concordat to give it effect. I say, even the mildest form of negative veto, for in the year 1805 Milner had a letter from the Holy See, in which he was informed that giving the English Government a positive power in the appointment of bishops was altogether out of the question; adding, at the same time, that a mere negative power would admit of fewer difficulties.[2]

Then, again, if Milner had not spoken to Ponsonby as he did, Ponsonby could never have ventured upon that

[1] The Hon. G. T. Kenyon, in his "Life of Lord Kenyon," p. 319, says, "Lord Clare, the Irish Chancellor, and it is generally supposed also Lord Loughborough, the English Chancellor, raised the first scruple in the mind of George III. on the subject of emancipation and the coronation oath. Lord Kenyon, the Lord Chief Justice, being asked for his advice by the King, gave it that his oath did not preclude him from signing an Emancipation Act, if in the opinion of the King such an Act would not destroy or essentially affect the government of the Established Church." And at pp. 306, 307 of the same Life, Mr. Kenyon observes, that "the King was peculiarly susceptible to anything which reflected, or might seem to the world to reflect, on his honour. And thus the idea that any concession to the Catholics would be an infringement of the oath, took so deep a root in an ill-regulated mind, enfeebled by disease, that no argument or persuasion, even from those whose opinions he most valued, could ever afterwards eradicate it. The motives, however mistaken, which guided him, must be universally held in respect, though they will now almost universally be acknowledged to have occasioned most deplorable results." We can say most happy results. The opinion which Lord Kenyon gave to George III. does great honour to his memory, as Lord Kenyon was himself very strongly opposed to the Catholic claims.

[2] "Supplementary Memoirs," p. 120.

gross exaggeration of Milner's words which caused the Catholics to understand the manner in which Lord Grenville and his followers meant to exercise the veto. And certainly it can hardly be doubted that the retractation by the Irish bishops of the resolutions of 1799, and Milner's condemnation of his "Letter to a Parish Priest," put both the bishops and Milner in a safer, a more defined, and in altogether a better position than if those resolutions had never been passed and the letter never written. This must be acknowledged, for it is proved by history, that our present freedom has lasted unimpaired by any change since the time when the mistakes of 1799 and 1808 were made and rectified. So that whatever faults were committed in the management of the Veto Question, it may be said of each one of them, *O felix culpa!* for each one was the occasion of greater good. Indeed, throughout the whole history of the second resurrection of the Church in England, nothing is so remarkable as the way in which Almighty God has brought good out of the crimes and the faults, the blunders and the mistakes of men. It looks like the pledge of a special Providence. We cannot expect that the third conversion of England should be brought about as quickly as the first and second under the Britons and Saxons. Hard will be the labour and long the work, and it may be the work of many decades to come. But the English Catholic must surely be blind who does not see that, though the work be slow, it is making steady advance. Long may the spirit which filled the Irish bishops and Milner in 1808, animate the Catholics of the United Kingdom; for that spirit may help to ensure for us the continued blessing of Heaven. And long may our freedom from State interference endure. Neither the welfare of the Church, nor the welfare of the State, demand a change.

"The Church," says Father Faber, "is less at her ease

in a concordat, than in a catacomb." What precisely was in the mind of the learned and devoted Oratorian when he wrote this, I will not venture to say. But it may be supposed that the reason of this is, that the Church can hope to escape from the catacombs, but can never expect to escape from a concordat. A right once surrendered by the Church to the State, is held by the State with at least as tight a hand as it holds the taxes and duties which have once been paid into its treasury. When an alliance between the Church and State may be compared to a happy marriage, it is a very pleasant state of things; husband and wife agree perfectly together, and children love father and mother as children ought. But unfortunately an alliance between Church and State formed by what is commonly called a concordat, may be compared to a mere *mariage de convenance*, in which the parties are forced together against their will; an unhappy marriage, one that does not turn out well. In the present state of things, the relations between the Church and the State in the United Kingdom cannot be compared to a marriage of any kind. But still the Church and the State on the whole live together on friendly terms: there is even a certain amount of mutual respect; things are going on smoothly. May this long continue; or rather, I will say, may it continue until the happiest of marriages can be contracted. One word more on this subject. There may be two opinions amongst the Catholics of the United Kingdom on the propriety of beginning diplomatic relations between the Holy Father and the Court of St. James: there can be but one opinion about a concordat.[1]

[1] By "diplomatic relations" is here meant the formal representation of each Court by an accredited minister; and not the informal representation of England in Rome which prevailed up to the year 1870, when Piedmont robbed the Pope of the States of the Church, and all representation of England at the Vatican ceased.

The action of Milner and the Irish bishops, as detailed in the last chapter, prevented the question of the veto from being immediately brought forward a second time. But Butler, and those who acted with him, were determined if possible to offer some concessions to the Government, to induce them to entertain the question of Catholic emancipation. The Vetoists, as those who advocated the veto were called, also thought it was necessary to do something in order to conciliate Lord Grenville and his party, disappointed and irritated by the bold measures which had been taken to stop all interference with the election of bishops. The position of the vetoists was somewhat difficult. The name of veto had been irrevocably fixed upon the scheme for State interference with the Government of the Catholic Church. But the word *veto* could not be pronounced without immediately raising a storm against those who uttered it. The vetoists were determined that some concession should be offered; and the veto was the only concession which could be tendered with any chance of its being accepted. They resolved, therefore, to get the English Catholics to vote a resolution, in which there should be no mention of the veto, but in which a desire to conciliate and make some concession should be expressed in such general and delicate terms, that while the scheme of the veto might be included, it should not be detected.

The year 1809 was allowed to pass without any active measures to obtain relief. There was no mention of emancipation in Parliament, and no public mention of the veto amongst Catholics.

In the year 1810 Grattan gave notice that he would again bring before Parliament the question of the Catholic claims. It was necessary, therefore, for the vetoists to mature their plans. They first determined to obtain an interview with Lord Grey.[1] Lord Grey consented to the interview, and it was accordingly held. Who the Catholic gentlemen were who attended it, Mr. Butler does not inform us.[2] The interview took place on January 29, 1810. Lord Grey was informed that a "Catholic petition" was to be presented to Parliament. His lordship said he thought it desirable that "the English Catholics should annex to their petition some general declaration of their willingness to give any reasonable pledge, not inconsistent with their religious principles, for the loyalty of the persons who should be appointed their bishops."[3] As Butler gives the above words in inverted commas, they were no doubt the exact words used by Lord Grey. Two days after this interview, another interview took place between a deputation of Catholic noblemen and gentlemen, and Earl Grey and Lord Grenville. The meeting was at the house of Earl Grey. But before giving an account of what took place at that meeting, the reader must be informed that on the 25th of January—that is, just four days before the interview on the 29th with Earl Grey—Lord Grenville wrote what was then his celebrated letter to the Earl of Fingall.

"Having premised in that letter that all due provision must be made for the inviolable maintenance of our (the Protestant) religious and civil establishments, and that he had pointed out the proposal of vesting in the Crown an effectual negative on the appointment of Catholic bishops (in other words, the veto), the noble lord goes on to say, 'that adequate arrangements may be made for all these purposes, consistently with the strictest adherence, on your part (that is, on the part of Catholics) to your

---

[1] This Lord Grey was the Lord Grey of the Reform Bill of 1832, and the father of the present Lord Grey. He was friendly to Catholics, but acted with Lord Grenville in requiring concessions from us.

[2] Mr. Butler merely says that "some Catholic gentlemen" met Lord Grey.

[3] Butler's "Historical Memoirs," vol. ii. p. 191. Edition of 1819.

religious tenets, is the persuasion we have long been labouring to establish. Were it otherwise, I should despair. But that these objects may be reconciled, in so far as respects the appointment of bishops, is known with undeniable certainty.'"[1]

From this extract it is perfectly clear what Lord Grenville's idea was, on the subject of the concession which the Catholics were to offer. He had not changed his opinion since the year 1808. The Catholics must offer "an effectual negative on the appointment of Catholic bishops." This, of course, was the old veto. An effectual negative and a veto are one and the same thing, and nothing else. But the word veto was not to be uttered, and nothing suggesting the veto could be proposed. Milner and the more loyal portion of the English Catholics would have fired up immediately if the odious word had been again brought forward. And besides this, the English Catholics had given a general pledge, which Butler says they held most sacred, "to adopt no measure, affecting the general interest of the two bodies, without the concurrence of their Roman Catholic brethren in Ireland."[2] When, therefore, the Catholic noblemen and gentlemen met Lords Grey and Grenville on the 31st of January, it was an interview between, on the one hand, two statesmen who thought that the Catholics must offer some security, and that the only security would be an effectual negative in the appointment of bishops; and on the other hand, Catholic gentlemen who had advocated the veto in 1808, who were vetoists still, but who knew that they could not propose to the Catholics of England, as the result of their interview with the friendly statesmen, anything which would even seem to suggest the obnoxious negative. The reader shall now have Mr. Butler's account of the meeting, and it may be

---

[1] Husenbeth's "Life of Milner," pp. 143, 144.
[2] "Historical Memoirs," pp. 192, 193.

taken for granted that either Butler was present at both this meeting and the previous one with Lord Grey (and most probably he was), or he had the account of what took place at the meetings from those who were present. "The subject," he says (that is, what concession the Catholics would make as the price of emancipation), "was revived; and it was most distinctly agreed, that no particular reference to the veto, or to any specific pledge, was intended; and that the only thing recommended to the English Catholics was, 'such a general expression of their wishes of mutual satisfaction and security, as existing circumstances made proper, to accompany their petition.' To this there would be no reasonable objection: and it is due to the two illustrious friends of the Catholics, to mention that they felt as strongly as the Catholics themselves could do, the propriety of their avoiding the slightest expression that might commit them with the Irish Catholics on the 'subject of the veto.'"[1] Such is Butler's account. The meeting between the Catholic gentlemen and the Protestant statesmen then broke up; all who had been present at it having agreed that there should be no "particular reference to the veto;" all having agreed that some security should be offered by the Catholics; all knowing that no other security would be accepted; and it may be added that no other security had ever entered the minds of any of them to offer or accept, except the royal negative upon the appointment of bishops—in other words, the veto.

The Catholic gentlemen then retired to draw up a resolution, which with some others was to be proposed at a public meeting of Catholics shortly to be held. It was a somewhat delicate matter to frame this resolution. It was to be so worded as to include the veto, in order to

[1] "Historical Memoirs," vol. ii. p. 193, second edition.

satisfy Lords Grenville and Grey and the Catholic vetoists; and at the same time, not to suggest, much less to mention the veto, for fear of rousing Milner and the Irish bishops. It was even intended to be so worded, that those who had drawn it up might afterwards be able to say that they had not so much as intended the veto. The resolution was drawn up in the following words:—" That the English Roman Catholics, in soliciting the attention of Parliament to their petition, are actuated, not more by a sense of hardships and disabilities, under which they labour, than by a desire to secure, on the most solid foundations, the peace and harmony of the British Empire; and to obtain for themselves opportunities of manifesting, by the most active exertions, their zeal and interest in the common cause, in which their country is engaged, for the maintenance of its freedom and independence; and that they are firmly persuaded, that adequate provision for the maintenance of the civil and religious establishment of this kingdom may be made, consistently with the strictest adherence, on their part, to the tenets and discipline of the Roman Catholic religion; and that any arrangement founded on this basis of mutual satisfaction and security, and extending to them the full enjoyment of the civil constitution of their country, will meet with their grateful concurrence." Such was the celebrated "fifth resolution." The reader will observe that some of the wording is taken literally from Lord Grenville's letter to Lord Fingall, and from what was said at the meeting on the 31st of January. It must be acknowledged that the resolution was cleverly worded. It was, in fact, a beautifully constructed capsule, apparently filled with sugar; but containing aconite. How not a few of the English Catholics, both clergy and laity, proved themselves to be "swell pill-takers," although they had previously suffered from the same doctor; and how the great analyst Milner detected the poison, the reader will presently see.[1]

In the first place, the reader must be told of the formation of what was called the "Catholic Board." Mr. Butler gives the 23rd of May, 1808, as the date of the commencement of the board. He says, "From the dissolution of the Catholic Committee in 1791, till the year 1808, the British Catholics had no point of union. On the 23rd of May in that year, a meeting of them, convened by public advertisement, was held; and unanimously resolved, 'that a subscription should be collected for the general benefit and advantage of the body, to be placed under the control of a certain number of noblemen and gentlemen, who should be requested to apply the same according to their judgment and discretion.'"[2] Mr. Edward Jerningham was appointed secretary to the board; and Mr. Butler says that an association of the most respectable description was formed, and finally organized in 1813.[3]

Dr. Milner, in his "Supplementary Memoirs," traces the origin of the board a little further back than Mr. Butler does. Milner says, "In 1807 certain lay Catholics, to the exclusion of their clergy, associated together as a literary club, for the purpose of defending their cause and religion against the shoals of pamphlets and paragraphs which the press poured out against them. It does not appear, however, that the association produced any work in support of their learned pretension; and it is probable that the ex-

---

[1] This sentence was written when everybody was talking of the cowardly murder for which Dr. Lamson was hanged. In order to induce his brother-in-law to take the capsule which contained the aconite, he encouraged him by telling him he was a "swell pill-taker."

[2] "Historical Memoirs," vol. ii. p. 202, second edition.

[3] When Butler says that the board was "finally organized" in 1813, the expression is rather loose, and calculated to mislead. The board was organized in 1808; in 1813 the organization was probably made more complete.

perienced gentleman who planned it, our present learned historian" (that is, Butler) "intended it for nothing else but the nucleus of a new Catholic Committee."[1] Accordingly this new committee formed itself the following year upon a larger scale, and with a more ample supply of ways and means, under the name of the "Catholic Board." Milner also says that he was "applied to from various parts of England, by the most respectable Catholics, for his advice, whether they should join the board or not. And his answer was given, though with doubts and fears, in the affirmative." The history of the board will prove that Milner's fears were amply justified. But the reader will notice that Milner makes no objection to the actual existence of the board as an organization of Catholics for the defence of their peculiar interests. He, indeed, condemns by implication the formation of what he calls the "literary club" in 1807, on account of the exclusion of the clergy. In this condemnation he was right, for certainly no association which has to deal with Catholic affairs can with any sort of propriety and without great danger be established, except under ecclesiastical sanction and with ecclesiastical co-operation. But when the Catholic Board, immediately on its formation in 1808, took a more proper and a more sensible course by inviting all the priests of Great Britain to be members, and by putting all the Vicars Apostolic upon the standing committee, we read of no condemnation by Milner or by any one else. The condemnation came some years after, when the outrageous conduct of the board made it a scandal rather than a help to the Catholic cause.

Milner does indeed charge Butler with having unduly swelled out the members of the board in order to give weight to its proceedings. He even says that the names

[1] "Historical Memoirs," pp. 135, 136.

of dead persons were entered, and also the names of the Catholic peers of Ireland and some Vicars Apostolic who never consented to belong to the board. At the same time he admits that "the society comprehends many orthodox, good, and pious Catholics."[1] The fair and just-minded Vicar Apostolic of the Midland District was therefore inclined to give the Catholic Board a fair trial. In the end the board proved a failure. But it must be remembered that the Catholic laity were only then being educated in the work of acting with their ecclesiastical superiors. As years went by, when the Catholic Association had succeeded to the Catholic Board, affairs were much better managed; and only a few other years later on, perhaps the very perfection of co-operation between the laity and the clergy was exhibited, when Bishops Griffiths and Walsh and Cardinal Wiseman were in London, and when Mr. Langdale was the acknowledged head of the English Catholics. As the proceedings relating to the veto, which I am now going to put before the reader, were in the main conducted by the Catholic Board, this short account of its formation was necessary as an introduction.

Bishop Milner had arrived in London on the 30th of January, 1810. He was aware that some of the Catholic laity were moving in the question of emancipation, and he came to London to do his duty both as a Vicar Apostolic and as agent of the Irish bishops, in watching over the interests of the Church. On the morning after his arrival, he received through Lord Clifford an invitation to dine with a Catholic baronet, to meet some friends at Doran's Hotel,

---

[1] "Supplementary Memoirs," p. 137. As an instance of what Milner calls the "swelling out" of the list of names, the author may perhaps mention that he sees in the list for 1808 the name of his own father, who was then a boy of sixteen years of age. Should Milner have noticed this, he may have consoled himself in this particular instance with the knowledge that the boy of sixteen was one of his "orthodox, good, and pious Catholics."

in Dover Street. He accepted the invitation, but before going to the dinner, he had an interview with Dr. Douglas, the Vicar Apostolic of the London District, and his coadjutor, Dr. Poynter. At this interview, "all the three prelates agreed that, while they owed to Government satisfaction as to loyalty, they should take care not to yield anything to it in spiritual concerns. Dr. Milner said, on leaving, 'At all events, let us prelates act in concert on this occasion.'"[1] He then went to Dover Street, and found upwards of a dozen Catholic gentlemen assembled to meet him. But it was not until the cloth was removed that the good bishop had any intimation of the real object of the party. Dr. Milner's own account of what followed is in several particulars of so great an interest, that I must give it in his own words. "The dinner was no sooner removed, and the waiters withdrawn, than the secretary stood up and read aloud the resolutions prepared for the next day's meeting, when several voices at once asked the writer, 'Dr. Milner, will you sign these resolutions?' He then perceived the object of this extraordinary dinner, and though taken by surprise, yet as he clearly saw the veto in its most hideous form, couched in the fifth and last of the resolutions, he immediately answered that he could not sign that particular resolution.[2] Much altercation on the subject took place, in the course of which the writer maintained, among other things, that *the signing of the fifth resolution by English Catholics would infallibly commit them with the Catholics of Ireland.* He was answered by an assertion, that *the case of the former stood on different grounds from that of the latter;* to which he replied, that, at all events, *Catholic bishops ought to hold the same language on a business of religion all the world over.* He

---

[1] Husenbeth's "Life of Milner," p. 143.
[2] The reader has already seen the fifth resolution at page 30.

was next interrogated whether, *in case he were a mere Vicar Apostolic, and not agent for the Irish prelates, he would sign the resolution?* To this he answered, that *he hoped to give an answer on this point, in common with his English brethren,* trusting to the engagements entered into that morning. He was then desired to promise that *he would not use any arguments to influence the opinions of his English brethren;* which proposal he indignantly rejected, saying that *when he met his brethren he would use such arguments as his conscience dictated.* In conclusion, one of the company cried out, 'May I sign the resolution?' to whom the writer, not by way of solving a case of conscience (for it is not over wine, and in promiscuous companies, that conscientious Catholics ask for spiritual advice), but merely to put an end to an importunate interrogatory, knowing, at the same time, that this lay personage's signature could have no effect in altering the discipline of the Church while the bishops continued firm in supporting it, as he had then reason to suppose they all would, he briefly answered, 'You may sign it if you will.' Had the question, instead of the former, been, '*May I sign a deed conveying away your land in Staffordshire?*' the writer would have given the same answer, 'You may sign it if you will;' adverting, in this case, to the inefficacy of the signature, not to the morality of it."[1]

For more than an hour Milner was, to use his own words, "baited and tortured on every side by the company present to make him consent to the *fifth resolution*, till he found relief in a flood of tears."[2] As Milner was one of the three greatest champions of the Church who have

---

[1] "Supplementary Memoirs," p. 148, *et seq.*

[2] Husenbeth, p. 144, quoting from Milner's "Letter to the Editor of an Apologetical Epistle," p. 335. This "baiting" was not the celebrated "Milner baiting." The latter took place in 1813, and we shall have to describe it in a subsequent chapter.

arisen in England during the time intended to be covered by this history, and as his conduct produced such great and enduring consequences, it is impossible to pass over what has just been written without some remarks.[1] The answer, "You may sign it if you will," was one of those unguarded expressions which not unfrequently fell from Milner. That he meant to approve of the fifth resolution, and to give his opinion that it might be signed with prudence, no one, of course, now would even profess to believe; and most probably no one who heard him give the answer did believe it at the time. It was an answer given in a moment of impatience, when the speaker was tired out by concurrent exclamations of many eager opponents; it was a sharp reply to a question which a man might think was put rather in a spirit of captiousness than with any serious desire of obtaining information and acting upon advice given; it was a smart way of getting rid of a bore. But the answer was an unguarded one, and, knowing the men who heard the answer as Milner knew them, it was unwisely spoken; for, both at the time and even years after, the great bishop had to lament that he allowed himself to utter the words. That sudden expression "You may sign it if you like" was asserted, by those who, to say the least, ought to have known better, to be a serious reply to a serious question, and it was made use of to justify the signing of the resolution by those who heard the words; and also to justify them in inducing others to sign it, on the ground that Dr. Milner had approved of such signature. And these very men who made the use we have stated of what Milner said,

[1] Of the other two great champions, one, of course, was Cardinal Wiseman; the other, thank God, still lives, the great leader of the "Oxford Movement," the pride not only of English Catholics, but of all England, and known and honoured over the whole world.

became henceforward the avowed enemies of the bishop, because he had in reality opposed the very resolution which for their own purposes they asserted he had approved. But this was not all the mischief which resulted from a few inconsiderate words. It is not my intention to enter, at least with any minuteness, into all the unfortunate disputes in which these words played a considerable figure, especially those disputes which unhappily occurred between Milner and the Vicar Apostolic of the London District. Suffice it to say here, that several years after, a gross misrepresentation of the unguarded answer, both of the words used and of the spirit in which they were spoken, was made as a formal charge against Milner to Monsignore Quarantotti, Secretary and Pro-Prefect of the Propaganda. The secretary believed what was told him, and actually informed Milner that he was charged with inconsistency of conduct in opposing the fifth resolution as schismatical, whereas at the dinner-party, having been consulted on the question, he had laid it down in the hearing of many credible witnesses that the resolution could be accepted by Catholics with a safe conscience.[1] In quoting this, Milner adds, "It is difficult to conceive a more dishonourable and immoral conduct than Mgr. Quarantotti's informant's, in representing the writer to him as deciding, at the public dinner in Dover Street, in favour of the fifth resolution, when they knew full well what disgrace he incurred with the heads of the dinner-party, from that day forwards, for having so firmly opposed it." While the firmness of Milner in opposing the veto is an example to every English Catholic, whether

[1] *Quinimo ille ipse D. M. pridie istius dici* (that is, the day before the meeting of the board—in other words, at the dinner-party) *illud* (that is, the fifth resolution) *salvâ conscientiâ à Catholicis accipi posse, multis fide dignis testibus audientibus, consultus statuit.* See "Supplementary Memoirs," p. 151, note.

a clergyman or a layman, the consequences of his unguarded expression is an example to all in authority or who have any influence over others, to be very cautious in what they say.

Though the reader may not have been altogether astonished that Bishop Milner should have spoken hastily and in a moment of impatience, he will no doubt have been surprised that he should have burst into "a flood of tears." But this apparent weakness was the effect of another characteristic of Milner which was as amiable as some of his other characteristics were dangerous to the possessor. Milner was a man of sound judgment, iron will, and determined perseverance. Strength of character was in him most conspicuous. How was it, then, that he burst into tears before men whom he was determined to conquer? The answer to this cannot be better given than in the words communicated to the author by one who as a boy knew Milner well, and who had special opportunities of hearing the bishop's character and conduct very frequently canvassed. "Milner," he says, "is one of the grand characters of English Catholic history. He was of a race of giants in the faith—strong and mighty—and, like such men often are, simple and imprudent as a child, and tender of heart as a woman." Here, then, we have the key to his whole character. In Washington Irving's "Conquest of Granada," he represents the mother of Boabdil as saying to her son, when they were taking their last look of Granada, "You do well to weep like a woman over what you were not able to defend like a man." Mark the difference between a strong character and a weak one. Milner could and did defend the rights of the Church like a man, and he was victorious in the fight; but the overflow of a tender heart found vent in tears at every wound which the Church received.

On the day following the evening of the dinner at Doran's Hotel, that is, on the 1st of February, 1810, the meeting was held at which were to be adopted the resolutions drawn up by the gentlemen who had the interview with Lords Grey and Grenville. Of the five resolutions the fifth only was objectionable.

Butler dismisses the account of the meeting in one sentence, as follows :—" At a numerous meeting of British Roman Catholics, held on the following day—the 1st of February—the resolution " (that is, the fifth resolution) " was, with the single exception of the Vicar Apostolic of the Midland District, agent of the Irish prelates, unanimously adopted." A few more particulars of the meeting must be added from Milner's account of it. The meeting, which Milner calls the " ever-to-be-lamented meeting," took place at St. Alban's Tavern. It was attended by about a hundred gentlemen, and amongst those present were Milner; Dr. Poynter, the coadjutor of Dr. Douglas, the Vicar Apostolic of the London District; and Dr. Collingridge, the Vicar Apostolic of the Western District. Before the proceedings commenced, Milner went up to the Bishops Poynter and Collingridge, and said to them, " Will you sign this (that is, the fifth) resolution ? " They both answered, " No." Milner then asked Dr. Poynter if he acted for Dr. Douglas as well as for himself, and Dr. Poynter said, " Yes." During the meeting, Milner, in consequence of some expressions which were used, thought it better that the bishops should retire, and he proposed to his two brethren that they should all three adjourn immediately to the house of Dr. Douglas, there to consider the whole business and take measures accordingly. Dr. Poynter objected to this course, but agreed to a meeting of the bishops on the following day for the discussion of the question as proposed by Milner. Before the fifth resolution was put to the meeting, Dr. Poynter suggested that before the Vicars Apostolic should be asked to sign it, it would be advisable to wait until Dr. Gibson, the Vicar Apostolic of the Northern District, should arrive in town, as, he said, "this resolution will probably involve in its consequences questions that would affect the spiritual interests of all the four districts."

When the fifth resolution was put, the bishops did not join in the vote. It is necessary to explain here that the four first resolutions which had been drawn up and which were adopted at this meeting, were to be put into the form of a petition to the Houses of Parliament from the general body of the Catholics of England. It was called the "General Petition." The fifth resolution was in a like manner to be drawn up as a petition, but it was to form a kind of addendum to the General Petition, and was called the "Supplementary Petition;" it was to be signed only by those present at the meeting, and perhaps some few others afterwards. Before the meeting broke up, the fifth resolution in the form of a petition had therefore to be signed. Having assured Milner they would not sign it; having appointed the following day to discuss it; without any further communication with Milner, Drs. Poynter and Collingridge both signed the fifth resolution. It was taken to Dr. Douglas, who also affixed his signature. When Dr. Gibson arrived in town, he also signed it, although he had just previously written to Milner, saying, "Take notice, that if anything is added to our petition" (the general one; that is, the four first resolutions), "all our signatures (those of the north) are withdrawn." If the reader wishes to know how it came to pass that the four bishops signed the obnoxious resolution, he cannot form a better judgment as to the reason than the one which will be immediately suggested to his mind, when he hears that a day or two after the meeting, a gentleman who had been present at it, happening to meet Milner, said to him, "Do not be angry with your brethren; they resisted as long as they could, but *we jockeyed them*."[1]

At the meeting at St. Alban's Tavern, there were present deputies who had been sent from the Catholics of Ireland; and during the meeting Milner moved an adjournment, till the decision of the Irish bishops should be known; but the motion was overruled. The Irish deputies sent off to Ireland on the day of the meeting an account of what had been done. "The fifth resolution was no sooner known there," says Husenbeth, "than nothing but execrations were heard, and complaints that the Irish Catholics had been deceived and betrayed by their brethren in England."

It happened that at that time fifteen of the Irish bishops were assembled in Dublin, with the proxies of the other twelve. The proceedings of the English Catholics in London were laid before their lordships, and they passed a resolution thanking Milner for "the faithful discharge of his duty" as their agent, and "particularly for his apostolic firmness" in opposing the fifth resolution.[2]

The two chief objections to the fifth resolution in itself were—First, that the word "security" included the veto, should that have been insisted upon by Parliament. The gentlemen who drew up the resolution, disclaimed any intention of suggesting the veto. But no security not including the veto would be accepted. When Lord Grey, on the 23rd of February, presented to the House of Lords the petition which had been founded on the fifth resolution, the words he used in his speech on that occasion clearly show that he understood the word "security" in the sense of

[1] "Supplementary Memoirs," p. 156, note.
[2] "Husenbeth," p. 182.

Lord Grenville's letter to the Earl of Fingall—that is, in the sense of an effectual negative in the Crown on the appointment of bishops; in other words, the veto.[1] And it is a curious circumstance that although Butler says that the veto was not intended in the fifth resolution, yet, having stated that the petitions founded on the fifth resolution were presented to both Houses of Parliament, he has the following words:—" In this single circumstance, the part which the English Roman Catholics, or any individual of their communion, took in the veto, began; with this it ended." [2]

The second objection made by Milner to the substance of the fifth resolution is stated by Husenbeth as follows:— " He considered that resolution as 'a pledge to concur in any measures which *Protestant politicians should judge necessary* for the security of their religion, and which they should say was not inconsistent with ours.' He argued that by the very words of it, the Catholic who adopts it says that he will *concur in arrangements for continuing the Protestant religious establishment of this kingdom;* and although he engages to concur only on condition that these arrangements shall be consistent with his religion, still the concurrence remains unlawful, because we may not do a lawful thing for a sinful purpose." [3]

But there was another objection to the fifth resolution which, though not appearing on the face of it, must have been pretty evident to all. This was the consequences which would flow from its adoption—the dissension it would cause amongst the Catholics of the United Kingdom. For these dissensions did follow. The matters I am writing about are past and gone. There are few Catholics,

---

[1] *Vide* "Husenbeth," p. 183.
[2] "Historical Memoirs," vol. ii. pp. 194, 195, second edition.
[3] "Husenbeth," p. 184.

unfortunately, who trouble themselves to become even superficially acquainted with our history during the last hundred years. But though seventy-five years have passed since these things happened, they have a great and abiding interest. A completely parallel case may not again arise. It may perhaps be held for certain that a case similar in its substance would not now be dealt with by the Catholic laity of England, as they dealt with the question of the veto in the year 1810. But who can tell that the veto question may never again arise? Who will be so bold as to affirm that no question is likely to be brought forward which may not, unless great care be taken, cause a serious difference between English and Irish Catholics, including the hierarchies of both countries, or between English Catholics in our own land? A great difference was caused in 1810, a great difference may be caused again. Let us, then, read as a warning what Milner says of the consequences of the fifth resolution. The words I am going to quote were not written in the heat of the controversy, but ten years later, when a cool judgment may be supposed to have succeeded to one under the influence of excitement. Writing in the year 1820, the great bishop says, "It" (the fifth resolution) "was a resolution which separated the Irish from the English Catholics, divided the last-mentioned among themselves, carried discord into the bosom of the sanctuary, distressed the See Apostolic beyond description, and at length brought forth the persecuting and schismatical bill of 1813. In short," he continues, "this pretended *conciliatory* measure has caused more dissension among the Catholics of England than any other measure (not excepting King James's oath and Mr. Butler's protestation) since the divorce of Henry VIII. from his Queen Catherine." It is not possible to read this without feeling our horror of dissension increased. The consequences of the fifth resolution are a lesson which should be well taught to the Catholic youth of England, and which those who are able to take part in Catholic affairs should ever remember.

At this time Providence, which has had such a watchful eye upon us, again came to our aid. The only thing that could stop the mischief from working out its malice to the bitter end was, that Parliament should refuse to give us emancipation upon any terms. Should they do that, the conditions upon which we were to be emancipated would cease to be a question urgent at the moment. God protected His Church in England, and made use of the bigotry and intolerance of Protestants to correct the mistakes and wilfulness of his own people. On the 18th of May, 1810, Grattan, having presented a petition for relief from the Catholics of Ireland, moved to refer the petition to a Committee. After a long debate, the House divided, the numbers being, in favour of referring the petition, 109; against it, 213, giving a majority of 104 against us. On the 6th of June, Lord Donoughmore made a similar motion in the House of Lords. On the division the contents were 58, the non-contents 154; the majority against the motion being, therefore, 86. Thus ended the Catholic question in the year 1810.[1] However mischievously people might talk and write on this side of St. George's Channel, no more mischief could at any rate for the present be done.

We have seen the evils which came from the mere passing of the fifth resolution, as described by Milner; but what a field for thought opens to us when we consider what those evils might have been, if the conditions expressed and implied

[1] It will interest the reader to know that the petition presented to the House of Commons by Grattan was drawn up by the man who was afterwards to become the great hero of emancipation, Daniel O'Connell.

in that resolution had been accepted by the Legislature, and Parliament had offered to relieve us on those terms! The state of things amongst the Catholics of the United Kingdom would have been this: on one side there would have been four English bishops, representing all England except the Midland District, together with the great bulk of the Catholic nobility and gentry in both Islands; and on the other side, Milner and the Catholics here, of the middle and lower classes, and in Ireland, all the rest of the Catholic people and the whole episcopate. And this division would have been not on a mere speculative question, but on a question eminently practical; not in a matter affecting only temporal rights, but dealing in a hostile way with the just claims of the Church in the United Kingdom, and with the rights of the Holy See; not a measure which could be easily amended or repealed, but one which, if once passed, would, in all probability, have remained on the statute-book for ever.

As the great question of emancipation was dealt with by Parliament chiefly as it affected the Irish people, and as the claims of us English Catholics were merely considered as a trifle to be thrown to a few harmless applicants, in a large distribution of relief to a multitude of men who were likely to be troublesome if denied, it might have happened that the refusal of Ireland to accept emancipation on the terms of the fifth resolution, would at once have settled the question for the whole kingdom. But even in that case, the dissention between the English and the Irish Catholics would have been more bitter than it was, and a great scandal would have been put before the whole Catholic world. We may imagine what Mr. Butler and his friends would have said and written, when, having emancipation within their grasp, it should have been moved beyond their reach, not by their English Protestant enemies, but by their Irish Catholic friends. It would have taxed Milner's powers to the utmost to have kept even a remnant of our grandfathers within decent bounds. The interposition of the Holy See would in all probability have been required to quell the storm. Great as the mischief would have been in the case we have supposed, it would, in another event, have been still worse. It is not outside possibility or even probability, that Lords Grey and Grenville would have accepted emancipation for the English Catholics alone, in the hope of establishing a precedent in subsequent relief to the Catholics of Ireland; and under the delusion that the Irish would eventually follow the lead which we had given them. Insignificant as we comparatively were at that time, we might have been made use of in the way I have supposed. I have said *under the delusion*, for in reality, if the two noble earls had entertained the idea I have imagined, they would have been in the position of men reckoning without their host. A power was just beginning to show itself in Ireland of which then they knew nothing. "God had visited his people;" O'Connell was just commencing "as a giant to run his course."[1] The result in the end would have been that the Irish Church would have remained free, and the Church in England have been fettered for ever by the State. But, thank God, these evils never came to pass. Thank God, Parliament did not grant us relief, when we were ready to accept it upon such disastrous conditions, and when we

---

[1] " Daniel O'Connell was to be the new leader of the Irish cause, and may be said to date the commencement of his wonderful career of agitation from the parliamentary defeat sustained by the petition of 1810. In a month after the rejection of that petition the general committee of the Catholics, after passing a vote of thanks to the worthy old John Keogh 'for his long and faithful services in the cause of Catholic Emancipation,' issued an address to all the Catholics of Ireland, urging upon them a new and more combined form of political action, and bearing the signature of ' Daniel O'Connell, chairman.' " *Vide* Mitchell's " History of Ireland," vol. ii. p. 265, second edition.

were so divided amongst ourselves. What took place in the year 1810 is a great example, teaching us, what indeed we might have known without it, that one great evil to be guarded against, and most carefully shunned by Catholics in the United Kingdom, is any serious difference between the Catholics of Great Britain and Ireland in any important matter equally affecting both countries. If on either side of the Channel a disposition should be shown to allow the prejudice of nationality to weaken the spirit of Catholic union, such a disposition would be but a poor counterfeit of patriotism, and it would be treason to the Church.

But another evil which came out in odious relief in 1810 was the difference amongst ourselves in England. Milner was in the right, and I suppose there are very few Catholics indeed who would now say that he was in the wrong. Our present happy state of freedom from State control is a lasting monument to the sagacity and firmness of the great bishop. All the other four bishops were ostensibly opposed to him. I say *ostensibly*, for in reality it is clear they thought as he did on the main question. They signed the fifth resolution, not because they liked it, but because they could not resist the pressure put upon them by the Catholic gentlemen. They did not want Milner's good intention; they were not altogether wanting in his discernment; but what they did want was his firmness.

With regard to the Catholic gentlemen themselves, they cannot be accused of having intentionally done anything which they knew would injure the Church. But they can be accused of having done, in a matter which clearly came under ecclesiastical authority, what one bishop most stoutly opposed, and what all the other bishops objected to, and to which they only reluctantly consented, in order to avoid annoying importunities. So that the most distressing part of the difference—that is, the division in the Episcopate—must be set down to the headstrong conduct of the laity and the weakness of the prelates themselves.

I will conclude with a few remarks on a subject which has been incidentally alluded to above. It is remarkable that throughout the whole action of English Catholics, from their first committee in 1778 down to 1829 and beyond that date, no word ever seems to have been uttered or written which would discourage the laity from forming an organized association for the protection of the interests of the Church. The only faults found with such organizations have been noticed when the laity have overstepped the bounds of their duty, and have presumed to settle matters which should have been left to the bishops. When men were banded together under Mr. Sheldon in 1778, and under Mr. Langdale in 1838, they received the direct thanks of the bishops. It is, indeed, the most natural thing in the world that our bishops should expect every layman to do his duty. But a layman does not do his duty unless he does what he can to protect the interests of the Church. If it is only the case of a single child in a workhouse, a Catholic layman should remember that an injury done to the meanest object is an injury done to the whole community; and if that one case should fall under his notice, he should use his influence to redress the wrong. In matters affecting general interests, or the interests of many, an organization is required; and the duty of English Catholics to possess one is as clear as it is the duty of any one person to act in any particular case. It is not right that English Catholic men should be content with the simplicity of the dove when the wisdom of the serpent is so much wanted. Is there any other class of men in England, having separate interests of their own, who have not an organized association to protect them? We

Catholics have many interests to be watched and protected. This is not the place to enter minutely into them; but this must be added, that by an organization is here meant one which is seen and known, and which works in the face of day; which can be used on an emergency; which every Catholic knows he can have recourse to; which is always ready to bring political power to a focus, in the various ways in which that can be done, and has been done in days gone by; which has an acting committee in London; which holds public meetings; which publishes to the world all its proceedings; and which is respected by Protestant Englishmen as the representation of Catholic Englishmen minding their own business in a business-like way, and working in their own interests as Englishmen are wont to work. The little interest which the Catholic young men of England take in Catholic affairs is a sad augury for the future. The present state of things will at some time or other produce the most baneful effects. Men not accustomed to work together, and unused to co-operate in public matters with their ecclesiastical superiors, will be likely, when the occasion shall arise, to be much more wilful and to deal much more roughly with those opposed to them, than the organized societies of former times. When, if a remedy is not soon applied, the evil time shall come, it will not be by good-humoured and gentlemanly importunities that spiritual directors will be induced to take their direction from laymen. In that evil day the laity will not *jockey* their bishops as they did in 1810; they will override them as they did in 1791: and the last stage in the history of English Catholics will be worse than the first.

CHAPTER XVI.

THE FIRST TEN YEARS OF THE CENTURY.

Attack on monastic institutions—The "King's speech" in 1802—Milner consecrated bishop—Pitt's second Ministry—Fox declines to move in the "Catholic Question," in 1806. In 1805, Lord Grenville presents a petition in the House of Lords and Mr. Fox in the House of Commons.

HAVING brought the history of the Veto Question down to the year 1810, it is now time to go back to the beginning of the century, and mention the principal events which affected Catholics during the first decade.

The session of Parliament, in the year 1800, closed on July 29, and in his speech, which he delivered in person, the King said, in allusion to the Act of Union, " This great measure I shall ever consider as the happiest event of my reign, being persuaded that nothing could so effectually contribute to extend to my Irish subjects the full participation of the blessings derived from the British Constitution." To these words, Lord Stanhope adds the following remark :—" The King's ready acquiescence in these last words when framed and recommended by his ministers, may have led Mr. Pitt, however erroneously, to think his Majesty's objections to the Roman Catholics were, in no small measure, modified."[1] Pitt, who was still in power, himself advised the words, and no doubt the great minister was perfectly sensible that it would be

[1] "Life of Pitt," vol. iii. p. 231.

absurdly unjust to maintain that the Irish were admitted to a full participation of the blessings of the English Constitution, while Catholics were excluded from Parliament. It is marvellous how George III. could bring himself to utter such words, when he well knew that he had irrevocably made up his mind never to consent that Catholics should possess one great blessing of the English Constitution, and have their share in making the laws. It shows the state of the Protestant mind with regard to Catholics. We were looked upon as outside all ordinary rules and principles of judgment; tyranny trampled not only on mercy, but upon common sense. That evil spirit which possessed almost all Englishmen in those days possesses many still. There are, indeed, signs that the process of exorcism is going on amongst the originally possessed; but there are indications that the ejected spirits have been sent into a herd of swine. If these creatures are not destined to destroy themselves, we should pray God that they may not destroy us.

In consequence of the return of the English Religious Houses to this country, some Protestants took alarm. Sir Henry Mildmay brought in a bill in 1800, "for the suppression of monastic institutions." The bill fell through. It is, however, to be regretted that some Catholics, who, Milner says, belonged to the Cisalpine Club, favoured the bill.[1] While it was before the House of Commons, Father Arthur O'Leary published "An address to the Lords spiritual and temporal" on the subject. In this, alluding to an exaggerated report that "two thousand of the common people, chiefly servant maids, were converted by the French clergy, in one part of London, in the space of two years," Father O'Leary writes as follows :—" That is to say, more than all the Catholic clergy of England have

[1] *Vide* vol. i. p. 226, note 2.

converted since the reign of Elizabeth. The French clergy, mostly half-starved and half-naked poor people, in spite of the generosity of Government, on account of the smallness of their allowance and the dearth of provisions, are ill-qualified for making converts. . . . I have preached in the chapels in London near twelve years, and I have not reconciled one single servant maid to the Catholic Church." But Father O'Leary did make conversions, though not amongst servant maids; for Bishop England says that the eloquent father's "controversial sermons were extremely valuable; and some very distinguished individuals could be named who were led by his doctrinal instructions to embrace the Catholic creed."[1]

In 1800, the King did one of those acts of personal kindness to Catholics for which, it must be acknowledged, the present royal family has almost always been known to us. "When, in 1800," says Lord Stanhope, "Cardinal York, in consequence of the French invasion, had found it requisite to leave Rome, and to forego his ecclesiastical revenues, the King, on the recommendation of Mr. Pitt, granted a yearly pension of £4000 to the last of the Stuarts."[2]

The beginning of the year 1801 will always possess a supreme interest for the Catholic Church in England; for on February 21, was born into the world that great man whose intellect, conscientiousness, hard work, and influence have been instruments in the hands of God to create a revolution in the Church of England which has brought thousands into the Church, and which, should it please Almighty God to convert all or a large proportion of our countrymen, will, in all human probability, have been the chief means by which so great an end will be brought about.

[1] England's "Life of Father O'Leary," p. 295.
[2] "Life of Pitt," vol. ii. p. 182.

In March, 1801, Pitt resigned because the King would not allow him to bring forward the Catholic question and admit Catholics into Parliament. The particulars of this resignation and reflections upon it have already been put before the reader. I need not, therefore, say more about it in this place. For some time at least after his resignation Pitt seems to have hoped that he might one day carry the question. On December 23, 1801, the Bishop of Lincoln, writing to Mr. Rose, says:

"Upon the Catholic question our conversation" (that is, between the bishop and Pitt) "was less satisfactory. He certainly looks forward to the time when he may carry that point; and I fear he does not wish to take office again, unless he would be permitted to bring it forward and to be properly supported. I endeavoured to convince him that he had been deceived by those on whom he relied on this question, as far as Ireland was concerned, and that the measure would be very unpopular in England. I did not seem to make much impression on this point, but I had not time to say all I wished."[1]

In 1802, Parliament met in January, and "on the 23rd, the King went down and delivered the opening speech." Amongst other things, "he exhorted the two Houses 'to maintain the true principles of the constitution in Church and State'—an allusion, as some persons deemed it, to the Roman Catholic claims. 'They have put *Church and State* into the speech; I think I guess why,' so wrote Mr. Canning from London. 'It could only be to revive what led to Mr. Pitt going out of office,' so said Mr. Rose at Bath."[2] Mr. Addington, who succeeded Pitt as prime minister, was a strong anti-Catholic, and was no doubt glad of an opportunity of showing both George III. and the people of England generally that he was opposed to

---

[1] "Life of Pitt," vol. iii. p. 364. [2] Ibid., p. 411.

any further concession. He did, however, one act of fairness, which proved he had no desire to deprive Catholics of the benefit of the Relief Acts already passed, but, on the contrary, wished us to have the full benefit of them. Those who took the oath prescribed in the first Relief Act of 1778 were exempted from certain penalties and disabilities imposed by the cruel Act of 11 and 12 William III. The second Relief Act of 1791 also prescribed an oath in order that Catholics might take the benefit of it. But those Catholics who took the oath of 1791, and not also the oath of 1778, still remained legally subject to all the penalties and disabilities of the atrocious Act of William. The practical result might have been this, that while under the Act of 1791 a priest who had taken the oath prescribed by it might say Mass, any common informer might have claimed £100 for proving against the priest that he had said Mass, if he had not taken the oath prescribed by the Act of 1778. Such a state of things was, of course, quite contrary to the intention of the legislature. An Act[1] was therefore passed in 1803, which entitled Roman Catholics taking and subscribing the declaration and oath contained in the Act of 1791, to the benefit of the Act of 1778. So Mr. Addington, by no means inclined to be generous, was ready, up to a certain point at least, to act with fairness.

The year 1803 is also remarkable as having been the year in which Milner was consecrated bishop. The consecration took place, on May 22, in Milner's own chapel at Winchester. The consecrating bishop was Dr. Douglas, Vicar Apostolic of the London District, assisted by Dr. Gibson, Vicar Apostolic of the Northern, and Dr. Sharrock, Vicar Apostolic of the Western District. Milner's title was Bishop of Castabala. He was appointed Vicar Apostolic of the Midland District. His predecessor was Dr. Gregory

[1] 43 George III. c. 30.

Stapleton, who died May 23, 1802, just a year before Milner's appointment. Thus began a glorious episcopate, in many ways remarkable, but chiefly to be remembered for the steady bravery with which the bishop defended the rights of the Church in England at a very critical portion of her history. Husenbeth, speaking of Milner's consecration, writes a few lines illustrating the state of Catholics at the time. He says:—

"There were few chapels out of London in which High Mass was ever celebrated; in the Midland District there was not one. It was only in private chapels that rich vestments were found, though a few others possessed one or two venerable old vestments preserved from Catholic times. There was only one cope in the Midland District: it belonged to Milner, but he hardly ever wore it. Catholics never spoke of Mass, but used the word *prayers* instead. The clergy had but recently ventured to dress in black."[1]

On May 15, 1804, Mr. Pitt returned to office and became prime minister.

"During his administration," says Mr. Therry, "individual differences of opinion on this subject" (*i.e.* the Catholic claims) "were kept in abeyance by one preponderating sentiment, in which there was a general agreement. . . . The scruple in the royal mind which Mr. Pitt determined to respect . . . was an insurmountable obstacle to the discussion of the Catholic claims."[2]

Pitt saw very clearly that difficulties would arise in the government of Ireland if the Catholic claims should be abandoned; on the other hand he knew, by a sad experience, that were he to take up those claims, George III. would certainly again become insane. It was a very hard case for the Catholics; but it is difficult to see what other conclusion Mr. Pitt could have come to, than to let the

---

[1] "Life of Milner," pp. 99, 100.
[2] "Canning's Speeches," edited by Therry, vol. v. pp. 359, 360.

claims stand over. In arranging for his return to power, Pitt, therefore, kept steadily in view that the composition of the Ministry should be such that the consideration of the claims should never become even an open question in the Cabinet. On May 2, a few days before he took office, in a long letter addressed to Lord Chancellor Eldon and to be laid before the King, he says, amongst other things :—

"The state of Ireland and the delicate and difficult questions which may arise respecting the internal condition of that country are scarcely less deserving attention. I need not repeat to your lordship what has long since been known to his Majesty, how fully my own determination has been formed to prevent his Majesty being ever disquieted for a moment, as far as depends on me, by a renewal of the proposition which was in question three years ago, respecting the extension of privileges to the Catholics; but I cannot help seeing that, although my conduct under all circumstances is fixed, there may arise moments of difficulty in which, if this country remains divided by powerful parties, the agitation of this question may be productive of great inconvenience and embarrassment. The formation of such a system, as I have supposed, would, I conceive, among other advantages, effectually remove this source of anxiety, as I certainly can never suppose or wish it to be formed on any other ground but that of all those who might form part of the Administration joining in the same determination with myself, to endeavour to prevent the renewal of any such discussion."[1]

As this letter was to be read to the King, it was necessary that Pitt should put very delicately his reason for engaging not to bring forward again the Catholic question. When Pitt says that he was determined to prevent His Majesty being disquieted for a moment, it must not be supposed that he would have been prevented from bringing forward what he thought a great measure,

[1] Stanhope's "Life of Pitt," vol. iv. appendix vi.

and one that he was almost pledged to, because it would cause mere disquiet in the mind of his Sovereign. Disquiet in Pitt's letter in reality meant insanity, and nothing short of the imminent danger of insanity would have prevented him from carrying out his views. And this reason seems to have weighed also with Fox, when on the death of Pitt in February, 1806, he 'became the Whig leader of the House of Commons. Mr. M'Cullagh Torrens, in his " Life of Lord Melbourne," writing of these times, says that Fox—

"Succeeded, when the new Administration was formed, in dissuading the Catholic leaders from presenting their petition during the session. If they did so, he would as usual support it with all his power; but he warned them that, if beaten, the government would be broken up, and another formed bent on their absolute exclusion. Instead of risking what may prove an abortive effort to grasp all they desired, he promised that measures should be brought forward to secure the Catholics in substance what they had then only in words—right to equal promotion in the army and to hold municipal offices, a revision of the local magistracy, and a bill for the commutation of tithes. 'The effect of these measures' (he wrote to Mr. Ryan) 'would be partly to make the Catholics generally more contented, partly to come with additional weight and strength when they again asserted their claims.'"[1]

And Lord Stanhope, quoting from the "Life of Lord Sidmouth," says that in the interview of Mr. Fox, at the Foreign Office, with Count Stahremberg, the Austrian Minister, the latter asked, "Have you no difficulty respecting the Roman Catholic question?" To this Fox answered, "None at all. I am determined not to annoy my Sovereign by bringing it forward."[2]

If Catholics, who then looked up to Charles James

[1] "Life of Lord Melbourne," vol. i. p. 61.
[2] "Life of Pitt," vol. iv. p. 391.

Fox as their boldest and staunchest advocate, could excuse him when he gave the "King's illness" as a reason for not bringing forward the Catholic claims, surely they can also excuse William Pitt when for the same reason he did the same thing.

But when, in the year before, Fox was in opposition and Pitt was in office, Fox stood nobly by us. On the 16th of February, 1805, a meeting of Catholics was held in Dublin, the result of which was that a deputation—

"Was appointed to wait upon Mr. Pitt, and ask him to present to Parliament a petition for emancipation. On the 12th of March eight deputies, namely, the Earl of Shrewsbury (Waterford and Wexford in Ireland), the Earl of Fingall, Viscount Gormanston, Lords Southwell and Trimleston, Sir Edward Bellew, Counsellor Denys Scully, and Mr. Ryan, had an interview with Mr. Pitt, who not only declined to present the petition, but said he should feel it his duty to resist it. . . . The Catholic delegates next applied to Mr. Fox and Lord Grenville, who agreed to present the petition, one in the Lords and the other in the Commons."[1]

Accordingly the two petitions were presented on the 25th of March.

"On the 10th of May," writes Lord Stanhope, "in due course, according to the notice given, Lord Grenville in the Peers, as on the 13th Mr. Fox in the Commons, moved to consider the petition. In the Peers there was a long and weighty debate of two nights, the last extending till near six in the morning. Lord Hawkesbury and Lord Sidmouth especially spoke of the question as one that at no time and under no circumstances ought to be conceded. The division gave, including proxies, only 49 Peers in favour of the motion, and 148 against it."[2]

In the Commons the petition fared no better than in

---

[1] Mitchell's "History of Ireland," vol. ii. p. 200; and Plowden's "Post-Union History."

[2] "Life of Pitt," vol. iv. p. 298. Lord Sidmouth was Addington raised to the Peerage.

the Lords. Fox moved "that the petition be referred to a Committee of the whole House." The debate lasted two nights, and Fox's motion was negatived; the numbers being: ayes, 124; noes, 336; majority against the motion, 212.[1] This motion was the first made since the Union for Catholic emancipation. Pitt, of course, opposed it, and he said in the debate that the prevailing sentiment amongst all classes was strongly against it.

[1] Butler, in his "Historical Memoirs," says that this motion in the Commons was made by Grattan. This is a mistake: it was made by Fox, and supported by Grattan.

CHAPTER XVII.

DISMISSAL OF LORD GRENVILLE'S ADMINISTRATION BY GEORGE III.

Army and Navy Bill—The "No-Popery" cry of 1807—Reflections on the dismissal of Lord Grenville's Ministry.

ONE of the most persistent opposers of Catholic emancipation was Lord Chancellor Eldon. The reader may be interested in knowing the arguments with which he combated the motion for the consideration of the Irish petition in 1805. I take the account from Lord Campbell's "Life of Lord Eldon :"—

"The question of Catholic emancipation being started, on a petition from the Roman Catholics of Ireland, he" (that is, Eldon) "made a long speech against it, bringing forward very boldly the religious principles to which he ever after most steadily adhered. He maintained that whatever was required of toleration had already been conceded to the Roman Catholics, and that their numbers should be disregarded, the Legislature looking only to the reasonableness of their demands. He argued that the Roman Catholics of Ireland were highly favoured, as they had a greater latitude in the form of their oath of allegiance than was allowed to the Protestant Dissenters of England; for the Irish Roman Catholics were required only to swear allegiance to the King and his family, whereas the form of the English oath was to the King and his family being Protestants. The British Constitution, he contended, was not based upon the principles of all men indiscriminately, but of equal rights to all men conforming to, and complying with, the tests which that constitution required for its security. By such arguments," says Lord Campbell, " he carried with him a majority of 178 against 49." [1]

William Pitt died on January 23, 1806. His spirit was crushed by the disastrous issue of the battle of Austerlitz. This battle was fought and won by Napoleon on December 2, 1805; and not all the glories of Trafalgar could buoy up the spirit of Pitt when he saw the break-up of the European coalition against the mighty Emperor.

On the death of Pitt, his Ministry came to an end: the King was reluctantly obliged to accept of Lord Grenville as prime minister, with Charles James Fox as leader of the House of Commons. This Ministry is known in history as the " Ministry of all the Talents." [2] Fox was in reality its head; he was not so nominally, because George III. would not endure it. But Fox did not long survive his great rival. He died on September 13, in the same year, 1806. The Ministry did not break up in consequence.

We have seen Pitt, in the fulness of his power, forced to resign on the Catholic question; we have now to see that same question break up the Ministry of all the Talents.

On March 5, 1807, Lord Howick[3] moved for leave to bring in a bill into the House of Commons " to enable his Majesty

---

[1] " Lives of the Chancellors," vol. vii. pp. 57, 58. What Lord Campbell meant to imply by "such arguments " is clear. He says somewhere, in his " Life of Eldon," that if two men condemned to death were offered a free pardon on the eve of their execution, on condition that they would read through two speeches of Lord Eldon against the Catholics, having eagerly accepted the condition, they would both of them, before they had got through one half of the first speech, throw it away, each of them exclaiming that he would sooner be hanged.

[2] When Fox agreed to join Lord Grenville, he did so on condition that every member of the Cabinet should be a man of first-rate talent: this was the origin of the name given to the Ministry.

[3] Lord Howick was afterwards Earl Grey, father of the present earl, and the reform minister of 1832.

to avail himself of the services of all his liege subjects, in his naval and military forces, in the manner therein mentioned." By the Irish Relief Act of 1793, Catholics in Ireland could hold any commission in the army up to the rank of colonel. But this Act did not extend to Great Britain. Lord Howick proposed, by his bill of 1807, to extend the Irish Act to Great Britain; and, further, to make provision that all who should enter his Majesty's service, whether in the army or in the navy, should not be hindered in their promotion on account of their religion. Spencer Perceval, a bitter enemy of Catholics, opposed the introduction of the bill: it was, nevertheless, introduced and read a first time. The King approved of the introduction of the measure; but after a short time he changed his mind and opposed it, and so also did some of the members of the Cabinet. In consequence of this opposition the bill was dropped. But George III. was not content with having induced his ministers to give up the bill. He went a step, or rather a long stride further, and did what has since always been considered an unconstitutional act: he required Lords Grenville and Howick to bind themselves never again to bring forward the measure, and never in future to advise his Majesty to make further concessions to the Catholics. This the noble lords, of course, refused to do; upon which the King dismissed all the ministers from their offices, and thus the Ministry of all the Talents came to an end. His Majesty then sent for the Duke of Portland, who formed what has been known as the "No-Popery Ministry." Perceval became chancellor of the exchequer. As a matter of course, Eldon was chancellor. Sir Arthur Wellesley, afterwards Duke of Wellington, was secretary for Ireland; Castlereagh, war and colonial secretary; the seals of the foreign office being held by one who afterwards, though always a Vetoist, became the most eloquent champion of emancipation, the great statesman and orator, George Canning.[1]

The consequence of these proceedings of the King was a disgraceful "No-Popery" cry over the whole country. Lord Campbell says that when the bill already alluded to was introduced, " a resolution was taken by the Tory leaders that it should be strenuously opposed, and that an alarm should be given of danger to the Established Church," and that Perceval, then in opposition, in his speech on the introduction of the bill, declared that "he felt himself bound to oppose its principle, and to call the attention of the House and of the public to one of the most important and most dangerous measures that had ever been submitted to the judgment of the Legislature ;" that " he then proceeded, in a very inflammatory harangue, to address himself with much dexterity to the religious prejudices of the nation, and foretold that, if the measure were agreed to, all our most valuable institutions must be swept away."[2]

This speech of Perceval caused a panic over the whole country. Lord Campbell says that " there is no reasonable proof that Lord Eldon suggested this most unconstitutional proceeding " (that is, the pledge required of the ministers by the King), " although he had the opportunity of doing so, in an interview which he then contrived to have with the King at Windsor ; but he certainly made himself responsible for it, by approving it and by taking advantage of it." The King's speech, at the close of the session, contained what Lord Campbell calls "a plain denunciation of the Catholics," and his lordship adds that it "was received with applause."

Parliament was then dissolved. At the general election

---

[1] *Vide* Butler's " Historical Memoirs," and Aikin's " Annals of the Reign of George III."

[2] " Life of Lord Eldon," p. 204, quoting 9 " Parl. Deb.," 9.

which followed, most of the candidates supposed to be favourable to Catholic claims were defeated.[1] The excitement in the country was intense, and the people disgraced themselves to such an extent that the year 1807 is one of those which not only Catholics, but all Englishmen, must look back to with regret. That this is true we can cite the authority of no less a person than Earl Russell, who ought indeed to be an excellent judge of a great storm of bigotry raised by a minister against the members of the Catholic Church in England.

"The 'No-Popery' cry of 1807, and the general election of that year," says the noble lord, "was the proceeding most discreditable to the English people of any that has occurred in my time. Several of the ablest men in Parliament, the chief ornaments of the House of Commons, were obliged to take refuge in small boroughs. Mr. Grey, then Lord Howick, went from Northumberland to Appleby; Mr. Windham went from Norwich to Romney. Mr. Perceval was the author of the "No-Popery" cry, and did his utmost to arouse the people to religious hatred. The flame did not subside until 1829, when O'Connell agitated the people of Ireland to assemble in their thousands, and impressed upon the Duke of Wellington the fear of civil war."[2]

These words of Earl Russell were published, and no doubt also written, many years after the year 1850. He says the "No-Popery" cry of 1807 was the proceeding most discreditable to the English people of any that had occurred in his time. But no man, according to the old saying, is a judge in his own cause. Catholics must decidedly differ from Lord Russell in his assertion. The proceeding the most discreditable to the English people which occurred during his life, and indeed since the Gordon riots, was the "No-Popery" cry which he himself raised,

---

[1] "Life of Lord Eldon," p. 215.
[2] Earl Russell's "Recollections," pp. 343, 344.

when Pope Pius IX., in the exercise of his undoubted right, established a hierarchy in England in 1850.

Mutatis mutandis, we can again use Earl Russell's own words about Mr. Perceval. Earl Russell was the author of the "No-Popery" cry of 1850, and he did his utmost to arouse the people to religious hatred. The flame did not subside for many years; indeed, it would be easy to show that the fire is not quite extinct, and that another Perceval or another Russell might, without difficulty, fan it into a blaze.

"When the 'No-Popery' Parliament met," says Lord Campbell, "the note of triumph was sounded in the royal speech, delivered by the lord chancellor, which boasted of 'the numerous addresses which his Majesty had received from his subjects, expressing their firm resolution to support him in defending the just rights of his crown, and the true principles of the constitution.' An amendment being moved, censuring the late dissolution, and the principles upon which the change of administration had taken place, 'the lord chancellor defended the dissolution, which had been found necessary for the safety of the Established Church.' The amendment was rejected in the Lords by a majority of 160 to 67, and in the Commons by 350 to 155."[1] This enormous majority in the House of Commons shows what a thoroughly anti-Catholic House had been returned.

We have now seen two Ministries overthrown by the Catholic question—the first Ministry of William Pitt, perhaps the strongest Ministry ever known; and the "Ministry of all the Talents," of which Lord Grenville was the head. In both instances, a sacrifice had to be made. No minister can resign because he is not allowed by his sovereign to fulfil his pledges, without great personal disappointment; no minister can be summarily turned

---

[1] "Life of Lord Eldon," p. 215; Aikin's "Annals," vol. ii. p. 222.

out of office by his sovereign, without great annoyance and great temptation to resentment. Pitt, however, had some consolation in his retirement from office: he thereby escaped the disagreeable duty of making peace with Napoleon. But Lords Grenville and Howick and their colleagues had no comfort in their ejectment; their feelings must have been those of pure unmitigated disgust.

The names of those who have served the Catholic cause should never be forgotten by us; the services they rendered should be written with red letters in our memory. Amongst us no distinction of Whig and Tory should make the smallest difference in the expression of our gratitude, indifferently to Whig and Tory ministers who have ever advocated our cause, or helped us in any way to stand in the position in which we now are. Pitt and Fox are both entitled to our gratitude—Pitt, for what he did in 1791, and for what he would have done in 1801, had he been allowed; Fox, for his bold, eloquent, and persistent advocacy of our claims, until the state of mind of George III. made it necessary he should desist. When a Catholic visits Westminster Abbey, his thoughts will be with its ancient glories, and as he moves from chapel to chapel his heart will still be drawn to the spot where the sainted confessor lies. But he will not forget others whose bodies repose in the sacred place. And amongst those whom a nation has placed there, are many to whom we owe gratitude, and we can pay it without compromising our opinions on any of those subjects which may not demand our thanks. The voice of our gratitude, like "the mournful requiem" of Sir Walter, may be uttered over the grave of Pitt, and it will be echoed in the tomb of Fox :—

> "O'er Pitt's the mournful requiem sound,
> And Fox's shall the notes rebound."[1]

---

[1] Introduction to First Canto of "Marmion."

Nor should the fact that some of our advocates demanded from us conditions which would have marred the gift, prevent kindly feelings on our part. Though we have a right to perfect freedom in the action of the Church, and should in season demand it, we cannot be surprised if Protestants, who are accustomed themselves to a state-slavery, should think little of fastening some of their chains upon us. And it must be remembered that those Protestant politicians, who were engaged in public affairs at the time of which I am writing, found helpers in their schemes for fettering us, to a certain extent, indeed, amongst bishops and clergy, and to the full extent, amongst many of the laity; so that, having condemned the Catholic gentlemen of 1807 for the part they took, we may very well discharge their Protestant friends, without calling them up for judgment. Another thing to be remembered is, that the chiefs of the Whig party in those days were different men from some of the chiefs of the Liberal party in our time. Lords Grenville and Howick were foiled in their designs in 1808 by the Irish bishops and Milner; yet they continued to be our friends, and to do all for us they could, until the passing of the Emancipation Act in 1829. In these days we have seen a Whig politician foiled in his plan to impose his English and Protestant ideas on education upon the Catholics of Ireland; and we have seen him resent the act by publicly accusing Catholics of disloyalty, and by trying, on the strength of his accusations, to raise a "No-Popery" cry over the United Kingdom. He was not successful: in the first place, he was not in power when he raised the cry; and in the second place, the English people detected the spite which was the motive, and, it would seem, rather pitied the accuser than attended to his accusations.

It is as well to note also that the Whig party, of the

time about which I am writing, was a very different party from what is called the Liberal party now. It was not until about 1819 that Radicals, then known as "Radical Reformers," were known in this country. French and German philosophy had not, in those days, so affected Englishmen as to make them give up old English traditions. Taking the whole body of politicians, and indeed the whole population, there was much more in them of sound English principle and, we may add, of Christian principle than there is now. Those English Catholics who, in matters of general politics and which do not affect the Church, ally themselves to the Tory, or, as it is now called, Conservative party, must not refuse their meed of praise to Fox and Grenville, Grey and Wyndham, because these men belonged to what would now be called the Liberal party. And in like manner, a Catholic who, when the interests of the Church are not in peril, would join the party which is called Liberal, cannot, in common justice, decline to respect the memory of men of the Tory party who have done a great deal for us—the memory of Pitt, of Canning, of Peel, and of George Bentinck.

If young English Catholics would study a little more the history of the last one hundred years, they would find men of both parties entitled to gratitude ; they would see that it is the good done to the Church which claims our thanks. And in this study, with the lessons learned from it, they might discover what it is that can unite all Catholics, no matter what their opinions on general politics may be, in endeavouring to obtain the great end, which should be common to all—the good of the Church in these islands.

CHAPTER XVIII.

CATHOLIC EMANCIPATION FROM 1811 TO 1812.

Grattan and Lord Donoughmore in 1811—Political parties—Lord Byron's vote—Letter of the Princess Charlotte—Canning's motion in the House of Commons—Lord Wellesley's motion in the House of Lords.

THE history of emancipation has now been brought up to the beginning of the year 1811. In that year there does not appear to have been much action on the part of English Catholics. But on the 20th of May, Mr. Grattan presented the Irish petition; and on the 31st of the same month, he moved that it should be read. In order to excite in the House a sense of shame that Catholics should be deprived of those rights which other Englishmen enjoyed, Grattan determined to bring forward, in a marked manner, the gallant conduct of the Irish troops in Spain. To do this with greater effect, he also moved that the votes of the House returning thanks to the armies under Wellington and Graham should be read by the clerk at the table. Grattan concluded one of his grand orations by moving that the petition be referred to a committee of the whole House. But the time had not come yet: the motion was lost by a majority of 63, the numbers being—for the motion, 83; against it, 146. Aikin says that—

"The motion was opposed on the grounds of a supposed inherent principle of intolerance in the religion of Rome, of the apprehension that Catholics would be still rising in their demands, and of danger to the Protestant establishment, should their claims be allowed."[1]

The Catholic petition was also introduced into the House of Lords by Lord Donoughmore, who moved that it should be referred to a committee. The motion was, of course, lost, the numbers being—contents, 62; non-contents, 121. It is somewhat remarkable that this division took place on the 18th of June, just four years before the celebrated 18th of June, 1815, on which hundreds of Irish Catholics, fighting for Protestant England, were shot down or sabred by the French troops at Waterloo.

Before following the progress of the Catholic question, it will be for the convenience of the reader to mention the state of political parties up to June, 1812. In the beginning of December, 1809, the Duke of Portland, on account of failing health, resigned the office of prime minister. He died a few weeks after. Spencer Perceval was his successor. Shortly before the resignation of the Duke of Portland, Canning and Castlereagh quarrelled and fought a duel, in which Canning was wounded; and both of them left the Ministry. On the 11th of May, 1812, Perceval was shot in the lobby of the House of Commons by Bellingham. After various attempts to form a new ministry, Lord Liverpool became prime minister, and thus began a tenure of office which lasted for fifteen years. This space of time covered one of the most brilliant periods of English history, including, as it did, all the principal battles of Wellington, and the final overthrow of the French Emperor. Canning refused to join Lord Liverpool's ministry. The seals of the foreign office were given to Lord Castlereagh; and Mr. M'Cullagh

[1] "Annals of the Reign of George III.," vol. ii. p. 114.

Torrens says that "although it was necessary in his" (Lord Castlereagh's) "case to treat Catholic emancipation as an open question, the Cabinet was emphatically constituted on the principle of resistance to all measures of civil and religious concession."[1] It would appear, however, that the Catholic question was only nominally an open question; for Mr. Therry, who was the friend of Canning, and edited his speeches, says that Canning refused to join the administration after the death of Perceval, "because the determination remained unaltered in the Cabinet to resist as one man the consideration of the Catholic question."[2] In fact, Canning, who had been a member of the Duke of Portland's "No-Popery" Ministry, now declared openly in favour of the Catholics. He had, most probably, always been at heart in favour of our emancipation; but, as we have seen, it was useless, in fact impossible, during the sanity of George III., for a Cabinet minister to advocate our claims. But towards the end of the year 1810, the "King's illness," as it was called, became permanent. The sad condition of the King was deeply lamented by the whole nation, and by none more than by Catholics. It was, however, always possible, during the regency of George IV., to bring forward the question, and ultimately it was during his reign that O'Connell forced the Legislature to grant our claims. But the Prince Regent himself (who up to the time of the regency had always sided with the Whig party on the Catholic question, as well as on other questions), when he became Regent, very soon deserted his old friends, supported the Tories, and opposed, as far as he could, all concessions to us. Canning seems to have made up his mind that he would devote himself to the emancipation

---

[1] "Life of Lord Melbourne," vol. i. p. 93.
[2] Canning's "Speeches," vol. v. p. 366.

of Catholics. He was quite as determined to force on our claims and to obtain relief, as his great master, William Pitt, had ever been. Unfortunately—but it was not entirely his own fault, as we shall see—he was a Vetoist, and a Vetoist of the most objectionable kind. He is, however, entitled to the gratitude of Catholics. Though he would have put new chains upon us, they were not chains that he or any Protestants in those days would have objected to if put upon their own Church. And it must be said of Canning, that for many years he exerted all his great powers, his mastery of parliamentary debate, his force of argument, his sparkling wit, and his brilliant eloquence, in order to strike off the old penal chains which still lay heavy upon the Catholics of the United Kingdom. Among the masterpieces of English oratory must always be included Canning's speeches on the Catholic claims.[1]

No sooner was the administration of Lord Liverpool formed, than Canning, though out of office, determined to force the question of emancipation upon the House of Commons. Accordingly, on the 22nd of June, 1812, he moved a resolution in the following words :—" That this House will, early in the next session of Parliament, take into its most serious consideration the state of the laws affecting his Majesty's Roman Catholic subjects in Great Britain and Ireland, with a view to such final and conciliatory adjustment as may be conducive to the peace and strength of the United Kingdom, to the stability of Protestant establishment, and to the general satisfaction and concord of all classes of his Majesty's subjects."[2]

[1] It would be impossible, perhaps, to find better examples of the difference between English and Irish eloquence, than by reading the speeches of Canning and Grattan on the Catholic question.
[2] *Vide* Canning's "Speeches," by Therry, vol. iv. p. 293; and Butler's "Historical Memoirs," vol. ii. p. 253, edition of 1819.

Canning introduced this motion in a long and interesting speech. After what has been said, the reader will be surprised to hear that the motion was carried by a large majority,—by no less than 129 votes, the numbers being—for Mr. Canning's motion, 235; against it, 106. It was the first time in this century that the Catholic question was victorious in Parliament, and the victory was owing mainly to the great influence of Canning, which he exercised during the negotiations for the formation of a Ministry after the death of Perceval, and also after the formation of Lord Liverpool's Cabinet. But we had not the same success in the House of Lords. On the 1st of July, the Marquis of Wellesley made in that House a motion similar to that of Mr. Canning in the Commons. Lord Eldon exerted himself strenuously to defeat the motion. But the sudden idea which seems to have seized upon Englishmen, that something must be done for the Catholics, had to such an extent affected even the House of Lords that the chancellor (Eldon) had to be very cautious. His lordship did not even dare to oppose the motion by either a direct negative or an amendment. He moved "the previous question." An active "whip" was made on both sides. Up to the moment of the division, messengers were sent all over London to bring in the peers. Eldon gained the day; but it was only by a majority of one! Lord Campbell, in his "Life of Lord Eldon," says that the latter was horrified at the result, and was observed to be deeply affected as he announced the division.

It will always be a matter of interest to Catholics to know how the celebrated men of England were disposed in the question of the Catholic claims. In the close division which has been mentioned above, Lord Byron gave his vote in favour of Lord Wellesley's motion. He was one of the peers sought out and brought down to the

House by the opposition "whip," and there is a rather amusing anecdote connected with his vote on this occasion. He says, "I was sent for in great haste to a ball, which I confess I quitted somewhat reluctantly, to emancipate five millions of people. I came in late, and did not go immediately into the body of the House, but stood just behind the woolsack. Lord Eldon turned round, and, catching my eye, immediately said to a peer, who had come to him for a few minutes on the woolsack, as is the custom of his friends, 'D—n them! they'll have it now! By —, the vote that has just come in will give it them!'"

Lord Campbell, who, quoting from Tom Moore's "Life of Byron," gives this anecdote in his "Life of Lord Eldon," adds, "that the noble poet afterwards, in some lines which he wrote as a continuation of the 'Devil's Walk,' showed that he had taken a very unfavourable view of the ex-chancellor's feelings and wishes on this subject"—that is, on a supposed intended rising of the Irish—

> "And he saw the tears in Eldon's eyes
> Because the Catholics would not rise,
> In spite of his tears and his prophecies." [1]

Lord Byron evidently thought that Eldon would have been delighted to see a rising in Ireland, in order that the Irish might have been effectually crushed by England; and that this would have been, in Eldon's judgment, by far the quickest and best means of putting down for many years to come the cry for emancipation. So great was the bigotry of the Eldon school, so intense was its hatred of everything Catholic, that the master of that school and his numerous followers would have taken as much pleasure in

---

[1] "Life of Eldon," p. 516. When Byron wrote those lines, it was many years after the vote in 1812, and when Eldon was ex-chancellor.

seeing the English soldiers shoot down the Irish, as they took in seeing the Irish soldiers shoot down the French in Spain and Belgium.

It is pleasant and refreshing to pass from the thoughts of such a man as Eldon to the thoughts of the royal Princess, who was then a young girl of sixteen, the presumptive heir to the throne, and who, if she had outlived her father, would have been Queen of England. The Princess Charlotte, writing to Lord Albemarle, in the year 1812, mentions—

Fox's "laudable exertions for universal toleration and comfort to our unfortunate and grossly abused sister kingdom, which," she says, "alas! were not crowned with success; and this is the man who, after devoting his time, health, and at length life, is called revolutionist. . . . Many there are who say they understand the word toleration . . . . There are dignitaries of the Church who pique themselves on their learning, but do not seem —no more than the temporal peers—to comprehend its meaning, or else they who are to preach meekness and charity would certainly not, I should conceive, seem to rejoice at the sufferings of Ireland, nor utter such virulent protests against their just claims . . . that God that they teach (or, at least, feign to do, who enjoins charitableness and forgiveness) is wholly forgotten in their rancorous hatred towards our oppressed and unfortunate people, whose crime is following other ceremonies, not owning these dignitaries, but above all having the name of Irishmen. It is with honest pride, the pride of a true-born English person, that I avow these sentiments—principles that I am convinced are the only true foundation of this country, and the spirit of the constitution, nor shall I be ashamed to broach them before the whole world, should I ever be called upon. Thank God, there are some young of both sexes, some that I have the happiness to know personally, as well as from report, that feel firm at this state of things, and that are, from their hearts and minds, followers of your late inestimable friend. Happy, thrice happy, will be the moment when the plans Mr. Fox pursued and planned are put into full force; then indeed England will have cause to rejoice, then she may lift up her head in conscious superiority and pre-eminence."[1]

Such were the sentiments of the Princess Charlotte; and to them it may be added, happy, thrice happy, would have been the moment when those who have governed the United Kingdom should have had the same wisdom and the same good feeling as the daughter of the Prince Regent, and when, having the power to act wisely and kindly, they should have made up their minds to do so. Is it not a shame that so many great statesmen who have lived since that letter was written, should have discarded all the lessons wisdom has taught and good feeling suggested in the government of Ireland? If a young woman of sixteen could see so plainly as the princess did, what were the sources of the misgovernment of Ireland, surely English statesmen must have seen them as plainly. And no doubt they did see them, and do see them still. The old saying is, "Where there's a will, there's a way." When wisdom points out the way, and the way is not followed, the inference is that there was no will to follow it. Hatred of the Catholic Church, jealousy of the prosperity of Ireland, did not blind the statesmen of the United Kingdom to the dictates of wisdom, but forced them to ignore them. If wisdom had been listened to and obeyed, the state of Ireland, and indeed the state of the United Kingdom, would be very different from what they are now. England beat the French; and she has beaten the Sikhs and the Afghans, some of the Africans, and last of all the Egyptians and the Arabs; but she has a terrible weight round her neck which prevents her from lifting "her head in conscious superiority and pre-eminence." And now it would require a political Hercules to raise

[1] "Fifty Years of my Life," by Lord Albemarle, vol. i. p. 332, *et seq*.

the load and hurl it into space. For what could have been easily done even so late as the year 1829, cannot be done now by one of ordinary strength. There would appear to be no probability that we shall see arise in this country a man of gigantic power, whose force of will will be equal to his wisdom. It would seem, indeed, that Englishmen are determined either not to learn the lesson of governing Ireland, or not to act upon it when learned. History has been read in vain; its instruction has been unheeded; the experience of two thousand years has been thrown away; and it may be that the very last of the Sybil's books has been cast into the fire!

CHAPTER XIX.

THE FIRST MEETING OF THE BISHOPS AT DURHAM IN 1812, AND THE BILL OF 1813.

The meeting of the bishops—The bill of 1813—Meeting of the Catholic Board—Unauthorized interference—The meeting at Lord Clifford's—Grattan's motion for a Committee of the whole House—Mr. Canning and Sir John Hippisley's motion—The Canning and Castlereagh clauses—The "Schismatical Bill."

IN the history of emancipation we have arrived at the year 1813. Our affairs during this year went through a most important crisis, and it is one of the memorable years in the course of the agitation for our relief.

Before narrating the proceedings in Parliament, the reader must be informed of some preliminary steps taken by Catholics and their supporters in the House of Commons. And first of all we must go back to the summer of 1812, at the latter end of which—namely, on the 21st of August—there was a meeting of Catholic bishops at Durham. The occasion of this meeting was as follows:— there were still in England many of what were called the *émigrés* priests, namely, those who had escaped to England from the persecution in France.[1] Amongst those who continued to reside here were many who adhered to the

[1] The great majority of the *émigrés* had returned to France on the signing of the preliminaries of peace with Napoleon in London in October, 1801, and on the signing of the treaty itself at Amiens on the 24th of March, 1802.

schism commonly known by the name of the *Petite Eglise*.[1]

And amongst those French priests who were conspicuous as abettors of the schism was the Abbé Trévaux, who, without having made a formal retractation, had been allowed the use of faculties in the London District. Dr. Milner strongly objected to this, and maintained that a formal retractation should be demanded. This very proper conduct on the part of Milner caused a considerable difference between him and Dr. Poynter, the Vicar Apostolic of the London District, and his vicar-general, Mr. Bramston. There was also another source of contention between Dr. Milner and the other vicars apostolic, and this was the continued adherence of all the vicars apostolic who had signed the Fifth Resolution, to that most objectionable instrument. This state of things in England was an embarrassment to the Irish bishops; and their lordships (I am now quoting the words of Canon Flanagan), being thus at some issue with a few English bishops upon the "Fifth Resolution," and with those of the London District upon Trévaux's case, now sought, while still maintaining truth, to win their English brethren to peace. They deputed Dr. Moylan, "the Bishop of Cork, to visit, on this errand of charity, all the English bishops. Dr. Moylan," continues Canon Flanagan, "was well adapted for so delicate a mission: he was not only firm, but so amiable in his manner that he was called the 'St. Francis of Sales of modern times.'"[2] Dr. Moylan was

[1] For the information of the reader, it may be stated that the Petite Eglise consisted of those French bishops and clergy who rebelled against the Act of Pope Pius VII., by which, in order to meet the views of Napoleon and thereby re-establish the Church in France, his Holiness suppressed all the old sees in France and established new ones. The most conspicuous among these schismatics in England was the Abbé Blanchard: hence they were commonly called here by the name of Blanchardists.

[2] "History of the Church in England," vol. ii. pp. 425, 426.

accompanied by the dean of his chapter, Dr. Macarthy. I cannot do better than give an account of Dr. Moylan's mission in the words of Dr. Milner :—

"He" (that is, the Bishop of Cork) "set sail from Ireland in July, 1812, and landed in the Western District of England, where he began his meritorious mission by treating with the pastor of it; but not meeting with a reception congenial to his own feelings, he proceeded to the capital, where he experienced, from the ecclesiastics in power, a quite different kind of reception—namely, the most courteous usage and the fairest promises; so that, writing to his friends, he expressed great confidence that he should be enabled to establish a right understanding in this important quarter. These hopes, however, proved delusive: for whereas his first and main object was to be able to assure his brethren in Ireland, from the testimony of his own senses, that the notorious schismatic, Abbé Trévaux, had retracted his schism—the act of which retractation, he was assured, lay in a bureau then before him—and though he was sometimes promised that this important document should be exhibited to him, he found in the end that no such satisfaction was to be afforded him; in fact, *the retractation of the schism itself* did not exist, but only a personal apology to the vicar apostolic. Coming into the Midland District, the venerable bishop had no terms to make there, he and the writer having been in all occurrences, for a long course of years, of one heart and one mind. To complete his mission it was necessary he should proceed into the north, as far as Durham, whither he begged the writer to accompany him and Dean Macarthy. The writer, however, would not accede to the request but upon condition that his western and southern brethren would be invited to the meeting; not wishing, as he declared, to form a party, but to investigate truth.

The invitation was accordingly given, and accepted by the southern prelate, who with his general vicar, the Rev. Mr. Bramston, met Bishop Moylan, Dean Macarthy, Dr. Milner, Bishop Gibson, Dr. Smith, and the Rev. Mr. Gillow, at Durham, on the 20th of August, 1812, in order to concoct with them a general plan of pacification. After much talk on both sides, it was at length agreed upon that each party should bring forward a project for the above-mentioned purpose. Accordingly, on the following day, the senior vicar apostolic produced the following brief formula :—'We, the undersigned, etc., are all of one faith and one communion.' To this proposal Bishop Moylan answered, that he could not carry back with him to Ireland so vague a declaration in answer to their specific complaints."[1]

This, so far as Dr. Milner relates, was all that Dr. Moylan said about the proposition of the senior vicar apostolic. Perhaps it was all that St. Francis of Sales would have said. But do those words contain all that Dr. Moylan thought, or all that St. Francis of Sales would have thought under the same circumstances? Most certainly not. The strongest terms consistent with charity, and which could have been uttered with temper, would have been justified on that occasion. It no doubt happens to most people, during the course of their lives, to have propositions made to them which may be viewed in two aspects, and which two aspects present themselves instantly and simultaneously ; one excessively insulting, the other supremely ridiculous. On occasions of this sort, we feel two interior motions, one to be angry, and the other to be amused ; we feel inclined to say sharp words ; and we feel inclined to laugh and to laugh out loud. These two motions clash, and if they be equal they neutralize each

[1] "Supplementary Memoirs," pp. 185-187.

other, and we may remain silent. Perhaps some such effect was produced in the bosom of the gentle Bishop of Cork, when he heard the proposition of the senior Vicar Apostolic. But still politeness required some answer, and as anger was engaged in its contest with absurdity, the spirit of St. Francis of Sales came forward and suggested the reply. So the good bishop said that the proposition was too vague to carry back to the twenty-seven Bishops of Ireland.

In a matter of importance like the subject we are now studying, it is well to understand clearly the true state of things. It was a matter of the greatest importance that there should be a good understanding and perfect unanimity between the Irish and English bishops, in the question as to whether any, and if any, what concessions should be made to the English Government in return for emancipation. It was known, from the result of Canning's motion, that the Catholic question would certainly come before Parliament early in the next session: it was also known that it would not be opposed by ministers, or at least not by a united Cabinet; and that it would be brought forward by powerful men who were determined, if possible, to carry it. Although it may not have been known to the bishops what condition would be asked of us, yet the fact that Grattan, Canning, and Castlereagh, all three vetoists, were interesting themselves in the question, was a sufficient index that some so-called securities would be demanded. Nor was it likely that without conditions any member of the Cabinet would vote for a measure of relief. The bishops also knew right well that Mr. Butler and his friends would not be idle during the recess, and that they would exert all their influence to carry out the principles of the Fifth Resolution, and make whatever concessions they possibly could. It must be remembered that all the vicars apostolic, with the exception of Milner, had signed the Fifth Resolution; and that the Irish bishops and Milner were determined that they would not accept any relief on conditions based upon that Fifth Resolution. As a political power working in fair and open constitutional fight, the English Catholics were of course very small in comparison with the Catholics of Ireland. But Charles Butler and his friends working on the spot in London, speaking for the bulk of the Catholic aristocracy, and supported by the adherence of all the vicars apostolic except Milner to the Fifth Resolution, were a power, and, as the sequel proved, a very dangerous power. It was not at all likely that the promoters of the promised Bill of Relief would have persevered in any obnoxious clauses, if they had been opposed by the united episcopacy of England and Ireland.

It became, therefore, really necessary that, if possible, the difference between Milner and the other vicars apostolic, and the difference between the Irish bishops with Milner and the bishops in England, should be arranged, and arranged in such a manner as to ensure union amongst them when the promised measure should be laid upon the table of the House.

The Irish bishops, therefore, having no mind that the affairs of the ancient and faithful Irish Church should be governed by English opinion, and that instead of arrangements for the government of their Church being made by themselves, they should be made by Mr. Charles Butler, Mr. George Canning, and Lord Viscount Castlereagh, deputed from their number the one whom they considered most qualified for the task, to go over to England, and to effect, if possible, a union where all ought to be united. The English bishops, with the exception of the Vicar Apostolic of the Western District, met the Right Rev. Irish

Deputy at Durham. As some of their lordships came a long journey, it may be supposed that they duly appreciated the importance of the occasion.[1] At any rate, we might have believed that something definite, specific, practical, and applicable to the grave state of affairs would have been resolved upon. An enthusiastic Catholic might have hoped that some grand resolution would have been come to which might have been handed down to future ages as a great principle of action. The bishops met and deliberated, they adjourned to think; they met again, and what was the result? The senior Vicar Apostolic proposed a resolution, declaring that they were all of one faith and one communion, which each one at the meeting knew perfectly well, when Dr. Moylan was at Cork, Dr. Poynter in London, and Dr. Milner at Wolverhampton. However, during the adjournment, Dr. Moylan and Dr. Milner had been thinking of something practically applicable to the existing circumstances.

When Dr. Moylan had meekly observed that the proposition of the senior Vicar Apostolic was too vague, his lordship produced two resolutions which he and Dr. Milner and Dean Macarthy had drawn up and agreed to that morning.[2]

The first of the resolutions protested against any change in the appointment of bishops, and was, of course, directed against the veto; the second resolution disposed satisfactorily of the Trévaux case. But both these resolutions were rejected by the meeting.

At this meeting of the bishops nothing, therefore, was done.

---

[1] How many nights the passengers by the stage-coach slept on the way from Town to Durham in the year 1812 I am not, at this moment, prepared to say, but it is not unlikely that some of the older passengers may have made their wills before starting.

[2] "Supplementary Memoirs," p. 187.

"Had these resolutions," says Milner, "proposed by the Bishop of Cork and his two friends, been adopted and adhered to by the senior vicar apostolic and his two friends, perfect peace and harmony would have been immediately restored among the Catholic pastors of the two islands; the mischievous resolution of the tavern-meeting would have been rendered innoxious; the schismatical clauses of the ensuing bill would not have been brought forward; the Blanchardist schism would have been suppressed, and hundreds, if not thousands, of the emigrant French, who, during the following six years, died in acknowledged schism, without any other chance for eternity but that which invincible ignorance afforded, would have died in the open communion of the Catholic Church. Unfortunately, the resolutions were not adopted, and the meeting broke up without anything taking place in it worth being recorded, excepting the apology printed in the appendix, which the writer made to those of his brethren who might be indisposed against him, and excepting an engagement, in a private letter, on their part, of being vigilant in preventing and firm in resisting any innovations or measures prejudicial to the unity or authority of the Catholic Church, to the sacred rights of the apostolic see, or to the integrity or security of our holy religion, in its faith, morality, or discipline. But, alas!" concludes Milner, "in rejecting the counter project" (that is, the two resolutions) "they rejected the means of accomplishing this."[1]

Such, then, was the end of the meeting of the bishops at Durham. All united action to oppose schismatical attempts against the Church was frustrated, and the Catholics of the United Kingdom were, as the reader will have to be presently told, left to the tender mercies of Mr. Charles Butler, Mr. George Canning, and Lord Viscount Castlereagh.

The apology referred to above was an apology which Milner wrote out and read at the Durham meeting. He afterwards printed it in his "Supplementary Memoirs."

[1] "Supplementary Memoirs," p. 189.

And what was this apology? Not meaning to retract any fact or reasoning contained in his different publications and writings within the three years previous to the meeting, until they should be disproved (which he thought none of them could be), Milner apologized for any expression he might have used which any of the bishops might have deemed offensive.[1] Milner mentions that some of his brethren had spoken and written and printed in a disrespectful manner of himself. No doubt they had shown their disrespect in more dulcet phrases than Milner would have thought it necessary to use.

No apology was offered to Milner; no regret expressed that more firmness had not been shown in presence of schism and unjustifiable lay interference.

What a sight is this! What matter it affords for reflection! Here we see the man who had been all along in the right, asking pardon for the roughness of his speech; but not a word of regret do we hear from those who in softer accents and in a milder way had been all the time in the wrong. Such is the way of the world. But how stands the case now? The names of those who sat silent when Milner had asked their forgiveness are fast fading in the twilight of history, and will soon be entirely forgotten. But the name of Milner is still a well-known and welcome sound. When that name falls upon our ears, our eyes are directed to a bright star whose cheering light shows us what dangers we must avoid, and in what path we must walk, if we would preserve the freedom of the Church in England. The name of Milner, like the names

---

[1] Dr. Weedall, who knew Milner well, was once asked by a young man if what he had heard was true, that Milner was rough and rude in his manner. Those who knew Dr. Weedall will recognize something characteristic in his answer. He said, "I should not say rough and rude, but I should say that he undervalued the little etiquettes of society."

of More and Fisher, will last during all time. Such is the way of Heaven.

On the separation of the vicars apostolic after their meeting at Durham, the prospect of Catholic affairs became very dreary. No union had been effected between the Irish and English bishops, and therefore there could be no united action of the Catholics of the United Kingdom. Milner was determined to do all he could to prevent mischief, and the Irish bishops were of course as staunch as ever. But Milner and the Irish bishops had not in their hands the preparation of the bill, nor were they consulted in the matter. Three Protestants were chiefly interested at this time in the advocacy of the Catholic claims—Grattan, Canning, and Castlereagh. Each one of these men had his own idea upon the subject. They do not seem to have acted in combination; but they did not oppose each other. The consequence was, as the reader will see, that the ideas of all three were contained in the bill; and a more monstrous production was never laid upon the table of the House. But if there was no combination between Grattan, Canning, and Castlereagh, there was combination between Canning and another gentleman, not a Protestant and not a member of Parliament: this gentleman was Mr. Charles Butler. Nearly two years before, Milner had prophesied that such would be the case. Writing to a Roman Catholic prelate in 1811, he said, "Mr. C. B., and two or three of his lay friends, will settle the arrangements (of the bill) with Protestant statesmen, and then he will write a new 'Red-book,' similar to that of 1789, to prove that 'he was most anxious to frame the arrangements in such manner as should not be thought objectionable by the venerable prelates.'"[1] These words of Milner were a comment on

[1] *Vide* "Supplementary Memoirs," p. 191.

a passage in a published letter from Butler "to an Irish Catholic gentleman," in which Butler said, "If Government should propose to us anything which affected our spiritual concerns, it would be our duty to submit that part of it to the Church." But Milner, in his "Supplementary Memoirs," says, "Our experienced manager knew full well that as this line of conduct never before had been observed by him and his Cabinet, so least of all was it their intention to observe it with respect to the bill then in contemplation. . . . In fact," says Milner, "*secrecy* was the very character of the bill in question." Milner positively asserts, and I do not know that his assertion has ever been contradicted, that "so far from being consulted on the *numerous and complicated arrangements* and changes in the Catholic discipline proposed to the Legislature in this bill, the bishops were not even informed of the tenor or nature of the oath containing a variety of doctrinal articles, which they themselves would have been required to take, under the expected Act; but the whole ecclesiastical as well as civil business of the bill, including a fresh profession of Catholic faith, was settled between Mr. C. Butler, with his two or three confidential lay friends and certain Protestant statesmen."[1]

While the bill of 1813 was thus being secretly prepared, a meeting of the Catholic Board was held in

---

[1] It has always appeared to me a very extraordinary thing that, as appears from what Dr. Milner says, Mr. Butler should have had no communication with Dr. Poynter on the subject of this bill. Dr. Poynter and Butler were great friends, besides the fact that Dr. Poynter was Butler's bishop. I cannot help thinking that there may have been some understanding between them which Milner was not aware of. If so, there is probably some kind of record of it in London, which may some day come to light. All who knew Dr. Poynter, including Milner himself, spoke in the highest terms of his goodness and piety. Any revelation of a secret understanding between Dr. Poynter and Butler would only prove weakness on the side of the bishop, while it would clear the character of the lawyer in rather a grave matter.

London. Several gentlemen came up from the country to attend it. Some of them, who were lodging at the same hotel, had their attention called to an article in the *Pilot* newspaper, intimating that Mr. Charles Butler was engaged with Mr. Canning in settling the terms of the expected Act for the Relief of the Catholics. They were rather astonished to see it asserted that one of their number had been acting for all of them behind their backs, and resolved to take action accordingly. One of them put the newspaper in his pocket, went down with the rest to the meeting, and, there and then producing the paper, read the article, and demanded of Mr. Butler, who was present, an explanation of his conduct, and an account of the terms he had been settling for them. It is not recorded that Butler made any reply to this most reasonable question. Indeed, it would appear that he had no time to answer; for as soon as the question was put, the chairman of the meeting rose and, addressing the gentleman who had dared to interrogate Mr. Butler, said, "Is not Mr. Butler at liberty to visit whom he pleases? Is he obliged to give to any one an account of his private conversations?" Now, this answer was, to say the least, very unbusinesslike. If Mr. Butler had called upon Mr. Canning as a matter of politeness, or to keep up social intercourse with a very desirable acquaintance, or to consult him on the various readings of some passage from a classical author, the chairman would have been certainly justified in asking if Mr. Butler was obliged to give an account of his private conversations at a meeting of the Catholic Board. But as it was, Mr. Butler was calling upon Mr. Canning to assist him in making arrangements for the future government of the Catholic Church in the United Kingdom; these arrangements involved some questions which came solely under ecclesiastical authority, and every matter spoken of concerned the whole body of which Butler was only one member. The Catholic Board professed to represent the Catholics of England, though in reality it did not; but only a very few of the members of the board knew what Butler was doing. Mr. Butler, too, was well aware that all the Irish bishops had opposed, and specifically condemned, the principle upon which he was ready to make concessions; he knew that Dr. Milner would fight to the last against his arrangements; and he must have known, also, that if the other vicars apostolic did not openly oppose him, it was not because they did not in their hearts disapprove of his action. To say that under these circumstances Mr. Butler's communications with Canning were private conversations, of which he might not be asked to give an account, was not only unbusinesslike, it was absurd, and against all common sense. It was not the gentleman who put the question to Butler, but the chairman, who said that Butler need not answer, who was unmannerly on that occasion. If Mr. Butler was not obliged to answer the question, it would seem to follow that, if two men are equally interested in some property, and one finds the other making arrangements for disposing of it behind his back, it would be an ungentlemanly thing to ask his friend what he was about.

I have dwelt longer upon this incident than I otherwise should have done, because, as has been more than once observed, history is read to no purpose if it does not teach a practical lesson for the present; and a very useful lesson may here be learned. I would say to our Catholic young men: Whenever you discover that any man, no matter who he may be, priest or layman, whether his domicile may be in the United Kingdom or in Rome, or sometimes in one place and sometimes in the other, is working in secret and alone in some matter that affects the interests of the Catholic Church, you may be pretty sure that mischief will follow, which it is your interest, if possible, to avert. What will bear the light should be done in the light; and if it is avoiding the light, it should be dragged into the light. Justice and prudence need not be overlooked in the matter. When a man has proper authority to act alone, justice demands that he should be let alone. When a matter requires secrecy, prudence dictates that it should not be made public. But the cases are generally very clear in which these two cardinal virtues should hold the sceptre. In all other matters where any one of you may have his opinion, and may make his voice heard, never let any one man arrange in secret for the whole body. This is a necessary caution, for as in the time we are writing about one man was arranging in secret for all, and, if Providence had not interfered, would, as we shall see, have succeeded in his designs; so in most, and perhaps in all other times, when some important question has to be decided affecting our Catholic interests, there will be found some one inclined, at least, to take the affair into his own hands, and work so that no one may know what he is doing, until we all know to our cost what he has done. There always are unauthorized individuals in the Catholic Church, and sometimes they practise in these islands, who seem to have "the solicitude of all the Churches" upon their minds. Macaulay says somewhere, that he could make a shift to live under a tyrant, but not under a busybody. It must not, however, for a moment be supposed that I intend the word "busybody" to apply to Mr. Butler. Though we may differ entirely from him in his views on the Catholic question, though we may think that he carried lay-interference in ecclesiastical matters to an outrageous extent, though we must most strongly condemn the course he took with regard to this bill, yet it was not as a busybody that he acted as he did. A man is not a busybody because in one matter he may act too independently and too secretly. Mr. Butler's general character and conduct entirely free him from any imputation of a disposition to be what is understood as a busybody. Men may take upon themselves more than they ought, or interfere where they have no right, from different motives and in different degrees. If any one should manifest a desire to manage alone the affairs of the English Catholics in both departments, ecclesiastical and lay, it would be pretty evident to all that such was the case, and those who are in a position to do so could act accordingly. Particular attention has been called to busybodies, because they are the persons against whom unsuspecting people should be especially warned.

We must now revert to the history of the bill of 1813. On the 19th of February, 1813, a meeting took place at Lord Clifford's house in Portman Square. A good many influential Catholic gentlemen were present, and amongst them Mr. Charles Butler. Dr. Milner also, by special invitation, was there.

"The real business of this meeting," says Husenbeth, "was to establish a right understanding and co-operation between the laity and the bishops and clergy and himself" (that is, Milner) "in particular, who had been exposed to obloquy and persecution from some of the leading Catholics ever since the year 1791. Dr. Milner," continues Husenbeth, "was satisfied with the assurances given him at the meeting that the grievances should be remedied, and understood those present to concur in the edifying sentiments, which Lord Clifford had often expressed to him, that he would oppose all further securities, except such an oath as should be approved by the bishops. . . . After this meeting, the best understanding existed between him and the lay personages present, who communicated with him in the kindest and most confidential manner."[1] Such is the statement of Husenbeth. If this meeting put a stop to open quarrelling or public difference of opinion between Milner and the Catholic gentlemen, it did so much good; but apparently it did no more good. At least, it did nothing towards stopping the progress of one of the most injurious bills against the Church in England that ever passed a second reading in the House of Commons.

The Catholic question was now engaging the attention of the country. Aikin, in his "Annals," says that "at this period, the question concerning the claims of the Roman Catholics became a matter of general interest, and the tables of both Houses of Parliament had been crowded at the close of the past and the beginning of the present year with petitions on the subject, of which a great majority were in opposition to their claims."[2]

The charges made against us at that time to inflame the public against the bill were, chiefly, that Catholics were seeking a civil establishment for their religion, and an alteration in the Act of Settlement, by which the Crown is limited to Protestants only; that we were merely looking for political power; that it was inconsistent with the principles of the British Constitution that Catholics should be capable of discharging legislative or executive functions; that Catholics formerly made a bad use of power; that the feelings of the public were against the Catholics. To these ridiculous charges was added the usual nonsense about the temporal power and the infallibility of the Pope.

Such being the state of things amongst Catholics and Protestants, Mr. Grattan, on the 25th of February, 1813, just seventy-two years ago, opened what Mr. Butler calls

[1] "Life of Milner," pp. 222, 223.   [2] Vol. ii. p. 284.

"the memorable campaign for Catholic emancipation," and moved in the House of Commons "that this House shall resolve itself into a committee of the whole House, to take into its most serious consideration the state of the laws affecting the Roman Catholic subjects in Great Britain and Ireland, with a view to such a final and conciliatory adjustment as may be conducive to the peace and strength of the United Kingdom, to the stability of the Protestant establishment, and to the general satisfaction and concord of all classes of his Majesty's subjects." The debate on this motion lasted during four nights: when the division was taken, the numbers were declared to be—for the motion, 264; against it, 224, thus giving Grattan a majority of 40.

On the 9th of March, the House, on the motion of Grattan, resolved itself into committee. Grattan then rose and moved the following resolution :—" That, with a view to such an adjustment as may be conducive to the peace and strength of the United Kingdom, to the security of the Established Church, and to the ultimate concord of all classes of his Majesty's subjects, it is highly advisable to provide for the removal of the civil and military disqualifications under which his Majesty's Roman Catholic subjects now labour, with such exceptions, and under such regulations, as may be found necessary for preserving unalterably the Protestant succession to the Crown, and better securing the rights and liberties of the subject, and for maintaining inviolate the Protestant episcopal Church of England and Ireland, and the doctrine, discipline, and government thereof; and the Church of Scotland, and the doctrine, worship, discipline, and government thereof, as the same are respectively by law established."

This resolution was carried by a majority of 67, the numbers being—for the resolution, 186; against it, 119.

Mr. Grattan's motion in favour of emancipation having been carried, Sir John Cox Hippisley gave notice, on the 24th of April, that on the 11th of May following he should move for a select committee to examine and report upon the laws in force against the Roman Catholics; on the state and number of their clergy; on their intercourse with the See of Rome; and on the appointment of their bishops. Three days after Sir John had given this notice, that is, on the 30th of April, 1813, Mr. Grattan introduced his bill. It was entitled "A bill to provide for the removal of the civil and military disabilities under which his Majesty's Roman Catholic subjects now labour." Grattan then moved that the bill should be read for the first time and printed. This was agreed to unanimously, and is a notable event, as it was the first time that a bill for our complete emancipation passed even a first reading. It would, perhaps, be impossible to frame a title to an Emancipation Bill which would better express what a Catholic Emancipation Bill should be. All that we ever wanted, and all that we ever asked for, was, that we should be put, by the laws of England, on a footing of complete political equality with all other Englishmen. This could only be done by removing all the obstacles to equality, for we could then advance to a level with others. The removal of civil and military disabilities was the removal of the obstacles which held us back. To be on a political level with others was our right; it was our right as Englishmen, and no one had any title to demand that we should pay any price for it. We were in the position of a person who had been wrongfully kept out of possession of his own, and the wrongful possessor had no right to impose any terms as a condition of restitution. On the night when the bill was read a first time, Mr. Canning, who was a most sincere and persevering advocate of emancipation, said that "there was nothing in the bill to which he did not most cordially agree." But, unfortunately, Mr. Canning thought that Catholics ought to pay for the removal of their disabilities. What the price was which he thought should be exacted we shall see by-and-by. It is a matter worthy of speculation, why Canning should have thought that Catholics should pay any price for those liberties which as Englishmen were their birthright. He was no bigot like Lord Eldon; he had no insane hatred of the Church; he was not a man to play fast and loose, to blow hot and cold in the same breath. Though in this instance he was in fact, yet certainly he was not in desire, one of those of whom it is said, *in quorum manibus iniquitates sunt, dextera eorum repleta est muneribus* (Ps. xxv.). He was a fair-minded, honourable man; one not afraid of his own thoughts, nor afraid of speaking them out before the world. He had set his heart on obtaining emancipation, and, to use a common phrase, he was determined, if he possibly could, to have it at any price. This is probably the solution of his conduct. He knew that it would be impossible to carry the bill unless it should be accompanied by what were called securities, and therefore he provided them. Grattan's bill would have struck off our chains, and left us free. But a majority of the House of Commons would not have been content with anything so liberal and fair. The Church was to be crippled in some way. It was not to be allowed free action. They were willing to strike the fetters off the left leg, but they would transfer them to the right leg. They would let the laity enter the Houses of Parliament; but they would have a veto upon the appointment of bishops, and examine and forbid or allow, as it pleased them, any communication between the bishops and Rome. It was with such men that Canning had to deal: he could not carry emancipation without concessions, and so he was willing to make them. It must be remembered, too, that he was a disciple of William Pitt, who was the first to negotiate for a veto. Therefore, when Mr. Canning had said that there was nothing in the bill to which he did not most cordially agree, he added that "at the same time there were some provisions—not in it—which he was desirous to introduce; not, indeed," he added, "conflicting with it, but carrying its spirit and principle still further;—clauses to this effect he wished to introduce, and to have them printed with the bill." Before the second reading of the bill, Sir John Cox Hippisley gave notice that he should insist on his committee, saying at the same time that "he hoped to lay before the committee such documents as would compel the majority of the members to postpone the measure, at least, for the present session." Sir John had hitherto been a good friend to Catholic emancipation. But now, when he seriously proposed to postpone the measure, in order to gratify a foolish notion of his own, every one in favour of emancipation deserted him. Even Butler turned against Hippisley, and tells us that the baronet gave the above notice to the infinite surprise and concern of every friend of Catholic emancipation. The impression made upon Butler must have been great, as in his mind it outweighed all Hippisley's past services, and, quoting Juvenal, he exclaims—

"*Servitii tunc perierunt tempora longi.*"

We shall see later on how Canning gave poor Sir John the *coup de grâce.*

Mr. Grattan then moved that the bill should be read on the 11th of May. This motion was carried. Mr. Butler tells us—

"On the 11th of May, Sir John Cox Hippisley made his promised motion for a committee. So far the conduct of the baronet was consistent, that on every former occasion on which the Catholic claims had been agitated in the House, he had avowed his intention of proceeding by a select committee; but on all these occasions the disposition of the House in respect to the measure was such as made all its friends favourable, and all its opposers hostile, to the appointment of such a committee. It was now directly the reverse; every friend of Catholic emancipation, considering a committee to be the most effectual mode that could be devised to injure the Catholic cause. The baronet prefaced his motion by a long speech, replete with curious and interesting matter. Mr. Grattan moved the order of the day. A debate of considerable length ensued: on a division, the votes appeared—for Sir John Cox Hippisley's motion, 184; for Mr. Grattan's amendment, 235. So that Sir John Cox Hippisley lost his motion by 48 votes: every member who opposed Catholic emancipation voted with him; Lord Castlereagh and Mr. Canning voted against him."[1]

Such is Mr. Butler's account of a debate which must have been well remembered by all who either heard it or read it in the newspapers of the day.

Canning, as every one knows, was a great wit. He had an extraordinary talent for ridicule, and on this occasion he seems to have given Sir John the full benefit of his powers. In the midst of peals of laughter from both sides of the House, he poured out a stream of ridicule, which, having effectually swamped Sir John's motion for a committee, floated off the unfortunate baronet himself, far away from all further public interference in Catholic affairs for the next two years. Dr. Milner defends Hippisley against Butler's charge of inconsistency. He says—

"It would not escape that author's" (that is, Butler's) "sagacity that, after all, Sir John and he were rival candidates for the same control over the Catholic clergy and religion—the former by means of the intended office of a Catholic commissary, which

---

[1] Butler's "Historical Memoirs," vol. ii. pp. 261, 262, edition of 1819.

he intended for himself; the latter by means of Mr. Canning's new board, proposed in the bill, of which board he foresaw that he would have, as usual, the chief management. No wonder, then," continues Milner, "that the baronet, seeing his own project, which he studied by day and dreamed of by night, in danger of being supplanted by Mr. Butler, should make all the opposition in his power against the latter, even at the risk of appearing to change sides on the main question."[1]

Milner seems to have thought that Sir John Hippisley wished to be appointed himself a sort of *ministre du culte*, for the special purpose of managing the affairs of the Catholic Church in England.

Sir John's motion having been disposed of, on the 13th of May Mr. Grattan moved the second reading, which he carried by a majority of 42. Dr. Duigenan had moved "that the bill be read this day three months." The numbers were—for Dr. Duigenan's motion, 203; against it, 245. Between the first and second reading, two sets of clauses, suggested by Canning, had been printed, and those clauses were to be discussed at the second reading. As it is a matter of importance that Catholics, especially our young men, should know to what lengths Protestant statesmen are prepared to go when, even in a friendly spirit and with an intention to serve us, they are handling the concerns of the Catholic Church, it will be no loss of time, and it should not be wearisome to the reader, if I give a full description of the clauses introduced by Mr. Canning and Lord Castlereagh into Grattan's bill of 1813. To do this is the more necessary because the unsuspecting have to be put upon their guard, not only against what Protestant statesmen can do, but against what Protestant statesmen can find influential Catholic laymen ready to help them to do. And let no young

[1] "Supplementary Memoirs," pp. 202, 203.

rising man amongst us suppose that because the state of things in 1813 will never return, therefore no practical lesson is to be learned. The state of things, such as they were in 1813, will never occur again; but it is very likely that a state of things will occur in which Protestant statesmen will deal with the affairs of the Catholic Church, and in such a case they are sure to find some at least among Catholics who will be ready to help them. It is not at all an improbable thing that some day the freedom of the Catholic Church in England will excite the envy, or even the unjust suspicions, of some statesman who may have the power to injure us. The lesson taught by the proceedings of 1850 and 1851 must not be lost upon us. Things are even going on now which, if not carefully watched by those whose business it is to watch, might very easily end in some proposal to give the English Government a voice in the elections of bishops.[1] Though we need not believe all that is written by newspaper correspondents, yet it would certainly appear that dangerous things are said where the saying of them may lead to mischief. We all know to what lengths English party-spirit will conduct party-men. When an English Catholic is a party-man, which he has a right to be if he chooses, he had much better, when he goes abroad, leave his party-spirit on this side of the Alps. Imprudence in this respect might lead to complications which would very materially affect the interests of the Church in England. But there are matters other than the appointment of bishops which, if not actually what are called "burning questions," may some day become such. The education question is not one that I have alluded to, but that question is a burning question, and we can all see how, notwithstanding the pastorals of bishops, the laity of England seem determined that *their* fingers at least shall

[1] This was written before the change of Ministry in June, 1885.

not be burned with it. We cannot expect that the peaceful tenor of the Church's way in England will long remain unmolested. We are reading about times when the lay Catholics of England were somewhat too active; we are now living in times when they are not active enough. But we are reading also about times when there was activity on the right side as well as on the wrong side. We have seen already some of the results, and we shall have to read of others as we proceed. The grand result, under a watchful Providence, is that the Church in England is the freest Church in Europe. And long may it remain so. But it will not long remain so, if the laity give themselves up to rest because they think there will never be another storm. It was when the labourers were asleep that the enemy sowed the cockle. We are not like the members of the establishment, who can take the warnings of their bishops or reject them, as they please. There is a time for rest and a time for action, and the time for action is when the watchman sounds the alarm. The reader may think that these remarks are a digression from the subject. But they are in reality, I presume to think, a proper introduction to what is now to follow. At the risk, therefore, of perhaps tiring some readers with a long extract, I will now give, in Butler's own words, an account of what well-meaning Protestant statesmen, with the help of some Catholic laymen, were prepared to impose upon the Church in England. At any rate, I hope to effect at least this result: that they who may read it will thank God that He delivered us from "the snare of the hunters and from the sharp word," and that while He has appointed bishops to rule over us, amongst those bishops, in the year of Our Lord 1813, was Bishop Milner.

Mr. Canning's clauses were as follows:—

"They first appointed a certain number of commissioners,

who were to profess the Catholic religion, and to be lay peers of Great Britain and Scotland, possessing a freehold estate of one thousand pounds a year; to be filled up from time to time by his Majesty, his heirs and successors. The commissioners were to take an oath, for the faithful discharge of their office, and the observance of secrecy, in all matters not thereby required to be disclosed, with power to appoint a secretary with a salary (proposed to be five hundred pounds a year) payable out of the consolidated fund. The secretary was to take an oath similar to that of the commissioners.

"It was then provided, that every person elected to the discharge of Roman Catholic episcopal functions in Great Britain or Scotland should, previously to the discharge of his office, notify his then election to the secretary; that the secretary should notify it to the commissioners, and they to the privy council, with a certificate, 'that they did not know or believe anything of the person nominated which tended to impeach his loyalty or peaceable conduct;' unless they had knowledge of the contrary, in which case they should refuse their certificate. Persons obtaining such a certificate were rendered capable of exercising episcopal functions within the United Kingdom; if they exercised them without a certificate, they were to be considered guilty of a misdemeanor, and liable to be sent out of the kingdom."

Similar provisions respecting Ireland were then introduced.

"The second set of clauses provided that the commissioners under the preceding clauses, with the addition, as to Great Britain, of the lord chancellor, or lord keeper, or first commissioner of the great seal for the time being, and of one of his Majesty's principal secretaries of state, being a Protestant, or such other Protestant member of his Majesty's privy council as his Majesty should appoint; and with a similar addition in respect to Ireland; and with the further addition, as to Great Britain, of the person then exercising episcopal functions among the Catholics in London,—and in respect to Ireland, of the titular Roman Catholic Archbishops of Armagh and Dublin, should be commissioners for the purposes thereinafter mentioned. The commissioners thus appointed were to take an oath for the discharge of their office and observance of secrecy, similar to the former; and employ the same secretary; and three of them were to form a quorum.

"The bill then provided that subjects of his Majesty receiving any bull, dispensation, or other instrument from the See of Rome, or any person in foreign parts acting under the authority of that See, should, within six weeks, send a copy of it, signed with his name, to the secretary of the commissioners; who should transmit the same to them, but with a proviso, that if the person receiving the same should deliver to the secretary of the commissioners, within the time before prescribed, a writing under his hand, certifying the fact of his having received such a bull, dispensation, or other instrument, and accompanying his certificate with an oath, declaring that 'it related, wholly and exclusively, to spiritual concerns, and that it did not contain or refer to any matter or thing which did or could, directly or indirectly, affect or interfere with the duty and allegiance which he owed to his Majesty's sacred person and government, or with the temporal, civil, and social rights, properties, or duties of any other of his Majesty's subjects,'—then the commissioners were, in their discretion, to receive such certificate and oath, in lieu of the copy of the bull, dispensation, or other instrument.

"Persons conforming to these provisions were to be exempted from all pains and penalties to which they would be liable under the existing statutes; otherwise, they were to be deemed guilty of a high misdemeanor, and, in lieu of the pains and penalties under the former statutes, be liable to be sent out of the kingdom.

"The third set of clauses provided that, within a time to be specified, the commissioners were to meet and appoint their secretary, and give notice of it to his Majesty's principal secretaries of state in Great Britain and Ireland; and the provisions of the Act were to be in force from that time."

Such were the clauses introduced to supplement Mr. Grattan's bill for unconditional relief—clauses which made the bill worthless, and, worse than worthless, mischievous in the extreme.

CHAPTER XX.

MILNER AND THE BILL OF 1813.

The Committee on the bill—Milner and Dr. Poynter—Milner on the bill—Milner left alone to oppose the bill—The bill abandoned—The expulsion of Milner from the Select Committee of the Catholic Board.

BESIDES the clauses which Canning proposed to introduce into Grattan's bill, there were others introduced by Lord Castlereagh. It does not appear in Butler's "Historical Memoirs," nor in Milner's "Supplementary Memoirs," which precisely were Lord Castlereagh's clauses; but I believe that the proposed additions to the bill, which were given in the last chapter, contained the clauses both of Canning and Castlereagh.

Mr. Butler, who no doubt was well informed in the matter, says that—

"It is understood that, between the division on the motion for the second reading of the bill and the motion for a committee, an interview had taken place at Mr. Ponsonby's house, between Lord Castlereagh and the principal advocates of the bill; that his lordship, at this interview, specified particularly the nature of the clauses which he had in contemplation, and that they were committed to writing by Sir Arthur Piggot."[1]

Mr. Butler does not tell us who the principal advocates of the bill were, who met at Mr. Ponsonby's house. We

---

[1] "Historical Memoirs," vol. ii. p. 266, edition of 1819.

may suppose that Grattan was one. But whether he was or was not there, it is unfortunately true that he made at least no public opposition to the introduction of the clauses which made his bill worthless. He was, in fact, a vetoist, and being such, notwithstanding his persevering and supremely eloquent advocacy of our claims, he must always stand second to Edmund Burke as a friend to Catholics.

On Wednesday, the 19th of May, the House, on the motion of Mr. Grattan, went into committee on the bill. On this day it would appear that nothing more was done than was necessary to bring the Canning and Castlereagh clauses up to a level in the proceedings with the rest of the bill. A motion was made that there should be a call of the House for the 24th of May, in order to proceed with the clauses in committee. Accordingly on that day the House was called over, and then resolved itself into a committee to consider the bill.

We must now turn our eyes to the great and only champion the Catholic Church possessed in England. No sooner did Milner become acquainted with the obnoxious clauses than he hastened to London. He went because it was necessary that one bishop at least should raise his voice; he went, as he himself tells us, openly to avow his opposition as a Catholic bishop to measures which were schismatical. Before starting, he wrote in very characteristic terms to the Rev. Thomas White, who was his successor at Winchester.

"I shall be baited like a bull," he says, "but I am ready to encounter the white bears of Hudson's Bay and the kangaroos of Botany Bay, rather than yield. I would willingly endure all sorts of sufferings for my own sins, but for the sins of the episcopacy I have nothing to answer."[1]

[1] Husenbeth's "Life of Milner," p. 231.

Milner arrived in London on the 19th of May. What immediately followed must be told in Milner's own words, or perhaps it would hardly be believed.

"The writer," he says, in his "Supplementary Memoirs," "the day after his arrival in London, sent a note to his brother prelate,[1] the contents of which are repeated in the answer to it, now before him : 'In reply to your note, by which you ask me *whether I will join you in openly opposing Mr. Canning's clauses*, I beg leave to say that I do not know what Mr. Canning's clauses are. May 20, 1813.' It is to be observed," continues Dr. Milner, "that at the date of this correspondence Mr. Canning's oppressive clauses had not only been printed, by order of the Commons, but also published in the newspapers : but, whereas Lord Castlereagh had proposed some further restrictions, it was ordered that the whole of the proposed restrictions should be incorporated in the bill and printed altogether. This was done, and the whole instrument, with its fresh terrors, was circulated in print on Friday, May the 21st, on which day the writer sent his brother a second letter, to the following purport :—'*As by this time you must have seen what the clauses are, will you now, at least, join me in openly opposing them ?*' To this question no answer whatever was given, which circumstance induced the writer hastily to draw up his BRIEF MEMORIAL. It was written, printed, and partly circulated among members of Parliament, on the same 21st of May."[2]

The provisions contained in the Canning clauses were of sufficient interest to excite the attention of every Catholic in the United Kingdom.

We learn from Mr. Butler that those clauses were printed a few days after the debate on Sir John Cox

---

[1] Dr. Poynter, Vicar Apostolic of the London District.
[2] "Supplementary Memoirs," pp. 204, 205.

Hippisley's motion on the 11th of May. At any rate, they were known to Dr. Milner at Wolverhampton before the 19th of May, as it was in consequence of the knowledge of them that he posted to London. What, then, must have been the thought of Milner, when, on his arrival in London, he received the letter from Dr. Poynter, saying that he did not know what Mr. Canning's clauses were? Supposing that on the evening of the 17th of June, just two years further on, that is in 1815, the Duke of Wellington had sent a message to Marshal Blucher, saying, " Can I rely on your joining me to-morrow to oppose Bonaparte, who is collecting his forces about a mile in front of me?" and had received for answer, " I am not aware that Bonaparte is in front of you," we can imagine Wellington's astonishment, and we can imagine his exclamations. Milner's exclamations were, no doubt, not exactly what the duke's would have been, but his astonishment could not have been less.

If there was anything in the steady and persevering determination of Milner to exclude the veto, which was like the same determination in the duke to beat back the French soldiers whenever he was told to do so, most certainly there was nothing in the good and pious Dr. Poynter which had the smallest resemblance to Marshal " Forwards."

We may now give the reader Dr. Milner's opinion of the bill of 1813. He says—

"The clauses of the bill, besides being generally injurious to the Catholic religion, were in some instances clearly *schismatical*, namely, where they attributed spiritual jurisdiction to a quarter in which it does not exist, and reject it in another where it does exist."[1]

---

[1] "Supplementary Memoirs," p. 203. This refers to the clauses which gave the commission power to reject a person nominated by the Pope to an episcopal see, and having the authority of a bishop or of a vicar apostolic in England.

He says it contained four or five different sets of galling restrictions so as to constitute it a bill of *pains and penalties* rather than that of relief; that there was reason to fear that the Bill of Relief, as it was termed, would turn out to be a bill of persecution, but no Catholic alarmist ever conceived it would be of so oppressive a nature as it proved to be. He moreover says that one of the six new oaths enjoined by the bill "contains alleged tenets of the Catholic faith on ten different articles, all of them more or less inaccurately, and some of them erroneously expressed;" and this oath every Catholic would have to take who wished to derive any advantage from the bill.

On the probable action of the committee, Milner writes strongly, but not too strongly. He says—

"The junta thus framed pronounces absolutely, yet secretly, on the character of the priest whose name is before them, and this without any fixed rule for guiding their decision, and *without any opportunity afforded the accused of vindicating his fair fame*, supposing it to be blasted at the board by calumny, or whispered away by malice; and yet the contriver of this scheme, as we have heard, *curses the Inquisition.*"[1]

He puts in a ridiculous light the effect of the clauses regulating the correspondence with Rome. He shows the inconsistency of those who framed the bill as it finally stood, in believing the bishop on his oath that the letter he has received from Rome *relates only to spiritual matters*, and at the same time not believing him on the other oath which they had just before extorted from him, that he would correspond with Rome *on no other but spiritual matters*. Milner concludes his description of the bill in words which show that he was not only a stout advocate of the rights of the Church, but a loyal and a chivalrous man. He says—

[1] "Supplementary Memoirs," p. 199. I suppose Milner here means Mr. Butler.

"The Legislature, by acting justly and consistently, ... will be more secure for their establishments against secret fraud and open force than by the complex oppression contained in the bill: that is to say, by trusting to the unsullied honour of conscientious men, and to the existing laws, which are as efficacious against treachery and disloyalty in the persons of Catholic bishops as against the same crimes in other subjects. Should sincere and intelligent Catholics be reduced to a choice among the three evils in question, they would prefer Sir John Hippisley's tribunal of a *ministre du culte*, to Mr. Butler's *domestic Committee of Inquisition;* and they would prefer Lord Grenville's *effectual negative in the Crown* to either of them. Yes, they would wisely 'fly from petty tyrants to the throne.'"

Milner was a staunch Catholic and a true Briton. He was a man in whose judgment the liberties of the Church and the liberties of England should afford mutual protection to each other. He knew that the Catholic religion was the best guarantee of civil loyalty, and on this ground alone he could appeal to the Legislature to protect the liberties of the Church.

In his Brief Memorial, which I have already noticed, and which was intended chiefly for the members of the House of Commons, Milner went through all the objections which a Catholic would naturally feel to the various provisions of the bill; and he asserts plainly that it would be an act of schism against the Catholic religion for any member of it, by word or act, to concur to the clause which declares that—

"Persons in Holy Orders, appointed, according to the usages of the Roman Catholic Church, to exercise episcopal duties, shall not be capable of exercising such duties—in whose favour a major part of the commissioners shall have refused to certify their loyalty and peaceable conduct."[1]

[1] "Supplementary Memoirs," Appendix F.

In a letter to the *Orthodox Journal*, in the year 1819, six years after the events here narrated, Milner reprobates the bill of 1813 in even stronger terms than I have quoted above, and says that—

"Upon the appearance of it, the prelates one and all were struck with horror, and one of them was reduced to death's door, from the dread of it."[1]

And yet, how strange! not one of the English bishops would help Milner openly to oppose the bill. The gallant bishop made a last attempt to induce his brethren to act.

"On the morning of the 24th of May, on the evening of which day the bill was to come on in committee, Dr. Milner" (I am now quoting Husenbeth) "held a conference with Dr. Collingridge and Dr. Poynter, in presence of two Catholic Lords and several gentlemen, in which he read three questions from a written paper, as to whether the bill contained anything contrary to Catholic doctrine or discipline; whether a Catholic could be a commissioner under the bill; and whether a vicar apostolic was not bound to speak out openly in opposition to the bill. The other two bishops refused to answer these questions, 'though I showed,' says Dr. Milner, 'that by doing this they might, through the weight of the company then present, prevent their (the clauses) passing that very night. The conclusion of the conference was, that I answered these questions for myself in the manner that you will suppose, and in the most emphatical terms that occurred to me, and I charged my brethren, before God and the Church, with all the mischief which would arise from the expected Act.'"[2]

Thus was Milner left completely alone to fight the battle

---

[1] Page 105, quoted by Husenbeth, p. 233.
[2] "Life of Milner," p. 233, quoting Encyclical Letter of the 22nd of November, 1813, addressed to the Catholics of the Midland District, p. 11.

of the Church. He was left alone when, if the other vicars apostolic had joined him in action, we now might have boasted that our bishops had saved us. Husenbeth omits in his "Life of Milner" one striking passage, which we read in the "Supplementary Memoirs." Milner, in giving his account of what he said at the meeting, the history of which I have given from Husenbeth, says—

"Lastly, he" (that is, Milner) "maintained it as incontestable, that if any two of the company present would go down to the House of Commons, and inform Mr. Grattan that the vicars apostolic had found clauses in the bill incompatible with the integrity or the safety of the Catholic religion, it would even then be stopped in its progress. However," adds Milner, "as this was the event which was dreaded by most of the company, much more than the religious evils with which it was pregnant, the writer's protestations and arguments were equally disregarded, and the instrument of schism was left to take its course."[1]

Milner had done what he could. His own unsupported appeal to Grattan would have been of no avail; for Grattan, Canning, Castlereagh, Ponsonby, and the other friends of emancipation, must have looked upon the question of the "clauses" as a party question amongst Catholics, in which Milner was on one side, and the other bishops and the great bulk of the aristocracy on the other.

What were Milner's thoughts and feelings when, after the meeting, he walked back to his lodgings in Titchfield Street? If we may compare the two situations, what would have been the thoughts and feelings of the duke if, on the morning of the 18th of June, 1815, every man under his command had marched off to Brussels, leaving him standing alone facing the French army? And let us remember that Milner loved his duty to the Church, threatened with a

[1] "Supplementary Memoirs," p. 208.

schismatical attack, far more even than Wellington loved his duty to England threatened with invasion. Milner was a man with strong feelings, and his suffering must have been acute. But he was also a man of strong convictions, and of a will immovable when he knew he was in the right. Opposition only made him more determined. The words in which Sir Walter sings the praises of the "evergreen pine" might be applied to Milner:

> "Moor'd in the rifted rock,
> Proof to the tempest's shock,
> Firmer he roots him the ruder it blow."[1]

This disposition in Milner must have greatly helped him through his many battles. And so the sturdy and disappointed bishop went to his home in London that evening, "the success of the bill, on its third reading, being," as he tells us, "as confidently anticipated to take place in the course of a few hours as the rising of the sun the next morning."

But that bill was never read a third time. What stopped it? Who stopped it? God stopped it. For it must be considered a providential interference, by which the bill never advanced even one step further. Perhaps the faith and fidelity of one man earned for the Catholic Church in England, that the bigotry of one other man should be the instrument by which we were saved. And, if it may be reverently said, what was done was done quickly. It is well known that when the House of Commons resolves itself into a Committee of the whole House, the speaker leaves the chair. The speaker at the time I am writing about was Abbot, a strong anti-Catholic. When the clerk read the first clause, Abbot rose in his place, and moved that the words in the first clause, *to sit*

---

[1] "Lady of the Lake," Canto II., Boatmen's Song.

and vote in either House of Parliament, should be left out of the bill. A long debate ensued ; the House divided, and Abbot gained his motion by four votes, the numbers being—for the clause, 247 ; against it, 251. The promoters of the bill then threw it up, and the Church in England was freed from Cisalpinism and degradation. Dr. Milner's opposition to the bill produced a greater effect than would appear at first sight. The manner in which he was shortly after treated by the Catholic Board shows that they were much more angry with him than they would have been if his opposition had been fruitless. He was well known amongst Protestants as a man of learning and of influence, and he was known also to speak for the Irish bishops. It was known that he and his Irish brethren were opposed to the bill. This and the Brief Memorial would give the waverers an excuse for voting with Abbot. Though it was known that many of the upper class of Catholic gentlemen were in favour of the clauses, it may also have been known that the great bulk of the Catholic middle class gave a hearty support to Milner. There is a passage in the "Diaries and Correspondence" of Abbot, the speaker, who was afterwards Lord Colchester, which shows the position in which Milner stood, in the opinion of some Protestants. Dr. Cyril Jackson, who was Dean of Christchurch, had a private conversation with Abbot, at the speaker's house, during which Dr. Jackson said that "he inclined to think that if our Roman Catholics claimed and maintained the same liberties as the Gallican Church, they might be admitted to political power. But this the Roman Catholics, and Dr. Milner at their head, positively disclaim."[1] Milner's opposition to the bill most likely turned the scale on the night of the division. Canning afterwards regretted that the bill had been thrown up. Twelve years

[1] Vol. ii. p. 526.

afterwards, speaking in the House of Commons on the 15th of February, 1825, he said, " In 1813 we might have carried a bill containing everything but seats in Parliament, but we threw it up in a pet. I have never ceased to regret that hasty determination.

> " Ex illo fluere, ac retro sublapsa referri
> Spes Danaüm.'

From that moment the Catholic question began to lose ground." Canning never ceased to regret the hasty determination : all loyal Catholics have never ceased to rejoice at it.

I have now to record the most disgraceful scene which has taken place amongst English Catholics during the last hundred years. In the Catholic Board there was what was called the *Select Committee*. Dr. Milner's name had been put upon this committee without his knowledge. But as his name was there, it afforded the members of the board an opportunity of expelling him from it, and thus punishing him for having opposed the bill of 1813. It is bad enough, and a sufficiently lamentable thing, when any number of Englishmen combine together to take revenge on a man for using his liberty to oppose a measure, merely because they, in the exercise of *their* liberty, are in favour of what he would reject ; but when it is the case of a high-minded, zealous bishop resisting a schismatical measure not only in his own name, but in the name of a whole hierarchy,[1] and, to punish him for his conduct, Catholic gentlemen endeavour publicly to disgrace him, the act may be said, without exaggeration, to be atrocious. But this the Catholic gentlemen determined to do.

The board continued to meet day after day succeeding

---

[1] The reader will remember that Milner acted as the agent of the Irish bishops.

the memorable 24th of May,[1] on which the bill was thrown up. At these meetings it was determined to expel Milner. But the members of the board were in such a state of continued irritation that they were not content that a resolution should be passed striking out Dr. Milner's name; they were resolved, if possible, to effect their object in the most personally offensive way that could be devised. They made various attempts to get Milner to attend the meetings, in order that they might see him leave the room after the resolution of expulsion; and (if all reports are true) there were some who were prepared to use physical force to eject him, if he showed any hesitation in his movement to the door.

At first Dr. Milner declined to attend the meetings of the board, and, as he says, "to hear the speeches and resolutions which its orators had prepared against him."[2] But at length he yielded. He tells us himself that, being solicited by a great personage whom he respected, and other well-disposed Catholics, he promised to attend a meeting which was fixed for the 29th of May.[3] Who this great personage was, I do not know. Late on the evening of the 28th, two of the bishop's friends called upon him. Who these two friends were, Dr. Milner does not tell us himself, and as Husenbeth does not mention their names, I suppose he did not know them. The object of their visit was to inform the bishop that at the meeting which he had promised to attend the next day, he was to be publicly expelled from the board, for having written and circulated his Brief Memorial. The reader will remember that this Brief Memorial was the circular against the bill, which Milner hastily wrote and distributed amongst the members

---

[1] The reader will not fail to notice that the schismatical bill was unexpectedly and providentially lost on the feast of the "Help of Christians."
[2] "Supplementary Memoirs," p. 210.   [3] Ibid., pp. 210, 211.

of the House of Commons. These two friends advised the bishop to avoid the blow by resigning his place upon the committee. Husenbeth's observation upon the advice of these gentlemen is, "They forgot to whom they were speaking. No man on earth was less likely to flinch before such a tribunal." To the last observation all will agree. But the first seems to imply that it would have been better if the two friends of the bishop had not gone to him with the advice they gave. Some, however, may think that the two gentlemen may be well excused for thinking that the boldness of the brave champion might this once be sacrificed, to prevent a great indignity to a bishop and a greater disgrace to the Catholic Board. But Milner took a different view. Not to go, he said, would be to disavow his cause. "He promised, however, to take no notice of any resolutions the board might pass against him, provided that they did not publish them; which compromise, however, the gentlemen said they were not authorized to enter into."[1] Milner then said, "Connected as I am with a great and sacred cause, if you publish against me, be assured that I will answer you."[2] Milner went to the meeting on the following day.[3]

It appears, as we shall see from a protest which Milner read at the meeting, that there were between sixty and seventy gentlemen present. Mr. Bodenham, who was present at this meeting, used to speak of Milner and

[1] "Supplementary Memoirs," p. 211.
[2] Husenbeth's "Life of Milner," p. 235.
[3] Milner gives a short account of this meeting in his "Supplementary Memoirs," and Husenbeth appears to have had some other information. Both sources have, of course, been made use of in this history; but in this account of it I chiefly rely partly on what I have myself heard from Mr. Charles Thomas Bodenham, of Rotherwas (father of the late Mr. De la Barr Bodenham), who was present on the occasion, and partly on the memory, better than mine, of Mr. Berington, of Little Malvern, who tells me that he has heard the story so often from Mr. Bodenham that he knows his words by heart.

Charles Butler as sitting at the same table, one at one end, and the other at the other end. Perhaps some of the members (possibly the members of the committee) were sitting round a table, while the other members were standing about. The proceedings commenced, and resolutions were passed condemning the Brief Memorial, declaring that the board was not responsible for Dr. Milner's political opinions or writings, and calling upon him to state whom he meant to designate by the expression "false brethren" in his Brief Memorial. While all this was passing, Milner says that he "listened with temper to the harangues." The expression "false brethren" does not occur in the Brief Memorial as published by Milner in his "Supplementary Memoirs," but it did occur in the original Brief Memorial which Milner sent to the members of Parliament.

In accordance with the resolution passed, the chairman rose, and addressing himself to Milner, asked him to point out whom he meant by "false brethren." Milner, pointing to Mr. Butler, who was sitting at the far end of the table, said, "There's Charles Butler there."[1] The scene which ensued when these words had been uttered was, by all accounts, something like the scene which, in the lower House of Parliament in France, follows the utterance of a piquant sentence which has smartly hit the extreme left. A state of wild excitement continued for some time, in the midst of which the first thing done was to propose and carry a vote of thanks to Mr. Butler, declaring at the same time that Dr. Milner's charge of being a false brother was a

[1] Husenbeth, in his "Life of Milner," p. 236, after mentioning that the bishop was called upon to designate whom he meant by "false brethren," says, "Dr. Milner at once declared that he had referred to Mr. Charles Butler." These words might include a very formal and solemn designation of a "false brother," so I have preferred to give the designation in the actual and very characteristic words and manner in which it was made.

"gross calumny." This was immediately followed by another resolution which, indeed, was the resolution all along intended, and which the bishop had been invited to the meeting on purpose to hear. Husenbeth gives it in these words: "That Dr. Milner cease to be a member of the private board or select committee appointed by the general Board of British Catholics."[1] This also was, of course, carried. I cannot say "unanimously carried," for two gentlemen, whose names will shortly appear, voted against this and the previous resolution. This sentence of exclusion, Milner also tells us, "he listened to with temper." There certainly are occasions when an insult, from its extreme grossness and injustice, serves more to steady than to excite the object of it. This seems to have been the case on the present occasion. Milner rose from his seat, and, standing at the table, took from his pocket a protest which he had previously prepared and read it, in the following words:—"My Brief Memorial was not published on behalf of the present company of sixty-five persons, nor of their constituents, they not being chosen to represent any other Catholics, nor does it profess to speak their sentiments. In short, I have spoken and acted on behalf of thirty bishops, and of more than five millions of Catholics, whom the bill concerns, and whose religious business I am authorized to transact." Dr. Milner, having read this protest, left the table; and, to use his own words, "moving to the door, instead of acting as he was authorized by his Master to act, on such an occasion, Matt. x. 14" (that is, instead of shaking the dust off his feet against them), "he satisfied himself with saying, 'I hope you will not turn me out of the Catholic Church, nor shut me out of the kingdom of heaven.'" Then, as he was on the point of leaving the

---

[1] "Life of Milner," p. 236.

room, he turned round and said his last words to his persecutors : " Gentlemen, you consider me unfit for your company on earth, may God make me fit for your company in heaven." Having said these words, the bishop left the room, followed, to their eternal honour, by Mr. Bodenham, of Rotherwas, and Mr. Weld, of Lulworth. In relating Milner's parting words, Mr. Bodenham used to say, " Then it was I saw that Milner was a saint."[1] Husenbeth says that Milner's conduct on that memorable occasion was described to him by one who was present as the grandest feature in his career. "If," said his informant, whose name he does not give, "I ever witnessed a manifestation of heroic fortitude inspired by religion, it was upon that occasion."

Such was the expulsion of Milner from the Catholic Board. Amongst Catholics it was spoken of at the time as "the Milner baiting."

As Milner's " Supplementary Memoirs " have been

[1] Mr. Weld was afterwards Cardinal Weld. With regard to Milner's words as he was moving to the door, I have followed what he himself, in the "Supplementary Memoirs," says they were. Husenbeth says that he began the sentence with the words, " You may expel me from this board ; but I hope," etc., etc. And Husenbeth says that he has often heard Milner repeat the words. The words which were traditional amongst Catholics many years ago, as having been used by Milner, were : "I thank God, gentlemen, that you cannot exclude me from the kingdom of heaven." These words are, it seems to me, more like what Milner might have been expected to say, than the words which he himself tells us he said ; and it may be added that the "Supplementary Memoirs " were written seven years after this meeting. With regard to the words which he said when he turned round just as he was leaving the room, I give them on the authority of Mr. Bodenham, who was present, and who frequently repeated them to Mr. Berington. It is hardly likely that Mr. Bodenham's memory would have failed him in a matter like this, especially when considering the special effect produced upon him by the words. For there was nothing in the first words, as the bishop was moving to the door, to prove extraordinary sanctity ; whereas the humility and charity implied in the words spoken as he was going to leave the room, certainly touched the heroic : nor is the fact that Milner does not mention these words any proof that he did not say them. He must have known that the mention of them would be self-praise, which he would have been the last man to put in print.

many years out of print, the reader will no doubt be glad to have, in the great bishop's own words, his comment on the disgraceful proceeding, and the recital of what afforded him consolation under the infliction. He writes as follows:—
"Thus ended this unparalleled scene of inconsistency and violence, which stands briefly thus. A society of Englishmen, having formed themselves to petition the Legislature against oppression and the denial of their civil rights, fall foul of their fellow-Englishman for exercising the common right of subjects, that of representing his case to Parliament! And, again, it stands thus. A society of Catholics, acknowledging their bishops to be the divinely constituted judges and guardians of their religion, publicly insult and persecute a bishop for doing his duty in these particulars! The writer's claim to speak on behalf of the prelates and Catholic millions of the kingdom was very soon justified. On the very day, and at the very hour, that about two dozen[1] out of an assembly of sixty-five Catholics were trying to disgrace Dr. Milner for defending the common religion, the bishops of Ireland, to the number of twenty-seven, being synodically assembled, were passing a vote of approbation in his favour, too lofty to be here inserted. Shortly after this the laity of Dublin, being assembled to the number of four thousand, bestowed upon him equal commendations; whose example was quickly followed by numerous other Catholic assemblies throughout other parts of Ireland. After this came an address of thanks to the writer from Liverpool, signed by above four thousand names. But what was of far greater consequence than all these praises was the decision of the above-mentioned prelates respecting the bill, three days before their commendatory resolution. In this they declare that 'certain

---

[1] This seems to imply that the majority allowed themselves to be ruled by a pugnacious minority.

ecclesiastical clauses or securities contained in the bill are utterly incompatible with the discipline of the Catholic Church,' and that they 'cannot assent to those regulations without incurring the heavy guilt of schism.'"[1]

The vote of approbation by the bishops of Ireland, which Milner says was too lofty to be inserted, was worded as follows:—"Resolved that the Right Rev. Dr. John Milner, Bishop of Castabala, our vigilant, incorruptible agent, the powerful and unwearied champion of the Catholic religion, continues to possess our esteem, our confidence, and our gratitude."[2]

On the 15th of June, a large meeting of the Catholics of Dublin was held in that city, and on the motion of O'Connell, who had been for about three years the acknowledged leader of the Catholics, a vote of thanks was passed to Dr. Milner, "for his manly, upright, and conscientious opposition" to the bill. In passing this vote, the whole assembly rose with loud demonstrations of applause, and Husenbeth, who, like Macaulay, enters into the particulars of such scenes, adds that "all hats were waved, and the ladies waved their handkerchiefs and curtsied in token of approbation."[3] Many other towns in Ireland followed the example of Dublin, each assembling to thank Milner for his services. The Catholics of the United Kingdom might have been divided, in 1813, into two parties. On one side was the greater part of the English Catholic and Irish aristocracy ; who else was with them does not now appear. Some day, no doubt, it will be known whether they were alone or not. On the other side was Milner, the bulk, perhaps the whole, of the English middle class, and the hierarchy and people of Ireland. After Dr. Poynter had written to Milner to say that he did not know what Mr.

---

[1] " Supplementary Memoirs," pp. 212, 213.
[2] Husenbeth, p. 237.   [3] " Life of Milner," p. 237.

Canning's clauses were, none of the vicars apostolic of Great Britain, with the exception of Milner, appear on the scene. I will conclude this account with a somewhat artful observation of Milner, with which he finishes his notice of the meeting I have described. He says it is remarkable that Mr. Butler should make no allusion whatever to this meeting in his " Historical Memoirs," especially considering that the gentlemen present at it passed a vote of thanks to himself.[1]

[1] In a subsequent edition of the "Historical Memoirs," Mr. Butler published a short account of the meeting. When this chapter first appeared in *Catholic Progress*, one of the Catholic weekly newspapers spoke of it as " not very edifying." This criticism appears to me to cover the account of the sufferings of any confessor for the faith or discipline of the Church ; indeed, it might extend much further, and be applied to the atrocious and murderous conduct of Messrs. Fitzurse, Tracy, de Moreville, and Brito in Canterbury Cathedral, on the 29th of December, in the year of our Lord 1170. Most of us, I presume, have been accustomed to think that the utility of reading the sufferings of a confessor is to be judged by the cause for which he has suffered, and by his behaviour under his sufferings ; and that they are not less edifying because we have to read at the same time the disedifying behaviour of those who were the persecutors. Milner was a confessor for the discipline of the Church ; for the same cause St. Thomas was a martyr. I should not have thought it worth while to notice the above criticism, except for the reason that it seems to be a symptom of that revulsion from the heroic which is one characteristic of the present generation.

CHAPTER XXI.

THE GRAND ATTACK ON MILNER.

The second meeting of the bishops at Durham—Milner's character.

DR. MILNER'S life and the history of Catholic emancipation are, at the time about which we are reading, so closely connected, that one cannot be separated from the other. The great question at this time, and for some years longer, was the question of the veto ; that is, what security for the loyalty of the bishops could be tolerated. History has proved that no security was needed. If any security had been given, it would merely have been the price of liberties which we were as much entitled to as all the other subjects of the Crown. If the conditions asked of us had been such as would not in any way have infringed upon the discipline of the Church, still they would have been unnecessary and degrading. But the conditions actually demanded were such that the Irish bishops decided, as we have seen, that they could not assent to them without incurring the heavy guilt of schism.

Milner was of the same opinion ; and he spoke in England not only for himself, but for all the bishops of Ireland. He opposed to the utmost of his power every endeavour to obtain emancipation on conditions of which the Church could not willingly approve. He was therefore directly opposed to all those Protestants who were in favour of emancipation accompanied with securities, and to all those over-eager Catholics who would have surrendered the rights of the Church in an important matter, in order to enjoy the liberty of sitting in the Houses of Parliament, and to possess the rights to which as Englishmen they were entitled. In the eyes, therefore, of these, both Catholics and Protestants, Milner stood as the head and front of the offence.

Hitherto Milner and his cause had been victorious. But those to whom he was opposed were able and determined men. They were not inclined to give up their cause because so far they had not been successful. Milner, on his side, was not a man likely to surrender or to cease fighting. The time had not arrived when a younger man, and a layman, loyal to the Church, was to appear upon the scene, and, with a strong political power to back him, was to force on the question of emancipation freed from conditions which interfered with ecclesiastical discipline. Ten years had to elapse before O'Connell should form his Catholic Association. Milner then was an old man. He had earned his laurels. The strength of his arm was not needed in the fray when, sixteen years after the time I am writing of, the great political Hercules, wielding his gigantic political club, bore down upon bigots and vetoists, and forced a way for himself and his followers to places from which Catholics had been so long shut out.[1]

In the mean time the war was to continue. The position of Milner had been greatly strengthened by the proceedings in Parliament, and the failure of the bill of 1813. He was strongly entrenched behind justice and the rights of the Church. He had no reason for quitting

[1] In using the word "club," no play upon the word was intended; but the reader is perfectly welcome, if he pleases, to take the word in its double sense.

his stronghold. An attack had therefore to be made upon him; and the attack was made. It was, to use a military phrase, an attack in force; fire was opened upon him along the whole line. Who was the schemer by whom the plan of attack was arranged or originally proposed, does not at present appear. It may have originated in one mind, or it may have simultaneously occurred to several. Although seventy-two years have elapsed since the year 1813, it may still be too soon to produce papers, if any exist, which would throw a light on what some future historian will undoubtedly ransack archives to discover. For all the important questions which have been debated amongst Catholics since the Reformation increase in importance as the Church gradually makes progress in England. But with whomsoever the plan of attack against Milner may have taken its rise, it was necessary that both clergy and laity should join in it.

To enter a little further into the particulars of Milner's position, I must note in the first place that the great bishop was strong in this—that he spoke for thirty other bishops. He was also strong in this—that he rejected every scheme of emancipation in which the principles of the Fifth resolution were to produce any effect. In the third place, he was strong because he was standing up for the rights of the Holy See; he was fighting in the cause of Rome. On each one, therefore, of these strong points of his position an attack was to be made. To weaken his authority as the spokesman of the Irish bishops, as many other bishops as possible must be got together to pronounce against him; to injure his influence in condemning the Fifth resolution, other bishops must be induced to support the principles of that resolution; to destroy the power which he had at Rome, as the defender of the rights of the Church, he must be denounced to Rome as a turbulent prelate, as a disturber of peace at home, and as one who was compromising the Holy See with an English Government willing to grant relief on reasonable terms. Such was the attack to be made upon Milner.

The reader will not object to have the plan repeated in a few words, written by Milner himself. "According to the present plan," he says, "there were three points to be carried: the first was to collect a synod of prelates, who by their number might in some degree equipoise the Irish prelature, for which purpose it was necessary to engage the two Scotch vicars apostolic to meet the three English vicars apostolic with their two coadjutors. The second was to get the parent stock of the late bill, namely, the Tavern Resolution, which had been censured by the thirty prelates, including the English agent, approved of and adopted by the British Synod. The last was, on the credit of this synod, to get the bill itself sanctioned by Monsignore Quarantotti, Secretary of the Propaganda, who, during the banishment of the Pope and cardinals from Rome, was supposed to possess sufficient authority for this purpose."[1]

With regard to the meeting of the bishops of Great Britain, in order to counteract the effect of the synodical action of the Irish prelates, a serious question arose as to the way in which the bishops should be got to meet together. In the days of the vicars apostolic, there was no such thing as a regular synod; and though Milner speaks of the meeting at Durham (of which I have now to give an account) as a "synod," it was only a *façon de parler* of what was, or rather would have been if all had been summoned, a *quasi* synod. A meeting of the vicars apostolic should have been, according to custom, summoned by the senior vicar apostolic. But the senior vicar apostolic,

[1] "Supplementary Memoirs," p. 214.

who was at this time Dr. Gibson, of the Northern District, could not well summon a meeting of the bishops without summoning all of them. It was determined that Milner should not be summoned: he was not to be invited; he was to be purposely excluded.[1] The object of the meeting was to thwart Milner, and therefore his presence would have been an embarrassment. Then, again, one of the vicars apostolic (Dr. Collingridge, of the Western District) had absolutely refused to meet Milner.[2] Moreover, it is very probable, indeed most probable, that some of the other vicars would have been glad to know that the doughty champion was not to make his appearance in the lists. But it was determined that there should be a meeting.

It was managed in this way: instead of being summoned to meet by the senior vicar apostolic, the bishops were severally to invite themselves to visit Dr. Gibson at Durham, at a time arranged amongst themselves. This was done, of course, behind the back of Dr. Milner. When Milner afterwards complained to the senior prelate that he had not been summoned in regular order by his lordship, Dr. Gibson wrote to Milner, and told him "that certain prelates wrote to tell him that *they were coming to pay him a visit* in the north, and that he could not refuse their company."[3] The difficulty as to the manner in which the bishops should be summoned having been got over in the way we have seen, there remained still another difficulty to be surmounted. Some of the British vicars apostolic might object to meet unless Milner were invited. But those who were equal to cope with the first difficulty were equal to cope with the second. There certainly was one British bishop who would

---

[1] Husenbeth, p. 242. [2] Ibid., 243.
[3] "Supplementary Memoirs," p. 215.

not knowingly join a meeting at which Milner was to be excluded. And it would appear from what Milner says, as I shall immediately quote, that there were more than one who would refuse to attend for the same reason. What, then, was to be done to secure a meeting?

The means were simple: the bishops who wished Milner to attend were to be given to understand that he would attend; and so they were given to understand. The reader may think this almost incredible. Whatever faults Milner may be charged with, most certainly deliberate falsehood was not one of them. In the opinion of some, his great fault was that he spoke truth too plainly. Nor was Milner a man who entertained animosity; angry passion never made him exaggerate. Yet, writing seven years after these events, he deliberately tells us in his "Supplementary Memoirs," that "certain other prelates, who made it the condition of their attending the meeting that the writer should be invited to it, were decoyed and imposed upon in that particular."[1] One of the bishops who had been decoyed and imposed upon was Dr. John Chisholm, Vicar Apostolic of the Highland District of Scotland. In a letter which he wrote to Milner after the meeting, Dr. Chisholm says, "Having only arrived here" (at Durham) "the night preceding, I was very much disappointed indeed when I did not find you here; having written to N.N. before I left home, expressing my most sincere wishes of your attending the meeting. On my arrival at Newcastle, I had the satisfaction to learn that you were here, and was only undeceived on my arrival. Though the Board had not used you as I wished, had not you a right to join your brethren wherever they happened to assemble? Agreeably to your request, I asked *why you had not been invited to this meeting*, and even took

[1] "Supplementary Memoirs," pp. 215, 216.

pen and ink to return you their precise answer. I received no explicit answer."[1]

Husenbeth says that when Dr. Gibson wrote to Milner to say that he could not refuse the company of the bishops, he at the same time assured Milner "that he had no objection whatever to his attendance."[2] And alluding to a passage in Dr. Poynter's "Apologetical Epistle," Husenbeth says, "Dr. Poynter adds that he himself had no objection to Dr. Milner's being present; but that it did not please the other bishops that he should be invited. Husenbeth then sums up the objectors as follows:—"This leaves," he says, "only Drs. Collingridge, Cameron,[3] and Smith[4] as objectors: for we have already seen that Drs. Gibson and Chisholm were not averse to Dr. Milner's attendance; and it can hardly be supposed that Dr. Smith would differ on the subject from his principal, Dr. Gibson. So that two only of the bishops probably objected, and perhaps only one, the Vicar Apostolic of the Western District."

In this summing up of Husenbeth's I cannot agree. I think it is against the weight of evidence. Dr. Poynter himself, as we have seen in his "Apologetical Epistle," which was expressly written for the information of Rome, says that "he had no objection to Dr. Milner being present, but that it did not please the other bishops that he should be invited." He does not say some of the other bishops, but "the other bishops." These words certainly mean all the other bishops, unless proof be forthcoming that there was an exception; and the words, "it did not please the other bishops" that he should be invited, also most clearly mean that they objected to his being invited. And

---

[1] "Supplementary Memoirs," p. 216.
[2] "Life of Milner," p. 244.
[3] Vicar Apostolic of the Lowland District of Scotland.
[4] Coadjutor to Dr. Gibson.

it may also be safely said that Dr. Poynter knew more about the whole proceeding than any other ecclesiastic knew.

With regard to Drs. Cameron and Smith, we have no evidence whatever except the words of Dr. Poynter, "the other bishops," to show what their wishes were. The only strong evidence we have, corroborated by the circumstances, that any one of the bishops was sincerely desirous that Milner should attend the meeting, is that which clearly shows that Dr. Chisholm, at least, was a lover of fair play.[1] By whomsoever the general plan of attack was devised, Husenbeth at any rate thinks that one of the vicars apostolic conceived the idea of the meeting at Durham. "The meeting," he says, "seems to have been projected by Dr. Poynter, and the prelates invited as early as August."[2]

Dr. Milner himself, in his "Supplementary Memoirs," does not venture to fix the blame of this particular attack on any one. He probably knew much more about it than he chose to publish. In introducing the matter, he speaks somewhat mysteriously. He says, "There always had been a party in the Board who were exceedingly desirous of following their pastors in matters of religion; but they, in fact, claimed to direct these pastors in the road by which they would be led; whereas our learned historian[3] and his little party with greater consistency took the crosier into their own hands on every occasion, and dictated equally to pastors and people new doctrinal oaths and resolutions, together with whatever changes of discipline it suited their

---

[1] But Milner says that "certain other prelates . . . made it the condition of their attending the meeting that the writer should be invited to it." It is not easy to reconcile the accounts. Perhaps the solution is that the Scotch bishops wished Milner to attend, and that the English bishops did not wish him to be present.

[2] "Life of Milner," p. 242.   [3] Mr. Butler.

politics to devise, without consulting with any ecclesiastical authority whatever. Whether the latter party yielded to the former spontaneously or by force is not known to the writer, nor does he know where or by what precise means it was planned to make ecclesiastical authority subservient to the purposes of worldly politics: all that he presumes to vouch for are the facts themselves, as they appeared in the face of the public, and all his reasoning on those facts is confined to the maxim of eternal truth: *The children of this world are wiser in their generation than the children of light* (Luke xvi. 8)." After these words, Milner begins the account of the plan of attack which I have quoted above.

As has been already noticed, the whole truth of this passage of history has most probably not yet come to light. A good deal must be left to surmise. "It was a suspicious circumstance," as Husenbeth remarks, "that the so-named Catholic Board had engaged to pay the expenses of the prelates who attended this meeting; though this engagement was not entirely fulfilled, for Dr. Chisholm complained that he was out of pocket."[1] It can, indeed, hardly be doubted that some members of the Board were connected with this attempt to ruin the influence of Milner. When the whole history of the battle, so far as it is known, shall have been before the reader, he will probably think that more heads than one were engaged in the plan of attack. Considering all the circumstances, it may be said to be probable that a very clever and a very determined lawyer, in conference with a very clever, pliant, and amiable bishop, decided upon the plan. I cannot assert this on positive knowledge. Some future historian may perhaps discover that Mr. Charles Butler and Dr. Poynter did not originate this combined attack upon the illustrious champion of religious liberty.

[1] "Life of Milner," p. 242.

According to arrangement, the vicars apostolic of Great Britain, with the exception of Milner, met at Durham towards the end of October in the year 1813. It is not my intention to enter into all that was done at the meeting, nor to enter into the subsequent differences between Bishops Milner and Poynter with more minuteness than will be necessary to follow the history of Catholic emancipation. This meeting, as might be supposed from the manner in which it was got up, led to no good, and to so little evil that Canon Flanagan, in his "History of the Church in England," does not even allude to it. Dr. Gibson, the senior vicar apostolic, issued a pastoral immediately after the meeting. It was dated the 27th of October; and on the 17th of November following, Dr. Poynter, adopting the pastoral of Dr. Gibson, published it for the London District.[1] The pastoral treated chiefly of the bill of 1813 and the Fifth resolution. Although Dr. Poynter professed to adopt the pastoral of Dr. Gibson, Dr. Milner expressed his belief that in reality it was originally composed by Dr. Poynter himself. This joint pastoral explains and justifies the Fifth resolution. In consequence of this and of other matters contained in the pastoral, Dr. Milner wrote an "Encyclical Letter" dated November 22, 1813. It was addressed to Catholics of the Midland District; but was not intended to be read publicly from the altar. In this letter Milner says he considers the joint pastoral of Bishops Gibson and Poynter to be a fresh attack upon the unanimous decision of the Irish bishops against the Fifth resolution, which it even renews and eulogizes. Dr. Poynter, in his once famous "Apologetical Epistle," complains that Dr. Milner had

---

[1] Vide Husenbeth's "Life of Milner," p. 245, *et seq.*, from which the account of the meeting and of the pastorals and Milner's "Encyclical Letter" is chiefly taken.

asserted that it was "a principal business of the Episcopal meeting to renew the Fifth resolution in opposition to the decisions of the Catholic prelates in Ireland on September 14, 1808, and Feburary 26, 1810." Dr. Milner afterwards retracted this assertion as made in the words just mentioned. But the reader has seen that, whether in opposition to the Irish bishops or not, the meeting did, as a matter of fact, justify and even eulogize the Fifth resolution. Milner, in his "Encyclical Letter," also complained of the indiscriminate praise bestowed in the pastoral upon the laity for "the Christian and Catholic sentiments which they have uniformly proclaimed, and for their willingness to refer all terms of emancipation of a religious nature to the judgment and decision of their pastors." Milner very justly, as the reader will most probably think, says that the public at large and the gentlemen themselves will understand their praises as "applying to those who, under the name of 'Protesting Catholic Dissenters,' endeavoured to force a heterodox oath upon the Catholic body, and who, under that of the *Cisalpine Club, professed to restrain the usurpation of the Pope* and the tyranny of the vicars apostolic, and who, lastly, having formed themselves into a *board of finance*, have laboured to give *securities to the Established Protestant Church*, and lately advertised against me in the most affronting terms for saving them from the actual guilt of schism." Milner also complains that the bill of 1813, which the Irish bishops and he himself had declared to contain clauses which could not be consented to "without the heavy guilt of schism," should be dismissed in the pastorals merely with an expression of "sorrow that it contained restrictions which," they say, "we cannot give our approbation or consent to, and which a British subject would feel a natural repugnance to submit to." It must be acknowledged that this very amiable and patriotic expression of opinion was, under the circumstances, very considerably wanting in energy and force.

With regard to the meeting itself, Milner condemned it and disposed of it in one word. He called it a *conciliabulum*. "After all," he writes in his "Supplementary Memoirs,"[1] "this far-fetched assembly was demonstratively not a *Canonical Synod*, but a party meeting, irregularly and fraudulently collected together, or, as theologians express it, a 'Conciliabulum.'" He justifies the use of this term on the grounds that it was not properly summoned, that he was not invited, though certain bishops made it a condition of attending that he should be invited. He was afterwards accused at Rome of having made use of this term Conciliabulum when he should not have done so. It was argued that there could be no such thing as a Conciliabulum in England, because there could be no such thing as a Council or Synod. He was, therefore, reproached with showing ignorance of canon law. Even Husenbeth seems inclined to think that Dr. Milner should not have called the meeting a Conciliabulum, for he says, "Granting, however, that Dr. Milner went too far in applying to a meeting of vicars apostolic those rules of canon law which refer only to canonical synods of bishops in ordinary, he had still ample cause to complain of being excluded."[2]

It certainly appears to me that Husenbeth to a certain extent deserts his hero in this passage when he might so easily have defended him. Milner probably knew as much about canon law as any bishop or priest in England; at any rate, he knew enough to know that, as there was no hierarchy in England, there could be no canonical synod. What he meant by using the obnoxious phrase was clearly this—that what a conciliabulum is to a council, that a

[1] p. 215.   [2] "Life of Milner," p. 244.

meeting of some of the vicars apostolic to the deliberate exclusion of one of them, when affairs relating to the whole country are to be discussed, is to a meeting of the vicars apostolic when all are summoned according to ancient and universal custom. Milner, therefore, protested against the meeting, "and against all the acts of it as null and void."[1] Certain it is that nothing done at that meeting could in any way bind Milner or fetter his action in the slightest degree. Indeed, with the exception of what he gathered from the two pastorals, he does not seem to have troubled himself about what passed at Durham. Thus we have seen that two of the three combined attacks which had been agreed upon were made. A meeting of the vicars apostolic was held to his exclusion, and at that meeting the Fifth resolution was upheld and defended. The reader will not be surprised to hear that no one ever for a moment looked upon the Durham meeting as raising "even in the estimation of a hair" the scale which contained the condemnation of the Fifth resolution by the Irish bishops. The attack at these two points most completely failed.

The third assault, as the reader will remember, was to undermine the reputation of Milner at Rome. The result of this action I must reserve for the next chapter.

We may stop here for a moment to consider why it was that Milner held the position which he did in the year 1813: how it came to pass that, as Husenbeth says, Dr. Milner had to defend single-handed the sacred interests of religion in England, and "to struggle for the safety of Catholic discipline in the face of open persecution on the part even of those who should have fought resolutely by his side."[2]

The fact is that Milner had an essentially orthodox

[1] "Life of Milner," p. 243. [2] Ibid., p. 250.

mind. I do not for a moment, of course, mean to insinuate that the other vicars apostolic at the time were not orthodox. But as a bishop or any other member of the Church may possess what I may call an ecclesiastical mind, without possessing it in the intense degree and with the all-pervading influence as it existed in the mind, for instance, of St. Gregory the Great; so a man may be orthodox without having that instinctive inclination to orthodoxy which makes the possessor instantly detect the most remote danger to the sacred treasure which he has in charge.[1]

They who have been engaged in the education of youth, and they who have been accustomed to direct others in matters of conscience, well know what a difference exists in the minds of men with regard to the perception of evil. There are some who cannot see evil until it is close upon them in unmistakable form. There are others who spy from afar the first movement of evil in their direction; and while another can see nothing, they see it just as, looking through a telescope, they might perceive an object in the distance by chance passing across the glass. What in this respect is true of morals is true also of doctrine. There is no doubt that, in matters of doctrine, some people are very short-sighted and others are very long-sighted. There are in the Catholic Church some who fight a good fight and keep the faith to the end; but during all their lives they have had a difficulty in squaring their ideas with the Church's measure, or, to change the simile,

---

[1] This sensitively orthodox mind has been noticed in St. Ignatius of Loyola: it is evident to those who have studied his Exercises; and Bouhours, speaking of the effect which the companionship of Ignatius had upon Francis Xavier, says that Xavier might perhaps have lost the faith if he had not fallen into the hands of a companion of the character of Ignatius, who abhorred everything which seemed like heresy, and who had an admirable discernment for recognizing heretics under whatsoever masks they might appear.—"Vie de S. François Xavier," vol. i.

in raising or lowering their note to the Church's pitch. It is a fact that there are some people so insensible in the matter of music, that they cannot perceive the difference between "God save the Queen" and "Rule Britannia." And as in melody so in harmony: harmony is a thing altogether beyond the perception of some people. So it is in matters touching faith and discipline: some will catch at once the mind of the Church; others can hardly perceive it, though it is placed clearly before them. In matters of faith and discipline the mind of Milner was most beautifully attuned to the grand note which the Church sounds through the world: he instantly perceived the slightest discord, he could detect the slightest variation from the proper pitch. This great quality, which Milner possessed, shows itself in all that he said and wrote and did. Milner had a great devotion to the Blessed Virgin Mary. This was evidenced, amongst other things, by his placing Oscott College, as soon as it came into his possession, under the protection of the Great Mother of God. Our Blessed Lady is addressed by the Church in her office in these words: "Thou alone hast destroyed all heresies in the whole world." It would seem that his great patroness had obtained for Milner that he should be a valiant helper in the use of this her privilege; and that she had also obtained for him that, in combating for the faith, he should have a large share of that gift which makes her "terrible as an army set in array." And this brings me to other qualities which Milner possessed, and which were necessary in the position in which he stood. He had the power and he had the will to be a stout champion of the truth. It would not be true to say that he was of a combative disposition, for that would imply that he loved fighting for fighting's sake. So far from being combative, he naturally loved nothing more than to be left alone to read and write. He loved peace; but "peace with honour." When circumstances called upon him to fight, there was no man who rushed into the fray with greater eagerness and greater bravery than he did. With this sensitiveness in everything which regarded doctrine and discipline, accompanied by the chief qualities required in one who has to keep guard over them in the time of danger, there was in Bishop Milner a total absence of human respect. If occasion required it, he could and did speak to a lord with twenty thousand a year in the same plain terms which he would use towards the poorest person in the congregation at Winchester or Wolverhampton.

But Milner had a fault—a small fault, if compared with what Father Faber, adopting an American expression, would call his "tall virtues," but still a fault—which made him enemies amongst more polished men, which was constantly getting him into scrapes, and which endangered the success of his gallant efforts when he was entirely in the right and those who were offended by him were entirely in the wrong. This was the fault which Dr. Weedall put so well and so delicately when, as I have mentioned in a former chapter, he said that Milner "undervalued the little etiquettes of society." In his fight for orthodoxy and union and discipline, Milner had to suffer both for his virtues and for his faults. The possession of a virtue or of a good quality, especially if it be possessed in an eminent degree, may itself be the cause of great suffering. For instance, if a person is naturally very compassionate, feeling intensely the suffering of others, the possession of this virtue must often cause great suffering to the owner of it, and even to such an extent that he may be more worthy of compassion than the object of his own compassion. In the same way, if a person has a very strong sense of justice, or if he has a quick perception of what trenches even by a hair's breadth upon that ground which is unknown to angels and forbidden to man, it is impossible that he should be able to pass through life without an immense amount of suffering which less sensitive people never feel. So Milner had to suffer, and to suffer much, because he possessed in an eminent degree what I have called an orthodox mind. He could detect the remotest suspicion of heresy or of schism long before any positive act of heresy or of schism had been committed. Therefore, having to work for emancipation with men, some of whom were Protestants lamentably ignorant of the dogmas and rights of the Church, others of whom were Catholics willing to surrender whatever they possibly could in order to obtain their civil rights, he must have lived in a continual state of anxiety and pain; for during the whole of his life from the year 1778, when he was twenty-six years of age, until the year 1826, when he died, the great battle for emancipation was being fought. With regard to the fault which he had, and which I have alluded to, probably the mere possession of it did not cause him much suffering, for the reason that he would hardly perceive it to be a fault. And though, weighed in the balances of men, undervaluing the little etiquettes of society is a fault, we may say with reverence that, weighed in the balance of the Sanctuary, it perhaps is none. But for this fault he was made to suffer by others: so often, unfortunately, does suavity of manner with a bad cause carry the day over brusqueness with a good cause.

The reader will pardon the amount of space which is given in this part of the history to the character of Milner; for it is a superficial reading of history not to dwell upon those characters, the study of which teaches a lesson. I believe it may be said with truth that no man has existed amongst English Catholics, during the last two hundred years, who during the last fifty years has been so often and so widely held up as a model in those matters which concern the public action of Catholics, as Bishop Milner.

In concluding these remarks upon Milner, I may allude to one other quality which he possessed, and which enabled him to bear the irritating conduct of others. He had the great and most enviable gift of strong nerves. A man of weaker nerves, however good his principles might have been, would have sunk, as many have sunk, under what Milner had to endure; but gifted as he was with the *mens sana in corpore sano*, he laboured on through all. If obedience ordered him to retire, he retired: when left free to act, as occasion required, he either stood his ground firmly under attack, or carried the war into the enemy's country. And thus he went bravely on through life, maintaining the right against all-comers, until, in his declining years, the great man of all in the cause of emancipation arose, who, unlike the men who deal in blows in these days, with one legitimate blow brought Protestant England to her knees.

CHAPTER XXII.

THE GRAND ATTACK ON MILNER (*continued*)—THE ATTEMPT TO DISCREDIT HIM IN ROME.

Monsignore Quarantotti—The Quarantotti rescript—Milner's journey to Rome—Milner in Rome—Address of the English Catholic Board to Pope Pius VII.—Pope Pius' answer to the address.

WHO, was Monsieur Quarantotti? Such was the question asked more than forty years ago by a young man who was lolling on a sofa reading, while four of his seniors were playing at whist in the same room. A game was just finished, and the question was received with a general burst of laughter. The young man who had put the question supposed that his friends were laughing at his ignorance. But what Catholic young man of twenty years old did then know who Monsieur Quarantotti was? The fact is, that the mention of the name suddenly brought to the recollection of the elders the memory of wordy battles and angry disputes amongst English Catholics in the stormy times when they were divided upon the Veto Question. Between twenty and thirty years had passed since the name of Quarantotti had the power to cause an instantaneous commotion amongst a party of British or Irish Catholics. But a calm had succeeded; and the name could now only raise good-natured merriment at the remembrance of the power which it at one time possessed. Each of the men who were at the whist-table appealed to one of the others to tell their young friend who Monsieur Quarantotti was. But it was voted that the explanation would at that moment be a great deal too long. One of the party engaged to answer the question when the party should have been broken up. Accordingly, when the question was afterwards repeated, the answer received was that Monsieur Quarantotti was a Roman monsignore who had written a letter which had set the Catholics of the United Kingdom by the ears.[1]

As no doubt the Catholic young men of these days are not very well up in the great Quarantotti disputes, and as it was a remarkable episode in the history of emancipation, it may be as well to answer as precisely as I can the question, Who was Monsignore Quarantotti? In a former chapter it was stated that Monsignore Quarantotti was secretary to the Propaganda. Canon Flanagan says that the monsignore was secretary and vice-prefect of the Propaganda;[2] Husenbeth calls him the pro-prefect of the Propaganda.[3] What is the precise difference between a vice-prefect and a pro-prefect need not be here discussed: the main thing to be established at starting is that the monsignore was neither Pope nor Prefect of the Propaganda. We advance a step further in our knowledge of Monsignore Quarantotti, when we see that, in his "Supplementary Memoirs," Milner speaks of him as "this pious and well-meaning secretary."[4] The reader may be pretty sure that when Milner calls a man with whom he has to transact Catholic business, "pious and well-meaning," the inevitable "but" is about to appear. It will appear in the course of this history. It will be well now to explain how

---

[1] The questioner no doubt committed a gross blunder in saying *Monsieur* and not *Monsignore* Quarantotti. But the fact is that in those days Englishmen were not so familiar with monsignori as they are now. The young man had certainly never seen a monsignore, and I doubt if he had ever heard of one.
[2] "History of the Church in England," vol. ii. p. 432.
[3] "Life of Milner," p. 243.   [4] p. 217.

it came to pass that Quarantotti held the position which he did in Rome. The holy confessor Pope Pius VII. had been a prisoner in the hands of Napoleon I., from the 6th of July in the year 1809; from the 10th of August in that year he was in prison at Savona. His place of confinement was afterwards changed. The Emperor had the Holy Father removed to Fontainebleau, where he arrived on the 19th of June, 1812. In the month of January, 1814, Napoleon released Pope Pius from captivity; and on the 23rd of that month his Holiness left Fontainebleau; but he did not arrive in Rome until the 24th of May, when, as the Roman Breviary recites the event, it came to pass that, the whole world greatly rejoicing, and as it were by the hands of all people, he was restored to the Pontifical throne. *Contigit ut ingenti plausu, ac veluti universi orbis manibus pontificio solio restitueretur.*

During the captivity of the Pope all the Cardinals had been expelled from Rome. From, therefore, the introduction of the Relief Bill of 1813 into the House of Commons until the 24th of May, 1814, there was neither Sovereign Pontiff nor Cardinal Prefect of the Propaganda in Rome. But as it was absolutely necessary for the carrying on of the routine business of the Church that some ecclesiastical authority should exist in the Holy City, the Emperor allowed a monsignore to remain for that purpose. Quarantotti, the secretary to the Propaganda, was appointed to the office, and, Canon Flanagan says, "was the only ecclesiastical authority left in Rome."[1]

The question now arises: What power had Monsignore Quarantotti in the government of the Church? Mr. Butler says that Pope Pius VII. "had invested Quarantotti with all the ecclesiastical and spiritual powers of the see of

[1] "History of the Church in England," vol. ii. p. 432.

Rome, the appointment of the episcopal order alone excepted."[1] Had such really been the case, his powers would have been great indeed. But Mr. Butler very considerably overrated Quarantotti's authority. Had the secretary to the Propaganda possessed all the powers attributed to him by Butler, he might have written a letter to an English vicar apostolic sanctioning the provisions of the bill of 1813. He did write such a letter, as we shall presently see; and the Holy Father told Dr. Milner that "Monsignore Quarantotti ought not to have written that letter without authority from the Holy See." Therefore Quarantotti had no authority in himself to write the letter; and therefore he did not possess all the power which Butler says he did. "The fact is," says Milner, "he (Quarantotti) had only the *ordinary powers* of the congregation, but was not authorized to change the canonical discipline of the Church of Ireland or the pontifical regulations of the English mission."

Having seen what the secretary's powers really were, we must now see what he actually did. But before coming to the famous rescript which fell like a bombshell amongst the Catholics of the United Kingdom, the reader must be told of another letter which the secretary wrote, which was a sort of *avant-courier* to the more celebrated rescript. In his "Supplementary Memoirs,"[2] Milner has the following passage:—"The writer had received a letter, dated February 15, 1813, from this pious and well-meaning secretary" (that is, of course, Quarantotti), "containing a catalogue of complaints, which had been forwarded to him from England, respecting certain differences between the writer and one of his brethren. These are detailed in his, unanswerable hitherto,[3] but unpublished work, 'The

---

[1] "Historical Memoirs," vol. ii. p. 196, edition of 1819.
[2] pp. 317, 318.
[3] The reader will remember that this was written in the year 1820.

Explanation with D. P.'[1] The secretary's letter was satisfactorily answered by the twenty-nine prelates of Ireland, in their synodical epistle of November 12, 1813, addressed to the then prefect of the Congregation, Cardinal di Pietro."[2] It is not necessary to enter here more particularly into the differences between Dr. Milner and Dr. Poynter. Dr. Poynter was, in the universal opinion of all who knew him, an amiable and polished man. But sometimes amiable and polished men can, when they put pen to paper, write very strongly. It is surprising what hard words can be written by persons whose spoken thoughts are such dulcet sounds that they suggest the idea vulgarly expressed in the saying, "Butter would not melt in their mouths."

Thus, while Milner was defending the Church in England with vigorous action and plain speaking, amiability was writing very strong things against him to Rome. If all that had been written to Quarantotti was confined to a personal attack upon Milner, it would not have caused the great bishop much anxiety; for he had a good cause and broad shoulders, and could easily have borne a rebuke. But we have seen that the third attack upon Milner's position was to lessen his influence in Rome, in order that the approbation of the Holy See might be more easily obtained for the bill of 1813. Dr. Poynter accordingly wrote to Rome to induce Quarantotti to approve of the bill. But a mere letter to Rome does not always produce much effect, unless it be backed up with the influence of some one present in the Holy City. Dr.

[1] Doctor Poynter.
[2] Milner gives the epistle in his "Supplementary Memoirs.". As the English vicar apostolic was writing to Quarantotti in Rome because he was in charge of the affairs of the Church, I am unable to explain why the Irish bishops should have written to Cardinal di Pietro. It does not appear from the epistle where the cardinal was in November, 1813—not, I imagine, in Rome.

Poynter's letter, therefore, was not left alone to attain its end. The means employed to support Dr. Poynter's letter were not creditable. Before mentioning them, I must say that I do not believe Dr. Poynter was mainly answerable for what was chiefly objectionable in the means used to influence Quarantotti. Dr. Poynter, no doubt, knew the chief actor in what I am about to mention, and approved of his action in general; but it is impossible to believe that he would have sanctioned all that was done. In a matter like this, when the character of others is concerned, I prefer to state the matter in the words of those who are competent authorities rather than in my own. At the risk, therefore, of a little repetition, I will quote a passage from Husenbeth's "Life of Milner"—a passage which will surprise those who have not already read it, and which ought to put all upon their guard.

"The partisans of the schismatical bill of 1813," says Husenbeth, "chagrined at its failure, and still eager for it to pass at least this year" (that is, 1814), "were anxious above all things to obtain some approval of it from the Holy See. The Pope was then a prisoner of Bonaparte at Fontainebleau; but it was thought that the secretary of the Propaganda, Monsignore Quarantotti, might be induced to give his sanction, and that he possessed the necessary powers delegated to him by the Sovereign Pontiff. Here the parties were under a serious mistake, for this secretary had only the *ordinary powers* of the Congregation. . . . Under this misapprehension, however, several letters were written to an agent in Rome, the Rev. P. Macpherson, President of the Scotch College, who, says Dr. Milner, 'through a series of gross falsehoods and malicious representations, which he professed to derive from high authority in England,'[1] fraudulently obtained

---

[1] "Supplementary Memoirs," p. 218.

a rescript in favour of the late bill from the unsuspecting good old man, a venerable prelate and afterwards a cardinal. . . .

"'Thus deceived,' continues Dr. Milner, 'in all the leading circumstances of the case, by letters which the Scotch agent professed to have received from the most respectable authority in England, . . . no wonder that the humane and pious old man should have been prevailed upon to outstep his authority and his province, and to sign his name to the document prepared for him.'[1] He had never even seen the bill, as Dr. Milner was informed by Cardinal Litta.[2] . . . The rescript itself," continues Husenbeth, "need not be given here, as it was irregular and of no authority from the beginning. It may be seen at length in Mr. C. Butler's 'Historical Memoirs of Catholics,' vol. iv., appendix, p. 518, and in the *Orthodox Journal* for 1814, p. 162. The sum of it was expressed in a single sentence, 'that the Catholics ought to receive and embrace with content and gratitude the law which was proposed last year for their emancipation, agreeably to the form received by us from your Lordship!' This refers to Dr. Poynter, to whom the rescript was addressed. Though dated at Rome, February 16, 1814, it did not reach England till the 28th of April."[3]

With regard to the words quoted above, when Milner says that the rescript was *prepared* for Monsignore Quarantotti, Canon Flanagan says, " Francis Plowden the barrister maintains that the rescript was both devised and 'modelled in the British metropolis.' His proofs, or rather collection of probabilities, are certainly remarkable."[4]

[1] "Supplementary Memoirs," p. 226.
[2] Ibid., additional notes, p. 335.   [3] "Life of Milner," pp. 268, 269.
[4] "History of the Church in England," vol. ii. p. 432, note, in which the reference is to Plowden's "Second Historical Letter to Sir J. C. Hippisley," p. 55 and *passim;* Paris, 1815.

It is now sixty-five years since Dr. Milner wrote and published the above account of the manner in which the secretary to the Propaganda was induced to approve of the bill of 1813. Forty-two years after the publication of the "Supplementary Memoirs," Husenbeth republished the account in his "Life of Milner." I am not aware that it has ever been contradicted. This passage of history shows what kind of information is sometimes conveyed to Rome, even on the most important affairs. The vetoists in this case obtained from the ecclesiastic who was left in charge of the affairs of the Church, his approbation by a rescript, of a measure declared by the whole Irish Hierarchy to be schismatical.

It is not necessary here, any more than in the "Life of Milner," to transcribe the particulars of the information which the "Scotch agent" said he had received from England. The reader may see it in Milner's "Supplementary Memoirs." It is on the very face of it worthless; but it is also amusing in its extreme absurdity : not a line of it reads like authentic history; the style of it would remind a reader in these days of *Punch's* "Essence of Parliament."

As we proceed with the history we shall see that the rescript was disavowed by the Holy Father. But in fact the rescript never was, in the technical sense of the word, "received" in the United Kingdom. To the vetoists in England it was, of course, a source of boasting and exultation ; to all other Catholics it was a matter of grief and sad reflection. But those who were staunch in their loyalty to the Holy See had this comfort, that it was not likely the rescript would ever be acted upon. It was, however, the cause of many disputes and angry words; it widened the breach between the two parties amongst us; and though it was speedily withdrawn, the fact of its having been sent was a source of contention for many years. The disputes to which the Veto Question gave rise were bad enough in England, but they were far worse in Ireland. The English Catholics were not a political power, and therefore there was no political power to be weakened by discord. It was far different in Ireland; the Irish were a strong political power; and at that time their power in the state was very materially weakened by their division on the Veto Question. Mr. Wyse, in his "Historical Sketch of the Catholic Association," says, writing about this matter, "The Irish Catholics were extremely divided: the clergy unanimously, and much the majority of the laity, still retained their opposition to the measure; but the aristocracy for the most part were favourable. . . . The dissensions of the body were seized and taken advantage of both by friends and opponents. Their friends in Parliament eulogized the measure; their enemies made it the *sine qua non* of their emancipation. . . . In 1812 and 1813," continues Mr. Wyse, "the same source of unavailing discord prevailed. Application was finally made to the Pope, and in his absence and detention in France, Monsignore, afterwards Cardinal, Quarantotti addressed, in 1814, his celebrated letter to Dr. Poynter, which, instead of calming, added only new fuel to their dissensions. Every bearing of the measure continued to be argued by Protestants and Catholics, both in and out of Parliament, with an acerbity scarcely known in the earliest discussions of the question. The anti-vetoists denounced, and the vetoists receded" (from the Irish Catholic Board). . . . "The very suspicion of vetoism was enough to blot the fairest actions and to render dubious the purest intentions. No compromise, no half-measure —an abjuration total and absolute of the obnoxious principle was alone accepted. The people became intolerant and despotic; reasoning was discarded. . . . The effect on the aristocracy was scarcely less pernicious. Instead of standing manfully at their posts and maintaining their opinions until they had been put to the test of sound logic and fair experience, and then nobly surrendering them if found inconsistent with public liberty and public good, they crept ingloriously away from the contest, and allowed themselves to be trampled into obscurity by numbers."[1]

Such was the state of things amongst the Irish Catholics after the rescript of Quarantotti. We have seen, as well as known facts enable us, how that rescript was obtained; the knowledge of it should produce its effect. Historical facts should teach a young man. To have the experience of others put before him is one of the tests to try whether a man is wise or foolish. A wise man will not wait to be taught by that personal "experience, which," to use an expression of Lord Brougham's, "is said to teach the most foolish of our foolish kind."

Monsignore Quarantotti's rescript in favour of the bill of 1813 having been obtained in the manner recounted, Dr. Milner determined at once to go to Rome and tell the truth. As Pope Pius had been liberated from captivity, Milner knew that on his arrival in the Holy City he should have to deal, not with a monsignore with limited powers, but with the Holy Father himself. He left Wolverhampton on May 2, 1814. "Landing on the opposite coast," he tells us in his "Supplementary Memoirs," "he passed through the several camps of the conquering armies from Boulogne to Parma—namely, the Russian, Prussian, Austrian, and English camps; and he viewed with horror the dire effects of war, which appeared throughout a great part of his journey—bridges broken

[1] Vol. i. pp. 181, *et seq.*

down, forests shot to shivers, villages laid in ruins, dead horses infecting the air, and human bodies floating down the rivers."[1] Milner arrived in Rome a few days after the Holy Father; that is, a few days after the ever memorable 24th of May, 1814. As regarded the main business on which he had made the journey, he found everything precisely as he could have wished. In his own characteristic style, he says, "Arriving at the Christian capital a few days after the Pope, he found all the four prelates and all the four theologians who had sanctioned the rescript, in disgrace and penance."[2] The disgrace and the penance were not only nor perhaps mainly on account of the rescript. "They had acted wrongly in that business," writes Milner, "for which they pleaded in excuse the wrong information they had received in the translated letters; and they had acted worse in taking the prohibited oath to the usurper, for which they had no excuse at all but human infirmity."[3] Pope Pius VII. seems to have been so offended with Monsignore Quarantotti, that, as Husenbeth says, "it was some time before he was admitted to the presence of his Holiness."[4] Quarantotti declined conversation with Milner on the subject of the letter of the 15th of February, 1813, and of the rescript. This, Milner says, "will be readily received." Milner must have felt very victorious when Quarantotti declined the conversation. But the other prelates and cardinals in Rome received Milner and conversed freely with him; "they were," as Milner says, "without exception, cheerful, communicative, and friendly."[5] While Quarantotti had to wait for

[1] Page 228. Milner's journey to Rome took place just after Napoleon had left France for Elba. The allies entered Paris on the 30th of March; Napoleon signed his abdication on the 11th of April, and left for Elba on the 26th. Louis XVIII. entered Paris on the 3rd of May, which was the day after Milner started for Rome.
[2] Ibid., pp. 228, 229. [3] Ibid. [4] "Life of Milner," p. 273.
[5] "Supplementary Memoirs," p. 229.

admission to the Holy Father, Milner was very soon admitted to an audience. Going into the presence of Pope Pius VII., Milner exclaimed, "As the hart panteth after the fountains of waters, so my soul hath panted to see your Holiness and kiss your feet." He was received by the Pope with more than his accustomed benevolence; his Holiness saying that he had heard much of him, and wished much to see him.[1] Pope Pius was not aware of the actual state of things in England regarding emancipation; for as soon as he had greeted Milner in the words recited above, he hastily exclaimed, "Has the Act of Parliament passed? Have the Catholics taken the oath?" The Pope then added the words already referred to: "He" (that is, Monsignore Quarantotti) "ought not to have written that letter without authority from the Holy See." To the questions of Pope Pius, Milner gave an answer showing the common sense and practical view which he took of the question of emancipation. "There is no question, Holy Father," he said, "about an oath or an Act of Parliament: the emancipation will take place; but not till there is a great change in his Majesty's counsels. In the mean time, schismatical measures have been carried on among our Catholics, as I am prepared to prove to your cardinals."[2] Milner then had some conversation with the Pope relating to the persons before whom his proofs were to be laid. On the restoration of Pope Pius VII., Cardinal Litta was made Prefect of the Propaganda, and before him, and some others joined with him, Milner was to expose his case. Cardinal Litta was a good and experienced man, and had already been employed in services requiring delicate management. The Pope spoke highly of him to Milner, and added that to his other qualifications, he possessed a knowledge of the English language.

[1] "Supplementary Memoirs," p. 229.   Ibid., pp. 229, 230.

As Milner's reception in Rome was, considering the position he held, an important event in the history of emancipation, and as it cannot be described better than in his own words, the reader will no doubt be pleased with the following extract from the "Supplementary Memoirs." Writing of himself in the third person, he says, "The writer had numerous interviews with this venerable cardinal" (that is, Cardinal Litta), "in one of the first of which he was directed to draw up a memorial of the whole case, to be laid before the Pope's council. This he executed in the course of two or three days, concluding his memorial in words to this effect: 'I know I have numerous and powerful enemies, Catholics as well as Protestants, whom I have provoked by my inflexibility in defending and securing our Holy Religion: if on this, or on any other account, the See Apostolic judge it to be for the advantage of religion that I should retire from my situation, I make an unreserved tender of resigning it.' A sufficient number of days for the examination of the memorial having elapsed, on the eve of SS. Peter and Paul's festival, the writer was summoned to an official audience, when he was assured that his *memorial had given great satisfaction, and that the writer of it was in high favour with the venerable College and the Holy Father himself; that he had well defended his cause and that of the Church, and this on its true ground;* finally, *that his resignation could not be accepted of.* On various other occasions it was signified to the writer, by the above-named and other personages of equal dignity, that *he had done his duty, and ought to proceed in the track he had hitherto pursued;* but it was added, that this *ought to be done with moderation, and without irritating the feelings of others.*"[1] Such is Milner's account of the reception of his

[1] "Supplementary Memoirs," pp. 230, 231. The italics in this passage are Milner's.

case in Rome: it was written six years after the event itself, and to it the sturdy champion of the Church appends the following note:—" In deference to so high an authority, the writer declares that if in defending the cause of religion, he should in any instance have exceeded the *moderamen justæ tutelæ*, he is sorry for it, and ready to make satisfaction to the injured party, at the discretion of an intelligent and conscientious arbiter, to be indifferently chosen. It appears to him that in the present work" (that is, the "Supplementary Memoirs," published in 1820) "and his other works, the writer has spared the character and feelings of his adversaries to the best of his power, with the exception of one domestic enemy of the Church, whom he despairs of reclaiming, and therefore thinks it his duty to disarm."[1]

From these extracts we see that Milner's view of the matters in dispute amongst English Catholics was the one taken in Rome; and further, that Milner's action in the cause was substantially approved of. The reader will see further proof of this later on. We also have another instance of the man substantially in the right, but accidentally in the wrong (so far as it is wrong to stand out for the right in an irritating way), offering to apologize to those who were substantially wrong, and indeed very wrong, but who spoke and did what was wrong in a manner polished and refined. How is it, I may, as on a former occasion, ask, that we have to look upon a spectacle of this kind? It is because the bold man was the humble man; because when in consequence of "undervaluing the little etiquettes of society" he had given pain, his first thought was to heal the wound which his

---

[1] The reader may here be reminded that Milner's "Supplementary Memoirs" were written in consequence of the publication, in 1819, of Charles Butler's "Historical Memoirs of the English, Irish, and Scotch Catholics."

inadvertence had caused. The "domestic enemy" whom Milner condemned to be still under his lash was, it may be presumed, Mr. Charles Butler. But Milner knew that Butler was a man well able to defend himself; and that the threat of Milner's continued severe criticism was not likely to produce such an alarming effect on the lawyer as to make it uncharitable to hold the prospect of it before him.[1]

We see also that Milner received a gentle reprimand from his superiors in Rome. He was told that he had done his duty, and that he ought to proceed in the way he had hitherto pursued; but at the same time that this was to be done with moderation and without irritating the feelings of others. This of course meant that he had not acted with moderation, and that he had unnecessarily irritated the feelings of others; otherwise the admonition would have been unreasonable. No doubt Milner felt this reproof; and though he submitted to it, as we have seen, with exemplary humility, and fully intended to act upon it, yet he must have known that it would be a very difficult thing for him to change his conduct. That the reproof must have caused him pain, that it was a sharp thorn in the crown of victory, we can easily conceive. If we imagine a general who by winning a great battle has for the time saved his country, received by his sovereign as such a man ought to be, honoured by a title and enriched by a pension, told that war is again imminent, and that he must fight other battles and win other victories, but at the same time admonished that he has

[1] If this history should advance to the year 1826, in which year Milner died, the writer, God willing, will dedicate a chapter to the consideration of Milner and Butler, when it will perhaps be seen that the two men had personally a great respect for each other, and that though they differed on a most vital question, there were points of resemblance between them which ought to be remembered as well as their contests.

been too hard with his officers and has unnecessarily irritated his men, we must suppose that he would retire from the royal presence in a state not completely satisfied. If such a man were conscious that the faults attributed to him were so connected with his natural disposition and his education that he would hardly be able to give an order, and certainly not one on the spur of the moment, without falling into the same faults again, he would undoubtedly feel a certain amount of discouragement, which would not be counteracted by the approbation of his deeds, but which would require very solid virtues in himself not to degenerate into disgust and despair. And so Milner in the midst of his triumph must have kept up his courage by the very highest motives, knowing, as he probably did by a bitter experience, that the uncatholic conduct of others would be far more irritating to him than any defect in moderation on his part could be to them.

It must not be supposed that the opponents of Milner in England were idle. On the 17th of June, 1814, a meeting of the General Board of British Catholics was held, at which an address to his Holiness Pope Pius VII. was voted. This address, which was signed on behalf of the meeting by the chairman and the secretary, was a long one, and, with the exception of one paragraph, an extremely good one. It may be found in Butler's "Historical Memoirs," and if part of it is to be read with shame, the greater portion of it may be perused with pride not only by an English Catholic, but by all Englishmen. But the objectionable paragraph is very bad. After speaking of the charges which Protestants bring against us, the paragraph proceeds to say—

"These imputations on our Church, from persons who had viewed her with those long-rooted prejudices which had prevented them from ever examining her doctrines, give us less pain, most

Holy Father, than the reproaches which were poured on us by some of our own brethren, who ceased not to accuse us as apostates and ready to sacrifice our faith to the acquisition of worldly advantages and for temporal to barter the eternal. . . . We were not affrighted by the menaces of those our bosom enemies."

When the resolution speaks of "some of our own brethren" and "our bosom enemies," if it alluded only to the action of Catholics in England, it might as well have used the singular number, and, pointing to Milner alone, have said "our own brother, our bosom enemy." But if the framers of the address meant to speak of the action of Catholics in the United Kingdom, " our own brethren" and "bosom enemies" included not Milner only, but the whole hierarchy of Ireland. If such was the meaning, a more monstrous thing was never written. It would be difficult to conceive a more daring compound of falsehood, presumption, and insolence than for those English Catholics who were for making unworthy concessions to the State, to give the name of "bosom enemies" to the staunch, the orthodox, the Catholic bishops of the Irish Church. The paragraph then goes on to mention "the unspeakable joy" with which the Catholic board "received the rescript" of Monsignore Quarantotti which approved of the bill of 1813; and concludes by expressing a confidence that, "on the return of his Holiness to the free exercise of his apostolic functions, they shall receive the assurance that these venerable depositories of his authority" (that is, Quarantotti and others) "during his captivity, have spoken the genuine and full sentiments of his Holiness' paternal heart towards the faithful of these countries." This resolution was passed in London when Quarantotti was doing penance in Rome for having amongst other things written the rescript alluded to—a singular instance of the truth of the saying,

"Man proposes, God disposes." The messenger chosen to take this letter to Rome and present it to Pope Pius was no other than the "Scotch agent" who had misrepresented to Monsignore Quarantotti the state of affairs in England. The agent had come to England with the rescript, and he was sent back again by the Catholic board, in order, as Milner tells us, to get the rescript renewed. The appointment of this particular messenger was a very impolitic measure on the part of the board; for they ought to have supposed that Milner would have exposed the fraud by which the rescript had been obtained. However, the address was presented to the Pope; but Milner says that Macpherson, "on his return to the Christian capital, had to digest many a severe mortification, in return for his agency."[1]

The address remained unanswered for six months; but at length the answer came, dated the 28th of December, 1814, though it did not reach England until February, 1815. In his answer, the Holy Father, after the thanks and congratulations which the first part of the address naturally elicited, proceeds to say—

"The rescript which, during our absence and the dispersion of our venerable council, was on the 16th of January last issued and sent to you by our beloved son the secretary of the Propaganda, inasmuch as it turns on a matter of the highest moment, we have given, as you already know, to those of the congregation of our venerable brethren, the cardinals, to whom matters of this nature are usually referred, in order to be examined by them maturely, and *ab integro*. We, however, entreat you to be persuaded that in this important matter we shall most willingly comply with your wishes, as far as the dignity, the purity, and the integrity of the Catholic religion will allow."[2]

Those members of the Catholic Board who had voted

[1] "Supplementary Memoirs," p. 234.
[2] Butler's "Historical Memoirs," vol. iv. p. 530, 2nd edition of 1822.

the address were in hopes that Pope Pius would immediately confirm the rescript of his "beloved son." The answer of his Holiness must have produced upon them much the same kind of effect which was produced upon the mayor and corporation of the City of London when, in answer to their loyal and "No-Popery" address in 1850, on the establishment of the Hierarchy, her gracious Majesty the Queen, after thanking them for their expressions of loyalty, reminded them that the City of London had always been conspicuous for upholding the principle of religious liberty.

CHAPTER XXIII.

"ROMA LOCUTA EST, CAUSA FINITA EST."

Cardinal Litta's letter to Dr. Poynter.

IN the last chapter the history of the Veto Question was brought down to the time when Pope Pius VII. informed the Catholic Board that he had referred Monsignor Quarantotti's rescript to certain cardinals, in order that it might be maturely and *ab integro* examined. Milner remained in Rome. As a man of an open, straightforward, truth-loving character is invaluable in the management of affairs, and, as he does as much good in Catholic business as one of an opposite character sooner or later does mischief, it will be well to hear the praise which Pope Pius bestowed upon the advocate of truth in Rome. Milner recounts it of himself; but it was not to satisfy vanity that he put it in print—it was to strengthen his position as a maintainer of the right. He thus writes in his "Supplementary Memoirs": "The writer had received many proofs of the favour and confidence of the Holy See during his residence there" (that is, in Rome), "none of which were so gratifying to him as the following :—There being question about the practice of English Catholics for a great number of years past, in order to settle an important point of discipline, some time about the beginning of March, when Rome was full of English Catholics, ecclesiastics as well as laics, the Pope said to the Cardinal Prefect of the Propaganda, as the latter said to the writer, 'Let us ask Dr. Milner; *he will tell us the truth.*'"

Quarantotti's rescript was examined by the cardinals. In due time they made their report to his Holiness, and Pope Pius then delivered his sentence in the matter, in a letter to Dr. Poynter, a copy of which was at the same time sent to Dr. Troy, the Archbishop of Dublin, and to Dr. Milner. The letter was actually written and signed by Cardinal Litta, he writing, of course, in the name of the Pope. It was dated from Genoa, April 26, 1815.

The reader will no doubt be glad to know how it was that the letter came to be addressed from Genoa. On the first day of the month of March in this ever-memorable year, 1815, Napoleon suddenly left Elba and landed in France at Antibes, near the town of Cannes. The history of the Emperor during what is called "the Hundred Days" may be passed over. His career was a splendid one, until he was checked on the 108th day at Quatre Bras, and finally overthrown on the 110th day by the Duke at Waterloo. One consequence of the escape of Napoleon from Elba was that Murat, whom the Emperor had made King of Naples, marched his army towards Rome. "The Pope therefore judged it advisable to quit his capital for greater security. He did so on the 22nd of March, and on the 3rd of April he made his solemn entry into Genoa. Thirteen cardinals arrived there on the following day."[1]

The affairs of England were not forgotten by the retirement of the Pope to Genoa, for, as we have seen, the letter to Dr. Poynter was written on the 26th of April. Milner followed his Holiness to Genoa. Some months after Milner's departure from England, and towards the close of the year 1814, Dr. Poynter also determined to go

[1] Husenbeth's "Life of Milner," p. 289.

to Rome. He accordingly went, and later on I shall have to speak of his visit to the Holy City. I presume that he followed the Pope; for Milner, speaking of the distribution of Cardinal Litta's letter, says "a third copy was delivered to Dr. Poynter, who was on the spot."[1] This letter of Cardinal Litta is so important that it is necessary to give a full account of its contents.

Although, as we shall see, the Pope did not wish the letter to be considered as "a final sentence," yet it does most decidedly settle some questions, and so far as I know, the Holy See has never up to this day expressed any other opinion on the subjects about which it is written. I give the first paragraph in full :—

"Most illustrious and most reverend Lord, your Lordship has lately informed me of your speedy return to England, earnestly entreating me, at the same time, to put you in possession of his Holiness' ideas respecting the conditions that would be allowed, with a view of enabling the Catholics to obtain from the Government the wished-for bill of emancipation. His Holiness, before whom, in compliance with my duty, I have laid the whole transaction, having been again compelled by the present unexpected conjuncture to absent himself from Rome before he was able to finish the examination of that affair, which he had begun a long time since, is unwilling, consistently with his eminent prudence, to pronounce his final sentence concerning a matter of such great moment. He has, however, been pleased to communicate to me his sentiments with regard to the only terms which, after rejecting all those that have been hitherto proposed,[2] his dear Catholic children of Great Britain may admit with a safe conscience, should the bill of emancipation, as has long been expected, have passed.[3] For his Holiness is confident that the

[1] "Supplementary Memoirs," p. 234.
[2] "Omnino rejectis aliis quibuscunque propositis."
[3] I take the translation from Butler. In the *Orthodox Journal* this passage is rendered, "in case the long hoped-for Act of their emancipation be passed." I have not seen the original. I take the meaning to be, "when it shall have passed."

august King of Great Britain, as well as the most serene Prince, son to the King,[1] agreeably to that signal clemency and wisdom with which they are endowed, and prompted by the native generosity of their minds, will doubtless add fresh favours and benefits to those already conferred upon the Catholics, particularly as they have always found them most loyal and most willing to suffer, under God's protection, the greatest dangers, rather than be anyways wanting in their duty to their renowned King."

On the words of this opening paragraph, "rejecting all those terms which have hitherto been proposed" (*omnino rejectis aliis quibuscunque propositis*), Milner makes the following clear, candid, and characteristic commentary.[2] "Namely," he says, "Sir John Throckmorton's *direct appointment by the Crown ;* Mr. Ponsonby's *unlimited negative, which would have had the effect of making the King head of the Catholic Church ;* the present writer's *limited negative, confined to avowed charges of disloyalty or sedition against the candidate ;* Mr. Charles Butler's Presbyterian scheme of a *lay domination in a divinely constituted Episcopal Church ;* and, lastly, the favourite *domestic nomination* of the Irish Catholics, which supposes a *concordatum between the Pope and the Catholic bishops."*

The second paragraph of the letter mentions the subjects which it says "the said" (that is, the English) "Government, for the tranquillity and security both of themselves and of the State, so far as the Catholic subjects are concerned, appear anxious to settle on a firm footing;" that is, "the oath of allegiance to be taken by them, the manner of appointing bishops to vacant sees, and the examination

---

[1] This was added because the Prince of Wales was then Prince Regent.
[2] I have taken the wording of the letter from Butler's "Historical Memoirs." Milner does not find fault with the translation. The translation, however, of the words "omnino rejectis aliis quibuscunque propositis" hardly does full justice to the Latin, which may be thus rendered: "entirely rejecting other propositions of what kind soever."

of all rescripts, or briefs, and ordinances from the supreme pontiff, previous to allowing them to be acted upon."

In the third paragraph of the letter, Cardinal Litta, on the part of his Holiness, proposes three different forms of the oath of allegiance which his Holiness will allow Catholics to take, "in the event of the emancipation, so it be favourable to the Catholics in general." One of the forms seems to be intended for bishops only, as it contains the words "in or out of my diocese." "It is much to be wished," says Milner, "that one of the three forms here proposed were substituted to the present oath of allegiance." But he adds the following words:—"at the same time it is to be regretted that the person who drew them up, for want of sufficient knowledge of the British Constitution, should propose in each one of them, to make us swear *obedience to the Sovereign*. Good subjects of this realm are *loyal to the King*, but they *only obey the laws*."[1]

On the subject of the appointment of bishops, the letter, after exhorting and ordering that none should be admitted into the number of candidates for the episcopacy but such as, besides the other pastoral virtues, possess in an eminent degree, prudence, love of quiet and loyalty, and after

---

[1] With all deference to the learned doctor of divinity, I think he is wrong in this question of law. This is a question of an oath of allegiance, and allegiance is always sworn to the Sovereign. Milner says that we only obey the laws, but in many matters obedience is due immediately to the Queen as the chief magistrate and executrix of the laws, as in the case of all writs. She has a right to command, and where there is a right to command there is a duty to obey. An order in Council, also, is theoretically an order of the Queen; and she can by an order in Council suspend in some cases the operation of the law. A good subject would be as much bound to obey an order in Council as an Act of Parliament. Milner puts the word *loyal* to the King in contradistinction to *obedience to* the laws. Johnson in his dictionary, under the word "loyal," gives as its first meaning "obedient; true to the prince." An Englishman is never required to swear obedience to the laws in general. Milner, however, was no radical; he never took part in politics, and "if," says Husenbeth (p. 548), "he inclined at any time to what is now called Conservatism, he did so purely because he wished to see religion and good order most effectually preserved."

observing that his Holiness considered the oath of allegiance taken by the bishops was quite sufficient security to the Government, proceeds in the following words :—

"Nevertheless, to their more ample satisfaction, his Holiness will feel no hesitation in allowing those to whom it appertains, to present to the King's ministers a list of candidates, in order that if any of them should be obnoxious or suspected, the Government may immediately point him out, so as that he may be expunged, care, however, being taken to leave a sufficient number for his Holiness to choose therefrom, individuals whom he may deem best qualified in the Lord for governing the vacant churches."

On the subject of subjecting the correspondence with Rome to Government inspection, the letter thus speaks :—

"As for the examination of the rescript, to which I have alluded above, or what is called the *Regium Exequatur*, it cannot even be made a subject of negotiation. For your lordship well knows, that as such a practice must essentially affect the free exercise of that supremacy of the Church which has been given in trust by God, it would assuredly be criminal to permit or transfer it to any lay power, and indeed such a permission has never anywhere been granted."

The letter also announces the intention of his Holiness, to address, when the Emancipation Act shall have passed, a brief to the bishops and Catholics of Great Britain—

"with the view of not only proclaiming to the whole world his grateful sense of the clemency and generosity displayed by the most powerful British Government, but of exhorting the Catholics themselves to exert their utmost endeavours in proving loyal subjects."

This letter was a most complete rejection of the decision which had been come to by Monsignore Quarantotti, and embodied in his famous letter to Dr. Poynter. The bill of 1813 provided that the name of any man elected a

Catholic bishop in the United Kingdom should be submitted to a Catholic lay-committee; which committee was, if it thought proper, to send a certificate of the loyalty of the bishop elect to the Privy Council. If any bishop elect were not to obtain such a certificate and were to exercise episcopal functions, he was to be considered guilty of a misdemeanour, and liable to be sent out of the country.

The bill of 1813 also provided that a copy of all instruments received from Rome should be sent to the secretary of a committee composed of clergy and laity, Protestants and Catholics, or in lieu of such copy, a notice that the ecclesiastic to whom it had been sent had received the instrument, accompanied by an affidavit that it related solely and entirely to spiritual affairs. Monsignore Quarantotti tells Dr. Poynter that the Catholics of the United Kingdom may accept such a bill with two such clauses "with satisfaction and gratitude." Pope Pius VII., through the Cardinal Secretary of the Propaganda, tells Dr. Poynter that he entirely rejects the first of those clauses; and that as to the second of those clauses, he will not even take it into consideration. A more complete triumph for Milner on the merits of the question can hardly be imagined; it must have enabled him to bear with patience the pain of the one thorn which he carried away from Rome. But the victory of Milner was not merely the victory of one man. It was indeed the victory of sound Catholic principles over schismatical attempts; it was the victory of the Church over the State, not in a battle in which the Church was an aggressor, but in a fight in which the Protestant State of England, having been led into the dominions of the Church by the Church's own sons, was repulsed by the Vicar of Jesus Christ. All honour, then, to Pope Pius VII. It is a curious circumstance that, as Milner observes, "the Pope and cardinals were then" (that is, when the letter was written) "completely in the power of the British Government, having been obliged to take refuge from the overwhelming arms of Murat, in a city defended by its troops and navy; nevertheless, no dereliction of principles, or other unworthy concession of Catholic principles to Protestant prejudice is to be found in that letter."[1] All honour, then, to the Holy Confessor, Pope Pius VII., and honour, too, to those English Protestant statesmen, who scorned to indulge in a spirit of spite and revenge because their measure was condemned by the Pope, and who never made that condemnation a motive for relaxing in their endeavours to emancipate their Catholic fellow-subjects.

Although it appears, from the letter of Cardinal Litta to Dr. Poynter, that Pope Pius VII. did not wish to pronounce "a final sentence" in "a matter of such great moment," yet the decisions announced in that letter must be considered to be final. The reluctance to come to a final decision must have been a reluctance to settle, at that time, the general relations of the Holy See with the court of S. James, and all the details which would have to be considered if the whole question were to be opened.

As to the specific questions contained in the cardinal's letter, his Eminence speaks of them as "the only terms which, after rejecting all those that have hitherto been proposed, his" (that is, the Holy Father's) "dear Catholic children of Great Britain may admit with a safe conscience." Those words have the stamp of finality upon them. The three questions decided in the letter were respecting the oath of allegiance, the interference of the English Government in the appointment of bishops, and the inspection of the correspondence between the English

---

[1] "Supplementary Memoirs," p. 234.

and Irish bishops and Rome. Since the letter was written, Rome, as was noticed in the former chapter, never has spoken, at least directly, on any one of those subjects. With regard to the oath of allegiance, the terms of the oath, which was taken up to a very late period, were settled in the English Parliament at the passing of the Emancipation Act, in the year 1829. I believe no communication was on that occasion made with the Holy See regarding the terms of the oath; and no bishop, as such, was obliged to take the oath. It used to be said by some, that Rome did indirectly sanction the oath prescribed by the Emancipation Act, not merely by silence in not condemning it, but in a particular instance, when the Holy Father, Pope Gregory XVI., sanctioned the appointment of Mr. Butt to the rectorship of the English Catholic college at Malta. Mr. Butt was appointed rector of the college by the late Lord Derby, on the recommendation of the late Rev. R. Lythgoe, S.J.; and Mr. Butt had to take the oath of allegiance before entering upon his office.

The late Mr. George Eyston, who was intimately acquainted with English Catholic affairs, and who frequently transacted business in relation to them with Dr. Griffiths, the Vicar Apostolic of the London District, always maintained that Rome never had directly sanctioned the oath of 1829.

It is true that the question of the oath of allegiance is now immaterial; but I have made these remarks for the purpose of impressing upon the mind of the reader the fact that since that letter, Rome has never spoken on the subjects contained in it, and it is now sixty-eight years since it was written.[1] The oath of allegiance has

---

[1] A letter written by Pope Pius VII. to the Irish bishops on the subject of the veto in 1816, and which will be mentioned in a succeeding chapter, was merely a defence of the plan proposed in the letter of Cardinal Litta.

now been settled in a form in which we may hope it will be allowed to remain; on this head, therefore, there is no likelihood that there will be in future any negotiation between England and the Holy See. With regard to the inspection of the correspondence between the Pope and the bishops, it is not probable that any question on this subject will soon arise. As, however, we cannot answer for what some future radical and infidel Government may attempt, it is well that the memory of those words in the letter of Cardinal Litta should be kept with care, in which he says, "As for the examination of the rescripts, or what is called the *Regium Exequatur*, it cannot even be made a subject of negotiation." These words, too, sound like a final decision. Let us hope that if any English statesman should be found to re-open the question, he will not find a Catholic to help him in his dirty work.

The remaining question treated of in the letter is that of the interference of Government in the appointment of bishops. It is in this matter that it is most important that the decision in the letter should be considered final. For it is precisely in this matter that almost all Governments show their jealousy of the legitimate power of Rome.

From the year 1815 down to the present day, it is, I believe, quite true to say that there never has been any formal re-opening of this question between Rome and England. I am not aware that the subject has ever even been mentioned by either the Church or the State.[1] That it was not made any condition of the Act of 1829, we owe to the previous wisdom and firmness of Milner and the Irish bishops, and to the loyalty and determination shown at the time by our great Emancipator.

[1] It has been mentioned more than once in Parliament, but has never, so far as I know, been made the subject of negotiation.

But it is not at all unlikely that at some future time, at no great distance, perhaps, from our own time, an attempt may be made to re-open the veto question. We should therefore be prepared for the occasion. In all matters which arise between the Church and States Catholics ought to have fixed principles of action, and be guided by certain axioms, in order that they may faithfully do their duty as worthy sons of both Church and country. In this question of the interference of the State in the appointment of bishops, it should be a fixed principle amongst us, that as a general rule the Church should be left absolutely and entirely free. I say, as a general rule, because there are conceivable cases in which the State would be justified in using strong remonstrance, and even a certain amount of pressure, in order to check an exercise of authority which the rulers of some particular country might know to be injurious to the welfare of the State. As we shall presently see, Rome seems to recognize that state of things in which the State might fairly complain of its action, and then Rome anticipates remonstrance by judicious action. But when the State has no serious complaint to make—serious both in the nature of the thing complained of and in its continuance—to insist upon interfering in ecclesiastical affairs so as to prevent the free action of the spiritual authority, is mere shameful tyranny; it is the stronger power forcing a surrender from a weaker power which is not willing to give; it is, in reality, something even worse: it is an act of revolt; it is acting on the old formula of rebellion, *non serviam*. That the Holy See has often, under compulsion, dealt with the State as if it were an equal power in ecclesiastical affairs, and entered upon what are called *concordats*, is no justification on the part of the State of any wish to interfere in a country where there is no concordat, and where there is no occasion to desire one, because things go on smoothly enough without one. Every loyal Catholic, therefore, should be more anxious to find reasons why there should not be, than why there should be any interference with the free action of the Church. But if circumstances should unfortunately make it prudent on the part of the Church to come to some formal agreement with the State in matters ecclesiastical, then it should be most certainly the object of every true Christian to fetter the action of the Holy See as little as possible.

Now, the great value of that part of Cardinal Litta's letter which treats of this subject is, that it lays down the least objectionable way in which State interference can be exercised, under a formal agreement between a secular power and the Holy See. And because it is the least objectionable way, we should look upon it as a final decision as to how much of a negative should be allowed to the English Government, should it ever—which may God avert—put pressure upon the Holy Father to come to any formal agreement upon the subject.

Let us now see in what the plan, laid down in Cardinal Litta's letter, differs from the least objectionable scheme which had been proposed in England. This least objectionable plan was the one advocated by Dr. Milner in his famous "Letter to a Parish Priest." As the reader will remember, the plan which Milner, to use his own words, only mooted, was one of those which were rejected by the Holy See. Milner's proposition was this: that one name only at a time should be presented to the English Government; that the Government should have no power to object to any name except for the reason to be assigned, that there existed a well-grounded doubt as to the candidate's loyalty and peaceable disposition; and that the right of objecting should be limited to a certain number of times,

—"for example," says Milner, "to three times."[1] In one respect, Milner's plan was the same as that contained in Cardinal Litta's letter. According to Milner, the objection to any one of the names proposed must have been that the loyalty and peaceable disposition of the person were suspected. In the cardinal's letter it is said that his Holiness will allow "a list of candidates" to be presented to the King's ministers, " in order that if any of them should be obnoxious or suspected, the Government may immediately point him out, so as that his name may be expunged;" which words, "obnoxious or suspected," may be taken to mean the same as suspicion of the person's loyalty and peaceable disposition.

But in the way in which the veto was to be exercised, and the way in which the names of the candidates were to be presented to the Government, there was a considerable difference between the two schemes.

Milner proposed that one candidate should be presented at a time. His reason for this course was, to use his own words, "to prevent the virtual choice of a Catholic bishop by a non-Catholic Ministry." The idea in Milner's mind was, I suppose, this: if, for instance, three names had been sent at once to the Government, and the minister objected to two of the names, only one name could have been sent to the Pope for appointment, which would have been a virtual selection of the person to be bishop by the British Government. Milner's scheme prevented any such virtual selection; as, after the minister had exhausted his veto, those appointed to send the names of the candidates to Rome might have sent as many as they pleased or as the canon law required. This plan of Milner's, however effective it might have been to attain the object he desired, would have led, it seems to me, to great in-

[1] "Supplementary Memoirs," p. 132.

convenience. The management of the sending of the names to the minister would have required very delicate manipulation. It might frequently, and certainly sometimes it would, have been a question whether those who had to send in the names should send the names of those they wished to be elected, or the names of those they did not wish to be elected, merely to exhaust the veto. There would have been at many elections endless questions, discussions, speculations, and diplomacy. All this would have been extremely annoying and inconvenient.

In the plan laid down in the cardinal's letter, all the names were to be sent in at once to the Government. How, then, was the evil to be avoided to prevent which Milner devised his scheme of sending only one name at a time? The case was provided for in this way: if the Government were to desire one or more names to be expunged, they might point out the name or names; but in doing so, they were "to leave a sufficient number for his Holiness to choose therefrom, individuals whom he might deem best qualified in the Lord for governing the vacant churches."[1] Under this provision, supposing three names had been sent up to Government, only one could have been objected to, otherwise no choice would have been left to the Pope. But probably, under this scheme, more names would have been sent to Government than it was intended to send to Rome. For instance, six names might have been forwarded to the minister; and if he objected to two names, only three of the remaining four might have been forwarded to his Holiness. This plan certainly went a long way towards avoiding the evil foreseen by Milner, and was a much more simple and convenient method than the one which Milner proposed. Under Milner's scheme, the

[1] See the letter of Cardinal Litta in Butler's "Historical Memoirs," vol. iv. p. 534, third edition.

Government could exercise the veto several times; whereas under that of Cardinal Litta, though with the above-mentioned restrictions they might exercise it on more than one person, they could only exercise it at one time. The scheme in the cardinal's letter seems to be the most simple and effectual way of giving to the Government the most limited right of veto. It may be called what Milner called his plan, "an iron-bound veto." It was, in fact, little more than putting into a formal agreement what is constantly done on the appointment of a bishop: it was a proposal on the part of the Holy See to bind itself to do in every case what in very many instances it does by courtesy. The Holy See is always anxious not to appoint any person bishop who is obnoxious to the English Government; and I have been informed by one likely to know, that before a bishop is appointed care is generally, if not always, taken to ascertain that the Government has no serious objection to the person selected by Rome. The case of Dr. MacHale alluded to in a former chapter was exceptional, and a good reason was given for not acceding to Lord Melbourne's earnest request.

The fact that the Holy See was willing, in the year 1815, to give this country a limited veto in the appointment of bishops, is no reason why any Catholic should wish that such a thing should actually come to pass. Besides our chief reason for wishing the Holy See to remain unfettered, namely, the preservation of the liberty of the Church, and which reason our Government is unfortunately not likely to listen to, we have that other reason contained in the advice given us by Edmund Burke in his letter to Lord Kenmare, which has been quoted in a former chapter. The advice amounts, in short, to this: the State does nothing towards the support of the Catholic Church, and therefore should not interfere in its affairs. This is a reason to which no Government can refuse its attention.

If, then, any attempt should ever be made to renew the veto question, the cry from all loyal Catholics should be "Hands off." If we should be forced to yield, we should give up as little as possible. The letter of Cardinal Litta contains the least offensive form of veto; let that letter, therefore, not be forgotten.

CHAPTER XXIV.

MILNER AND O'CONNELL.

Dr. Moylan's letter to Milner—Dr. Murray in Rome—Proceedings in Ireland—Resolutions of the Irish bishops—O'Connell's attack upon Milner—O'Connell apologizes—Rev. Mr. Hayes' letter—The two Irish bishops in Rome—Letter of Pope Pius VII. to the Irish bishops—End of the veto question—Sir Robert Peel on the veto—The victory.

CARDINAL LITTA'S letter was by no means favourably received in Ireland. To explain what happened in the sister island, it is necessary to go back to the year 1814. On May 25, in that year, the Irish bishops assembled at Maynooth. Amongst other things, they determined to send two prelates to Rome for the purpose of remonstrating against the rescript of Monsignore Quarantotti. "Only one Irish bishop, however," says Husenbeth, "was thus commissioned, who was the most Rev. Dr. Murray, coadjutor of the Archbishop of Dublin, Dr. Troy; the other deputy was their long-tried and faithful agent, Dr. Milner."[1] It appears that at this meeting of the Irish bishops some of their lordships were not for immediate action in the matter of Quarantotti's letter. "Some of the prelates," says Husenbeth, "were recommending the expediency of a little delay, when Dr. Moylan rose, and brought them at once to a unanimous decision by these memorable words: 'Let us put expediency out of consideration; let us

[1] "Life of Milner," p. 276.

consider what is *right,* and *let us act like Irish bishops.'*" Dr. Moylan was Bishop of Cork, and an intimate friend of Milner; it was he who, as the reader will recollect, made an ineffectual attempt, at the Durham meeting in 1812, to bring about a good understanding between the Irish bishops with their agent, Dr. Milner, and the three other English vicars apostolic, on the veto and the Blanchardist questions. Before parting with Dr. Moylan, I cannot refrain from quoting a passage from a letter which he wrote to Dr. Milner when the latter was in Rome. The letter was dated from Cork, December 7, 1814; Milner received it early in the year 1815. The preservation of the entire liberty of the Church was an object dear to the heart of Bishop Moylan. When he wrote the letter to Milner he was in the eightieth year of his age. The letter begins in the following words:—" My dear and honoured lord, I am the oldest of the Catholic prelates in this kingdom, and expect soon to appear before the awful tribunal of the Almighty Judge, in whose sacred presence I solemnly declare that *any compromise made or control whatever given* to our Protestant Government or ministers, in the appointment or nomination of the Catholic bishops or clergy of this kingdom, *or any interference whatsoever* or influence over them in the exercise of their spiritual functions, will eventually lead *to the subversion of our venerable hierarchy,* and, in consequence, to the *ruin of the Catholic religion* in this long-suffering and oppressed Catholic country. It would certainly cause the greatest dissatisfaction in the minds of the Catholic body, lessen their attachment and respect to the Holy See, and by degrees dispose them for every bad change."[1] Two months after writing this letter, namely on February 10,

---

[1] The remainder of the letter, which is not a long one, may be seen in Husenbeth's "Life of Milner," p. 285.

1815, the staunch and holy Bishop of Cork went to his eternal reward.

Dr. Murray arrived in Rome about a month after Dr. Milner, and had several audiences of the Pope, along with the latter bishop.[1] I have no record of what Dr. Murray said to his Holiness on the subject of the veto; but there can be no doubt that he represented as faithfully as did his fellow-deputy Dr. Milner, the decision of the Irish bishops, which was against any interference of the English Government with the discipline of the Church. But Dr. Murray did not remain in Rome as long as Dr. Milner did. He had returned to Dublin before February 15, 1815, for on that day he received a deputation from the Irish Catholic Association, sent to him to obtain information relative to the state of the veto question. Dr. Murray told the deputation the history of the proceedings in Rome, up to the time when Pope Pius referred Quarantotti's letter to the special congregation. As the reader has already had an account of this, it is not necessary to repeat it. Dr. Murray, however, added, "that Milner had protested against Mr. Macpherson as the English agent, and also against the Board being considered to represent the English Catholics."[2]

Dr. Milner arrived in London on his return from Rome on June 2, 1815. He rejected many offers of presents and addresses. He was satisfied with having done his duty, and with the approbation of the Holy Father. In a letter to the *Orthodox Journal*, writing in the third person, he says, "His conduct in opposition to the schismatical bill and the fatal pledge, which he so often foretold would lead to some such measure, has been approved in that quarter, to which alone he looks for a decision on theological questions previously to the sentence of the great Master,

---

[1] "Life of Milner," p. 276.   [2] Ibid., p. 286.

who can adequately reward as well as infallibly judge of the right behaviour of His ministers."[1]

It appears, however, that one address was sent to the victorious bishop, signed by four thousand English Catholics, and some of those who had previously opposed his conduct expressed their concern at having done so.

At this time the contents of Cardinal Litta's letter were not known to the public either in England or in Ireland, it never having been published. Husenbeth says that both Dr. Murray and Dr. Milner refused to convey the letter to Ireland.[2]

Although the letter of Litta had not been published, "it began to be whispered about that his Holiness had approved of such arrangements in the bill of 1813, as the prelates of Ireland and Dr. Milner had condemned. Mr. Eneas McDonnell wrote on the subject to Archbishop Troy, imploring his Grace to inform him of the real truth of the matter; and Dr. Troy, in his answer of August the 9th, assured him that his Holiness had not approved of the bill of 1813, and that he would determine nothing till emancipation had been granted."[3] No doubt very exaggerated reports had been spread about respecting the nature of the letter, and in consequence of this, considerable irritation had been excited in the minds of all who were opposed to any interference of the English Government in the affairs of the Irish Church. The bishops, however, thought it most prudent not to publish the document until

---

[1] "Life of Milner," quoting *Orthodox Journal* for June, 1815.

[2] Ibid., p. 295. But this appears to be a mistake as far as Dr. Murray is concerned, because, as we have seen, he left Rome very early in the year, and the letter was not written until the 26th of April. It is possible, however, that he may have known before starting on his journey what the nature of the letter was to be. With regard to Dr. Milner, Husenbeth may have had some special knowledge that he declined to send the letter to Ireland.

[3] Ibid., pp. 295, 296.

they should have met together and considered it themselves. The meeting of the bishops took place on the 23rd and 24th of August, 1815. After passing two resolutions, in which they condemned all interference of the crown of Great Britain in the appointment of Catholic bishops, and recorded their determination to resist such interference in "every canonical and constitutional way," they proceeded to pass a third resolution, in which their lordships went perhaps as far as they could without disrespect to the Holy See, in expressing their disapprobation of what Pope Pius had done. The words of the resolution as given by Husenbeth are as follows:—

"Resolved—That though we sincerely venerate the Supreme Pontiff as visible head of the Church, we do not conceive that our apprehensions for the safety of the Roman Catholic Church in Ireland can or ought to be removed by any determination of his Holiness adopted, or intended to be adopted, not only without our concurrence, but in direct opposition to our repeated resolutions and the very energetic memorial presented on our behalf, and so ably supported by our deputy, the most Rev. Dr. Murray, who in that quality was more competent to inform his Holiness of the real state and interests of the Roman Catholic Church in Ireland than any other with whom he is said to have consulted."[2]

The fourth and fifth resolutions are important, in view of future remarks I shall have to make. I give them, therefore, to the reader as follows:—

"Resolved—That a declaration of these our sentiments, respectful, firm, and decided, be transmitted to the Holy See, which, we trust, will engage his Holiness to feel and acknowledge the justness and propriety of this our determination." "Re-

---

[1] Who this other person may have been, I do not know. Most likely some meddling individual, forcing himself into notice and thinking that he understood the interests of the Irish Church much better than the bishops did.

solved—That our grateful thanks are due and hereby given to the most Rev. Dr. Murray and the Right Rev. Dr. Milner, our late deputies to Rome, for their zealous and able discharge of the trust reposed in them."[1]

The reader will no doubt think these resolutions sufficiently strong. The most useful lesson which they teach to our generation is not to purchase the favour of Government and the good-will of the English people by any concession which would weaken the independence of the Church. The resolutions were signed by the four archbishops, the coadjutors of two of them, and the Warden of Galway. Their lordships also determined to send another deputation to Rome on the subject of the veto. Dr. Murray and Dr. Murphy, the Bishop of Cork, were selected for the mission.

We now come to an attack, much spoken of at the time, which O'Connell made upon Dr. Milner. In the agitation for emancipation, O'Connell was now what Edmund Burke would have called "Lord of the ascendant." He was beginning to see his way towards that glorious work which he afterwards accomplished, of uniting the Catholics of Ireland in a determination to force the British to yield emancipation. Anything, therefore, which he thought would prevent or disturb that union was, in his mind, an obstacle he was resolved to overcome. The chief obstacle at this time towards the union of all Irish Catholics was the difference of opinion which existed amongst them on the question of the veto. The strength of the two parties in Ireland on this question may be stated in the words of Mr. Wyse, which have been already quoted from his "History of the Catholic Association:" "The Irish Catholics were extremely divided ; the clergy unanimously, and much the majority of the laity, still retained their

[1] "Life of Milner," pp. 296, 297.

opposition to the measure, but the aristocracy for the most part were favourable." All the world knows that O'Connell was in religion a thorough Catholic, and that in politics he was, in the whole history of Christianity, the greatest creator and the ablest commander of moral force. He therefore, wisely as a Catholic, and, as the event proved, prudently as a politician, stood firmly by the bishops, the priests, and the great bulk of the people. We have seen that the bishops of Ireland met on the 23rd and 24th of August. During the meeting one of the bishops read a letter which he had received from Dr. Milner. This letter "which," Bishop Milner says, "was a very long one, was also," he says, "*a confidential one*, and was *stated to be such in the body of it;*" nor, he continues, "will I easily believe that any one of my honoured and venerable friends was capable of betraying such confidence."[1] From this it appears that it was Milner's intention that the letter should be read to the assembled bishops, but only to them, and in confidence. One of the bishops spoke to O'Connell about this letter, and his lordship must have spoken pretty freely, for, as the reader will see, O'Connell said he could give an abstract of it. But, most unfortunately, a very wrong impression was left upon the mind of O'Connell of the real meaning of the letter.

On the 29th of August, 1815, an "Aggregate Meeting" was held in Dublin.[2] At that meeting O'Connell, having made some previous remarks, proceeded as follows:—

"The next class in the arrangement of the veto are the English Catholic bishops. First of all, I must mention a name

[1] *Orthodox Journal* for September, 1815, p. 338.
[2] The reader will remember that after Government had put down the Irish Catholic Board in 1814, on the ground that it was against the "Convention Act," O'Connell changed his tactics, and held what were called "Aggregate Meetings."

that ought not, perhaps, though it will, surprise you—Dr. Milner. Yes, Dr. Milner has performed another truly English revolution. He was the first to broach the veto. He came to Ireland on a vetoistical mission; the Irish rejected the mission and the missionary: he then recanted his errors, renounced his first opinions—abjured them, and brought no small discredit on himself by the flat contradiction under which he laboured.[1] We, however, thought his repentance sincere, and leaving him to decide his personal quarrel as he could, sustained him for his anti-vetoistical principle. Well, what has occurred now? Why, this identical Dr. Milner has gone round again, and has actually written to the bishops to accede to Litta's plan of veto.[2] Milner's letter was read at the synod. It was, I understand, an official document: of its contents I can give you certainly an abstract, because its contents have been communicated to me by one of our prelates, whose name, if necessary, I am at full liberty to use. His letter requested of the bishops to accede to the new plan of veto." O'Connell made some other remarks upon Dr. Milner's letter, during the course of which he gave, according to the report in the *Orthodox Journal*, some verbal extracts, and applied to Dr. Milner's words the terms "flimsy and unmanly sophistry;" and concludes his observations by saying, "I trust that it is the intellect, not the integrity, of this prelate that has been thus affected."[3]

From the account in former chapters of Milner's action with regard to the veto, the reader will know how ex-

[1] This statement of O'Connell's, that Milner went to Ireland on a vetoistical mission which was rejected by the Irish, was not fair. In his tour in Ireland in 1807, Milner warned the bishops against the veto; in his second tour in Ireland in 1808, I cannot find what he spoke about the veto. But from what follows he must have done so; and the tour was made immediately after Milner had written his "Letter to a Parish Priest." He went to Ireland in August, 1808. On the 14th of September in the same year, the celebrated meeting of twenty-nine bishops took place in Dublin, at which meeting their lordships unanimously resolved that Dr. Milner's account of his conduct as their agent was satisfactory. This does not look like a rejection by the Irish of the mission and the missionary.

[2] It may be proper to remark here, that though O'Connell knew something about Cardinal Litta's letter, the people whom he was addressing most probably knew nothing of its contents.

[3] Andrew's *Orthodox Journal*, September, 1815, p. 336.

tremely unjust this accusation against Milner was. In a moment of irritation, O'Connell allowed himself to attack, without any justification, an advocate of the independence of the Church than whom no one was more staunch, the episcopal character of the advocate not saving him from bitterly sarcastic words, unworthy insinuations, and disrespectful language. When O'Connell applied to Milner the epithet "unmanly," he said it of one who was to the full as manly as himself. What O'Connell meant by calling Milner's supposed change of opinion about the veto question a "truly English revolution," it is not easy to imagine. Among the three great divisions of the United Kingdom, England is not the one pre-eminently notorious for fickleness and instability. O'Connell afterwards made amends for this ungracious attack, as the reader will presently see; for full justice must be dealt out to all, and in the case of O'Connell, gratitude leads justice forward by the hand. And in justice to Dr. Milner, the reader shall see what the two bishops, who had started for Rome, thought of O'Connell's charge against him. "One of them," says Husenbeth, "probably Dr. Murphy, in a letter to a priest in Dublin, dated from Dover, September 14, said, 'We passed Sunday night with Dr. Milner, whose heart is with us most fervently, notwithstanding all the cruel calumnies that have been uttered against him. My heart bleeds to see him so foully traduced as an enemy to our cause.'"[1]

In answer to O'Connell's charges, Dr. Milner wrote a letter to the Editor of the *Dublin Chronicle*. It is not necessary to give the letter here; it belongs more to a life of Milner than to a history of emancipation; and, moreover, the nature of the answer must be pretty evident to any one who has read these pages, and O'Connell afterwards fully

[1] "Life of Milner," p. 298.

and handsomely withdrew the charge. But justice to the Liberator obliges me to give his withdrawal as it is recorded in the "Life of Milner." "After a time," says Husenbeth, "O'Connell was satisfied that he had been mistaken; and then, with the frankness of a just and generous spirit, he made an ample and public retractation and apology. At an aggregate meeting in Dublin, on March 5, in the year following" (that is, in 1816), "Mr. O'Connell stated that he felt it a duty which he owed to that learned prelate" (that is, Milner) "to admit most distinctly that he had wrongfully accused him of having returned to the approval of any vetoistical arrangements, and he felt much pleasure in doing so in the face of his countrymen, now so numerously assembled.[1] He had seen a letter written by the Rev. Mr. Hayes (the Irish deputy of the lay Catholics to Rome), in which the unaltered detestation of the veto by that worthy prelate is incontestably established; and he felt personally grateful to the rev. gentleman for having disabused his mind of such unfavourable impressions, and enabled him to announce to his countrymen that Dr. Milner continues to be the same decided, determined anti-vetoist that he had proved himself to be under the most painful and discouraging circumstances."[2] At the same aggregate meeting, another speaker alluded to a circumstance which, though not necessary to mention here, yet contains so useful a lesson to those honestly engaged in Catholic affairs, that I cannot pass it over without remark. When O'Connell had sat down, Mr. Eneas McDonnell rose to address the meeting,

---

[1] As O'Connell's words imply that Milner had once approved of vetoistical arrangements, the reader must remember that Milner had never even advocated, in what he called a "mooting essay," a more stringent veto than that which the Irish bishops themselves had proposed to Lord Castlereagh.

[2] "Life of Milner," p. 299, quoting *Orthodox Journal* for March, 1816, p. 115.

and he also apologized "for having in some degree aided in the circulation of the opinion injurious to Dr. Milner. He read a portion of the letter from the Rev. Mr. Hayes, alluded to by Mr. O'Connell, which was as follows:—' In justice to this worthy prelate (Dr. Milner), I think myself bound to state that he opposed the veto with all his might at Rome and at Genoa; and that, when unsupported by his friends, overwhelmed by the calumny of his foes, and threatened with immediate deposition from his episcopal functions, he found that all his opposition was in vain, he then, without at all *approving*, softened down the evil he could not prevent, and to him alone are we indebted for the mild *permissive*, indecisive tone and tenor of the Genoese letter. Nay, however he may have acted under certain difficulties since that epoch, this I know, that down to the present moment his letters to the Holy See bitterly lament the treachery practised on his Holiness, and bespeak him still the warm hater and opposer of all veto-istical arrangements.'"[1] The words "however he may have acted under certain difficulties since that epoch" (that is, since Cardinal Litta's letter was written), seem to apply to Milner's letter to the Irish bishops at their meeting in August, 1815. I do not know to what else they can apply. The letter itself was never published. Dr. Troy, in a letter to the editor of the *Dublin Chronicle*, says that he "was instructed by the prelates assembled not to give a copy or an extract of Cardinal Litta's or Dr. Milner's letter to any person."

With regard to that part of Mr. Hayes' letter in which he says that Milner was threatened with immediate deposition if he continued his opposition to the veto, it would certainly seem that there is here some exaggeration. He could not have been threatened with immediate de-

---

[1] 'Life of Milner," p. 300.

position for combating a veto which was more objectionable than the one which the Pope himself devised; his opposition to the veto which the Pope proposed could not have been very obstinate, for he himself speaks of the proposed change in the discipline of the Church as regards the appointment of bishops, in Cardinal Litta's letter, as "*slight in itself* and *safe in its consequences.*"[1] It may be that when Milner first went to Rome, he inveighed in very strong terms against any interference whatever of the English Government in the election of bishops. If so, when his Holiness had made up his mind to surrender some of his liberty, he may have looked upon Milner's strong views as an obstacle to the settlement of the question with the English Government, and to the arrangement of a *modus vivendi* between Milner and the other vicars apostolic in England. If this supposition be true, then Pope Pius might perhaps have delicately hinted to Milner that his resignation of office would be better than continued opposition. But it is difficult to suppose that Milner carried firmness into obstinacy, which could only be overcome by a threat of immediate dismissal. But supposing that Mr. Hayes was correct in what he said, or supposing even that a considerable amount of pressure was put upon Milner, but short of a threat of instant dismissal, still Milner's position, and the way in which he conducted himself in it, was one which teaches a great and most useful lesson. For what was that position? It was one which, no doubt from his infancy, he had learned, is the fate of most men who steadily pursue the course which they believe to be right; and how to act in that position, he must have learned from the old fable of "the man and his son and the donkey." The moral of that fable is sometimes hastily summed up in a very summary way: "You cannot

[1] *Vide infra*, p. 195.

expect to please everybody." But the lesson extends further. You must sometimes pursue your own course, though you may have reason to believe you will please nobody.

Now, if Mr. Hayes was right, or even nearly right, what, it may be asked again, was Dr. Milner's position at this time? He was admonished by Pope Pius for not yielding; and he was roundly abused by O'Connell for having yielded. Milner's action was honest and straightforward all the way through. He was honest; he was one of those men who could have said of himself what Cardinal Newman has said[1] of himself, in words which are like honey in the mouth: "I never had any suspicion of my own honesty." It is a grand thing for a foremost man in a great cause to be able to say that. It is not every man who can say it. As there are men in private life, in the ordinary business of life, who know that they are not honest, so there are men in public life, in the management of public business, who know that they are not honest. There must be many men who have the most important affairs in their hands, who live for years with the gravest possible suspicion that their motives are not honest. But when one who has never had a suspicion of his own honesty, has also a well-founded conviction that he is in the right, but, at the same time, has not the courage of his conviction, his weakness, when there is a question of mportance, may lead to very disastrous results. It is quite possible that a man may feel certain that his view of a question is a right one, even when almost every one else is against him, or at least apathetic in the matter. The wise maxim, "Rely not upon your own prudence," is not forgotten; but it does sometimes happen, still bearing this advice in mind, that a man may also very profitably

---

[1] "History of my Religious Opinions," p. 165, edition of 1849.

remember another lesson taught in a fable so well known under the title of "The Dog and the Shadow," and not let his own prudence drop, lest in doing so the seeming prudence of others should vanish, and leave only their imprudence behind.

Milner was a Catholic bishop, with no suspicion of his own honesty. Neither ambition, nor spite, nor jealousy, nor human respect provided any motive of action for his use. He knew he was right, and he had the courage of his convictions. It would certainly seem that God blessed his work. The Catholics of the United Kingdom were emancipated, and no voice in the appointment of bishops was offered to, or even asked for by the State. Milner was straightforward in action. He opposed the veto in Rome, and all the world knew it. It may be said indeed of him that if he held a strong opinion about anything, he was not content until he had seen it in print. When Pope Pius positively desired to give the English Government a very limited veto, Milner yielded and defended the action of his Holiness. The reader will not have failed to remark the exceptional candour, openness, and straightforwardness of Milner's conduct in the whole history of his differences with his colleagues in the episcopacy and with Catholic committees and Catholic boards And for his admirable conduct, though he was blamed by many at the time, he is held in universal benediction now. To Milner, under God, we owe, in great measure, the freedom of the Church in these realms. He had none of that human respect which sometimes, as a blight, prevents honesty from bearing fruit. The good of the Church was Milner's aim, and he despised those weaknesses which sometimes destroy a moral strength, which in its kind might be compared to the physical strength of Sampson. In what a position should we be now if Milner had been a weaker man : if, during his services to the Church, he had been constantly saying to himself, "What will the senior vicar apostolic think; what will Dr. Poynter think; what will Dr. Colingridge think; what will Charles Butler think; what will Counsellor O'Connell think?" What would have been our position in England now if all English Catholics had been vetoists, it is impossible to say. We might have been free in consequence of being included, as a body not worth much notice, in an Emancipation Act won by the Irish people, who were determined to steal nothing from the Church to pay for their just rights; or we might have been emancipated by a separate Act, framed to suit our peculiar English tastes in the matter of Church government. But if there was in reality any danger of such a calamity, we were saved from it by the sagacity and firmness of one bishop, who, with the great majority of the Catholic upper class against him, but supported by the great bulk of the middle class, stood up bravely in defence of the Church's rights.

Another lesson to be learned from the proceedings which have been narrated is the very extreme caution which a person, especially in an important affair, must use if he wishes a secret to be kept. If a man wants a secret to be kept, he should tell *absolutely no one*, except when circumstances make it *absolutely necessary* that he should tell some one. Milner wishes to "make a communication to the Irish bishops in meeting assembled, but he wishes no one else to be admitted to the knowledge; he states in his letter that it is a confidential communication.[1] Dr. Troy refuses, upon strong pressure, to give even an extract from the letter. But one of their lordships tells the con-

---

[1] *Orthodox Journal* for September, 1815, p. 338.

tents of the letter to the very man from whom Milner would have wished to conceal it. This man takes a wrong impression from what he hears, and a few days afterwards publishes it to the whole of Ireland, with remarks which give great pain to an exemplary bishop, and hold him up to reprobation for his conduct in a matter where he had done nothing but good, and should have received nothing but praise. And the mistaken orator has afterwards to retract every word he had uttered. A man may sometimes wish to write or to speak what he does not want the whole world to know; let him remember that sometimes telling to one is telling to all. O'Connell's speech caused a great deal of ill-will on both sides of St. George's Channel; it made the Irish very angry with Dr. Milner; and it made Milner's supporters in England very angry with O'Connell. It rendered more difficult what has always been difficult enough—that is, a good understanding between English and Irish Catholics. And all this was caused through the indiscretion of the bishop who told the secret to only one man. But Milner himself at least completely forgave O'Connell, in proof of which the reader will forgive a short extract from Husenbeth's Life of the great bishop. "Dr. Milner had presided as usual," he says, "on one occasion at the Midsummer Exhibition at Oscott College, and the writer" (that is, Husenbeth) "was standing by him afterwards in the ambulacrum, when a fine Irish youth passed by. The bishop called him, and asked him if he should soon see Mr. O'Connell, as the boy was going home to Dublin. He replied that he should see him shortly. 'Then,' said Dr. Milner, 'tell him from me, that if he were not a Catholic I would erect a statue of brass in his honour; but since he is a Catholic, I will do something far better—I will offer the adorable sacrifice of the Mass for him, that God may give him every blessing in this world and the next.'"[1]

Dr. Murray and Dr. Murphy, the two deputies from the Irish bishops, having arrived in Rome, obtained an audience of Pope Pius VII. on the 5th of November, 1815. They presented to his Holiness the resolutions which had been passed at the meeting of the bishops in the previous month of August, as already related. Husenbeth says, but without mentioning his authority, that "Dr. Murray, with great energy and emphasis, addressed a few words to the Holy Father, in support of the remonstrance; and was followed at greater length by Dr. Murphy, who, in an affecting strain, conjured the Pope not to sanction any measure destructive to religion, and showed the evil tendency of the proposed arrangements."[2] The result, however, of this deputation to Rome was, that Pope Pius addressed a long letter to the Irish bishops in defence of the arrangements proposed in the letter of Cardinal Litta. His Holiness was evidently not very well pleased with the reception which the Cardinal's letter had received in Ireland. The letter of Pope Pius to the bishops says that the letter which the bishops addressed to him impressed his mind "with a deep sense of concern," and also speaks of the "pain" which one portion of it caused him.

The letter of his Holiness is a great deal too long to insert, but a general description of it must be given, and also a few extracts which the reader will be pleased to see. Any one who may take an interest in this question (and there should be many who would do so) ought to read the whole letter as it is given at the end of the fourth volume of Mr. Butler's "Historical Memoirs." It is a very valuable

---

[1] As Milner died in the year 1826, he must have said this some years before the "Agitator" earned for himself the title of "Liberator."

[2] "Life of Milner," p. 310.

"State paper." It is dated from St. Mary Major, February 1, 1816. Preserving the complete independence of the Holy See, it shows from reason, from authority, and the custom of the Church, how the Holy See has always acted in the nomination of bishops, on the principle of not appointing any one who might be obnoxious to the respective Governments. The words are remarkable, and therefore may be inserted here. "It is unquestionably evident that what we have done" (that is, in the letter of Cardinal Litta) "amounts only to this: we have agreed to act steadily towards the British Government, according to the same rule, useful in itself, founded in prudence, which our predecessors the Roman pontiffs, even before those times when the nomination of bishops was granted to princes, determined in their wisdom to maintain as effectually as might be; that is, not to promote to vacant sees any persons whom they might know to be unpleasing to the powers under whom the dioceses to be administered by them were situated—which rule, far from being considered injurious to the Church, and far from having brought any evil on it, is justly approved of and praised by all." The letter shows how the proposal in Cardinal Litta's letter was altogether unobjectionable. Milner's account of this portion of the letter is as follows:—"His Holiness proves that he has not conferred any power of nomination, presentation, or postulation on the British Government contrary to the terms of the declaration of Benedict XIV., made to the King of Prussia; but that he had barely signified to the prelates themselves how far, and no farther, he was willing to proceed in the event of a complete emancipation taking place, namely, that when they themselves had in each instance made out lists of clergymen qualified in every respect for the episcopal functions and dignity, the civil Government, if it suspected the principles of any of them, might object to the promotion of a certain number of them, yet so as to leave a sufficient number of names on the list for the Holy See to exercise its judgment in the appointment of one of them. His Holiness strongly argues that as *all the candidates are to be chosen by the Catholic prelates, and as the ultimate appointment of some one among them in every instance will rest with himself*, there can be no danger of unfit or unworthy candidates being promoted to the detriment of the Catholic Religion."[1]

The whole of this letter of Pope Pius shows great firmness, and a very paternal feeling towards the Irish bishops. It is clear and argumentative, and contains a passage expressing the gratitude of his Holiness to England which I cannot omit, and the latter words of which we should never forget. "Remember," says Pope Pius, "that the Government which, under other circumstances, might be suspected of entertaining projects hostile to the Catholic religion, is the same which by laws, especially those passed in the years 1774, 1778, 1791, and 1793,[2] repealed a great part of those penal statutes by which the Catholics of the British empire were so grievously oppressed; remember how often your most excellent King George III., and his illustrious son, have extended their protection to Catholics, and that the British Government was amongst the chief of our supporters in procuring our return to the pontifical chair, and our restoration to our ancient independence in the exercise of those spiritual rights which the hand of violence had wrested from us."[3] These last words are our pride as Englishmen; and as Catholics, they are one

---

[1] "Supplementary Memoirs," p. 238.

[2] The two first years as given in Mr. Butler's copy of the English translation of the letter are 1773 and 1788; but as this is evidently a mistake made either in Rome or by the London printer, I have made the correction as seen in the text.

[3] "Historical Memoirs," vol. iv. p. 540.

anchor of our hope that the greatest of all blessings may be showered upon our countrymen.

In concluding his remarks upon this letter of Pope Pius to the Irish bishops, Milner says : " Thus this grand cause is at last settled, as far as concerns Catholics, by the only power competent to make a change in their discipline, and the change which it eventually engages to make is seen to be slight in itself and safe in its consequences. But," he adds, " as Protestant statesmen do not acknowledge that power, it will require all the firmness of the Catholics, in the event of a new Emancipation Bill, to save themselves from being hurried away by those statesmen, beyond the bounds marked out in the letters just mentioned. In proof of this, it may be mentioned that when the present plan was first made known to the writer at Rome, by the eminent personage who wrote the letter from Genoa, he observed what had happened at the late restoration of the Church of France. His Holiness entered into a concordat with Napoleon, highly beneficial to religion, when presently the latter tacked to it 'the organic laws,' exceedingly injurious to religion."[1] No further

---

[1] " Supplementary Memoirs," p. 239. In Mr. Ornsby's " Life of Mr. Hope Scott," there is mention of another case exactly in point, illustrating how effectually the State can, when it pleases, counteract the effect of its own agreements with the Holy See. The passage is as follows :—

" The condition of the Church in Bavaria is determined in its chief features by the concordat of 1817, and by a subsequent religious edict of the State. Of these the former is printed in the appendix to Eichhorn's ' Kirchenrecht,' and both in a small " Bibliothek of Bavarian Law," which I purchased (quod vide). The terms of the concordat are considered by W. (Dr. Windischmann) a masterpiece of Papal policy, as there was a strong Jacobin party about the then King, and he was himself not well disposed to the Church. His minister, who conducted the transaction at Rome, was also a man of indifferent character, but at the same time he seems to have had sufficient feeling for his own order (he was a bishop) to dispose him to assist the Church. It is said that the greatest surprise was created by the concordat being such as it was, under the circumstances ; but the adverse party contrived to procure a law of the State very shortly afterwards, which has materially impaired its efficacy. Under the

negotiations took place on the subject of the veto with Rome. It was occasionally mentioned in Parliament, and I shall have to remark on what was said; and at least once a formal motion was made in the House of Commons in favour of a check on the appointment of bishops, but little attention was paid to it, and it was immediately rejected. The subject still continued to be discussed among both English and Irish Catholics. The differences on this question caused unhappy divisions; but the whole history of it, so far as Catholics were concerned, up to about the year 1823, may be summed up in two words: mischievous talk. O'Connell did his utmost to prevent the subject from being even mentioned, so important was it that for the great object he had in view all should be united. When the great agitator established the Catholic Association, the question of the veto was practically quashed; at last it completely died out.

The bold stand which Milner and the Irish bishops made against State interference with the affairs of the Church, and the deference to the Holy See with which the final decision was received, were well rewarded. When, fourteen years after the letter of Cardinal Litta was written, emancipation was at last extorted, the question of the veto was deliberately set aside. Though it will be somewhat anticipating the history of emancipation to quote from Mr. Peel's speech when he introduced the measure in 1829, yet his words will be a fitting termination of the history of the veto. "A veto on the nomination of the Catholic bishops," said Mr. Peel, "was another security which had been contained in former proposed bills; but that, too, he would give up. His objection to it was, that it would be considered, and not unjustly, as the com-

latter, the royal assent became necessary to Church edicts." See Ornsby's "Life of Hope Scott," vol. i. p. 223, extracting from Diary of Tour in Germany.

mencement of a qualified establishment with regard to the Roman Catholic Church. He objected to it, not that he thought this an unreasonable demand on the part of the Crown, but because he thought that, if we had sent to us a list of the names of candidates for the dignity of Catholic bishops in Ireland, it would be extremely difficult to free ourselves from the responsibility that must attach to our choice. We, in fact, would thus be parties to the nomination of Roman Catholic bishops, and would commence a qualified establishment for that Church, which, above all things, under existing circumstances, it was desirable to avoid. At once, then, he abandoned the idea of a veto—first, because it afforded no rational security; and in the second place, because objections might possibly be made by the Roman Catholics towards our exercise of such a power, which objections it was not worth while to raise."[1] These last words of Mr. Peel are a grand testimony to the victory which had been won by Milner and the Irish bishops, and finally by O'Connell. It was most certainly not worth Mr. Peel's while to raise objections. He was determined to pass emancipation. The choice of the English minister lay between emancipation and civil war, and he knew that O'Connell would not accept the veto as a condition. Peel, in fact, was under pressure. He was overcome on this question of the veto, and compelled to abandon all thought of it, by the determination of the great bulk of the Irish and English Catholics, not to listen to any terms which would have given the Government a right to interfere in the appointment of bishops.

This was a great Catholic victory; this was the result of the hard fight which Milner and the Irish bishops had fought, and the history of which has occupied so many

[1] "Annual Register" for 1829, pp. 24, 25.

pages of this history: it was the result, also, of that grand organization of moral force by O'Connell, which followed the fighting days of Milner, and which has still to be recounted. This victory is one of the events in later history to which we Catholics of the United Kingdom can look back with pride. It is the victory which, after Milner's death, enthroned his memory in the minds of all English Catholics, and placed him as the greatest of all the vicars apostolic who have governed our Church since the evil days when our old hierarchy was destroyed. The name of Wiseman is a welcome sound, but it does not make the name of Milner less pleasing to our ears. The glories of the first Archbishop of Westminster have not dimmed the brightness of the guiding star. Milner and Wiseman were both great, but each in his own sphere. The time will come, if the world shall last so long, when those two names will be pronounced together. They will be evidence of the providence of God over the seed which fell on to the ground when the good old tree planted by our Saxon forefathers was torn up by the roots.

But one other reflection remains. Let the Catholics of the United Kingdom remember that the victory gained by the steadfast loyalty to the Church of Milner and the Irish bishops and O'Connell, was won by hard fighting in the days before emancipation. Unemancipated Catholics fought the battle, and fought it against fearful odds; in England an unemancipated bishop who could not even vote at an election, withstood the great statesmen of the day—statesmen compared with whom, Lord Brougham said in his day, "we are mere pigmies," and these statesmen backed by our Catholic aristocracy. In Ireland an unemancipated Catholic, who could vote indeed at an election, but who could not make his voice heard in Parliament, created an organization before which the strongest phalanx of bigotry which the Christian world has ever seen, gave way. We now are living when only the older ones amongst us can remember the passing of the Act of Emancipation. Young men ask us when the Act was passed, as they would ask us when the trial of Queen Caroline came on. Though there have been gusts of wintry weather, we have had sunshine enough during the last fifty-five years to take a good deal of exercise and warm our limbs, cold and cramped by the chains which O'Connell struck off, and yet we Catholics in England cannot, for the benefit of the poor and the young amongst us, come up, in the matter of useful organization, to the standard of Wesleyan Methodists. And what is to be said of Ireland? O'Connell was the only man who ever united the whole Catholic population; and O'Connell comes once in a thousand years.

CHAPTER XXV.

PROGRESS OF AGITATION FOR RELIEF.

Proceedings in 1814—O'Connell and Grattan—Meetings in Ireland—Speech of O'Connell—Sir Henry Parnell presents the petitions—His motion defeated—Mr. Daly's speech—The debate in the Commons in 1815—The debate in the Lords in 1815.

HAVING disposed of the veto question except so far as it may incidentally arise in the course of this history, it is necessary now to speak of the progress of the general question of emancipation. We have already seen that Canning, speaking in the House of Commons in the year 1825, and alluding to the failure of the bill of 1813, said that from that time the Catholic question began to lose ground. This was perfectly true as far as Parliament was concerned. Though, as we shall see, the question was frequently brought forward, the house refused to give it a favourable reception until the year 1821, when Mr. Plunket obtained a majority of six, the numbers in favour of his motion being 227 against 221. There were several reasons for the decline of our cause in Parliament. It has been noticed in an early part of this history that fear was the chief motive which induced the Legislature to give us relief. During the whole time that we were at war with France, it was a great object of those English statesmen who were not thoroughly steeped in bigotry and hatred of the Catholic Church, to conciliate the Irish. Some few, indeed, of those statesmen—as, for instance, Lords Grenville and Grey—supported our claims on broad liberal grounds;[1] but the bulk of our friends gave a favourable hearing to our complaints, and would have given us relief merely in order to secure the enlistment of the Irish in our armies to enable us to beat the French. When the news of the victory at Waterloo had caused all fear to vanish, and when all sorrow was turned into joy, the House of Commons became comparatively indifferent to our wrongs. Nor were our representatives thoroughly roused from their apathy until alarming sounds were heard from Ireland. Then, as the distant rumblings swelled into loud thunder, not only Commons, but King, Lords, and Commons were forced to yield in presence of a power which they were obliged to confess was greater than their own. Another reason why there was a change in our favour in the year 1821, may have been that in the previous year, 1820, a new reign began on the death of King George III. on the 29th of January. It is true that when, in the year 1810, the old King's "illness," as it was called, became permanent, and his eldest son became Regent without restrictions, statesmen did not consider themselves bound by their humane resolve not to endanger the sanity of their Sovereign by bringing forward the Catholic question. Still, it may be supposed that many Englishmen had determined that they would not entertain a proposal for our relief until the beginning of a new reign. At any rate, such an epoch would afford a favourable opportunity for reconsidering the matter.

But it must unfortunately be admitted that another reason why, between the session of 1813 and the session of

[1] The reader must understand that the word "liberal," applied to statesmen who acted their part many years ago, does not include those revolutionary and irreligious opinions which now it often does.

1820-21, there was less anxiety in Parliament to listen to us, was the notorious divisions amongst ourselves on the question of veto. In the "Annual Register" for the year 1814 the following words occur:—"It was observed, in relating the proceedings of the Irish Roman Catholics during the last year" (that is, 1813) "that a spirit of disunion had manifested itself in that body, which had operated upon the efforts towards an improvement of their situation ; and the same remark will apply to the present year."[1] The "Annual Register" then goes on to relate the proceedings in Ireland in regard to the veto question. From this it is pretty plain what was the effect produced in England by disunion amongst the Irish Catholics.[2]

In the year 1820, the disgraceful proceedings in Parliament, commonly called the "Trial of Queen Caroline," set on foot by the man whom Lord Byron most appropriately calls "the double tyrant," so engrossed public attention that no place was left for the grievances of his Majesty's Roman Catholic subjects. And so it was not until the year 1821 that the successful fight began which, after eight years of hard campaigning, resulted in the victory of 1829.

But though the general question of emancipation was making no progress in Parliament between the end of the year 1813 and the commencement of the year 1821, yet, as it was discussed in Parliament and out-of-doors, it was progressing in this sense—that O'Connell was advancing his reputation as the prince of agitators, and gradually acquiring that power which enabled him ultimately to win the day.

During these intermediate years, however, several things

[1] Chapter xix. p. 215.
[2] It would be well worth some one's while to write a book on the misery of disunion, illustrated solely by examples taken from the history of the Catholics of the United Kingdom.

took place both in and out of Parliament which I must now proceed to relate.

In the year 1814, the British Catholics were not idle. "On the 17th of February, a general meeting of the English Catholics was held at the house of the Earl of Shrewsbury, in Stanhope Street,[1] and a form of a petition to both Houses of Parliament was resolved upon. It referred to their former petitions, and prayed the House to 'take into consideration the many pains and disabilities under which they laboured, and to adopt measures for their relief.' It was also resolved that a deputation should wait upon Earl Grey and the Right Hon. William Elliot, and request that they would present the petition of the Catholics to the respective Houses of Parliament, and express to those gentlemen 'the wish of the board that they should have the advantage of a separate and distinct discussion.'

"At a subsequent meeting it was resolved, that 'their parliamentary friends should be requested to obtain, if possible, the repeal of all remaining restrictions on the religious observances of the Catholics, particularly with respect to their marriages.'

"On the 28th of the following June, the British Catholic petition was presented to the House of Lords; and on the 1st of the following July, a similar petition was presented to the House of Commons by Mr. Elliot."[2]

I do not find mention of any discussion upon the presentation of either of these two petitions.

In Ireland there was little mention at public meetings of anything connected with emancipation, except the question of the veto. O'Connell was now the great

---

[1] This is a well-known house; walking up Stanhope Street towards the Park, it is the last house on the left-hand side, at the corner of the street and Park Lane, with a verandah facing towards the Park.

[2] Butler's "Historical Memoirs," vol. iv. p. 272.

champion in Ireland of the freedom of the Church, and through his influence the Catholic Board, previous to its dissolution in this year by the Government, induced Lord Donoughmore in the House of Lords and Grattan in the Commons to present petitions for unqualified emancipation.

But Grattan declined to discuss the merits of the question. Of this refusal of Grattan's, O'Connell, in a speech which he made in Dublin on the 16th of June, 1815, spoke as follows:—"Mr. Grattan took charge of our petition last year; he presented it to the House, but he refused to discuss its merits. No reason was given for this refusal, other than the reason which silences, though it cannot satisfy, the slaves of despots. It consisted singly of the phrase '*Stat pro ratione voluntas.*' We were deeply impressed with the conviction that the discussion of our grievances and claims in the last session—indeed, every session—could produce nothing but advantages. Our cause is founded on eternal justice and plain right; therefore, so long as there remains one particle of common sense amongst men, discussion must advance that cause. The Catholic Board called on Mr. Grattan to bring forward our question; he again refused. The board a second time entreated of him to do so; he once more refused. We then called another aggregate meeting, and that meeting requested from Mr. Grattan a discussion. Strange to say, he still persevered in his refusal—a perseverance unexampled in the history of Parliament."[1] The reason of Grattan's refusal was that he was a very decided vetoist; and when we come to the discussion in Parliament in the year 1816, we shall see that not only did he think *securities* desirable, but he thought emancipation could not be obtained without them. Entertaining the views he did, he

---

[1] "O'Connell's Speeches," edited by his son, vol. i. pp. 452, 453.

would not found a motion on a petition for unqualified emancipation.

In the year 1815 there was a Catholic meeting in Dublin on the 23rd of February. At this meeting, says Canon O'Rourke, O'Connell made his first public appearance after his duel with Mr. D'Esterre. "He" (that is, O'Connell) "submitted to that meeting a resolution, calling on the different counties and cities of Ireland to petition for *unqualified* emancipation. The Catholics," continues Canon O'Rourke, "at this time were feeble on account of their divisions. Those who were satisfied to give the Government *securities* (that is, who were willing to agree to the veto), had retired from public agitation, amongst them Mr. Sheil and Lord Fingall. Those who acted thus were called the Seceders." Canon O'Rourke then makes a somewhat long extract from the speech which O'Connell made at the meeting. As this extract contains words which not only throw a light on the history of the agitation in Ireland at this time, but which teach, from the mouth of the great master of constitutional agitation, sound principles and most useful lessons, the reader will no doubt be glad to peruse it.

"After speaking of the value of discussion and of persevering in sending petitions to Parliament, O'Connell continued to say, 'The great advantages of discussion being thus apparent, the efficacy of repeating and repeating, and repeating again our petitions, being thus demonstrated by notorious facts, the Catholics of Ireland must be sunk in criminal apathy, if they neglect the use of an instrument so efficacious for their emancipation. There is further encouragement at this particular crisis. Dissension has ceased in the Catholic body. Those who paralyzed our efforts, and gave our conduct the appearance and reality of weakness and wavering and inconsistency, have all retired. Those who were ready to place the entire of the Catholic feelings and dignity, and some *of the Catholic religion too*, under the feet of every man who pleased to call himself our friend, and to prove himself our friend by praising on every occasion, and upon no occasion, the oppressors of the Catholics, and by abusing the Catholics themselves; the men who would link the Catholic cause to *this* patron and to *that*, and sacrifice it at one time to the minister, and at another to the opposition, and make it this day the tool of one party and the next the instrument of another party; the men, in fine, who hoped to traffic upon our country and our religion—who would buy honours, and titles, and places, and pensions, at the price of the *purity* and *dignity* and *safety* of the Catholic Church in Ireland;—all those men have, thank God, quitted us, I hope, for ever. They have returned into silence and secession, or have frankly or covertly gone over to our enemies. I regret deeply and bitterly that they have carried with them some few who, like my Lord Fingall, entertain no other motives than those of purity and integrity, and who, like that noble lord, are merely mistaken. But I rejoice at this separation. I rejoice that they have left the simple-hearted, and the disinterested, and the indefatigable, and the independent, and the numerous, and the sincere Catholics to work out their emancipation unclogged, unshackled, and undismayed.'"[1]

On the 16th of June, 1815, an adjourned meeting of the Catholics of Ireland was held at Clarendon Street Chapel. In the course of his speech at this meeting, O'Connell maintained that it was necessary to find some other member of Parliament than Grattan to present their petition. "You must have a new selection made," he said; "you must have a man selected who *will* consent to receive your instructions: who, in short, will seek to obtain for the Catholics of Ireland that which the Catholics of Ireland deserve, and not get up a plan of his own, in which he may be the principal figure, and the Catholics secondary objects. . . . We must seek for an Englishman, for I know of no Irish member to whom you can now commit your petition." And he concluded his speech with the

[1] Centenary "Life of O'Connell," p. 91.

following motion :—"That the Catholic Association[1] be requested to send a delegation to London, in order to procure a member of the House of Commons to present our petition, and apply for unqualified emancipation." At the request of some members of the association, this motion was deferred until the 23rd of June. Of the meeting held on that day I have no record, but Grattan did not present the Irish petition in that year, 1815. It was presented by Sir Henry Parnell, the historian of the penal laws, and one of the best supporters of the Catholic claims.

I will now give the progress of the Catholic question in Parliament for this year from the "Annual Register."[2] "It was remarked in the history of the last year," says the writer in the "Annual Register" for 1815, "that the cause of Catholic emancipation had been injured by the dissensions which took place among the persons of that persuasion in Ireland, and by the violence displayed at their public meetings against any attempts to reconcile them with Government." I may interrupt the quotation to notice that reconciliation with Government meant a surrender of the rights of the Church; and the

[1] What O'Connell here calls the "Catholic Association" was little more than a nominal organization.
[2] In the proceedings on the Catholic Question during the year 1815 there is a discrepancy in the matter of dates, which, with the materials before me, I am not able to solve. In the account given above, the motion of O'Connell to seek some other member instead of Grattan to present the Irish petition, was stated to have been made on the 16th of June. This statement was made on the authority of Mr. John O'Connell in his edition of his father's speeches, vol. i. p. 452. The "Annual Register," as the reader will see, puts the presentation of the Irish petition by Sir H. Parnell on the 11th of May, that is, nearly five weeks, according to Mr. John O'Connell, before it was determined that Grattan should not do it. The discrepancy is not a matter of much importance as far as the general history of the question is concerned, but it impairs the accuracy of the account. The main point to be remembered is that one of the most eloquent and most persevering Protestant advocates of emancipation was rejected by O'Connell because he was a vetoist.

"violence" was the enthusiastic determination of the Irish people not to make such surrender. I may also add that when Englishmen read accounts of what takes place in Ireland, they should always remember that the phraseology used is descriptive of the idea in the English mind as to what has been done, and by no means a description of the thing as done in Ireland. Enthusiastic opposition to a veto is called in England "violence" and "a want of the spirit of conciliation."[1]

"They" (that is, the Irish Catholics), continues the "Annual Register," "agreed, however, upon a new petition to Parliament; and on the 11th of May, a paper to that effect was presented to the House of Commons by Sir Henry Parnell, which he stated to contain the unequivocal opinion of the mass of the Roman Catholics of Ireland. It was read, and concluded with imploring the House 'to grant to them the redress of the oppressive grievances of which they so justly complain; and to restore to them the full and unrestricted enjoyment of the rank of free subjects of the Empire.' On the 18th, the same hon. member rose to submit to the House certain resolutions with respect to the claims of the Roman Catholics of Ireland. These resolutions were read, and after some discussion relative to form, the first of them was moved; upon the suggestion, however, of Mr. Banks, the motion was withdrawn."

The Catholics of England, or some of them at least, were not inactive during this session: for the "Annual Register" continues to say that, "on the 30th" (that is, of May), Sir H. Parnell presented a petition signed by 6000 Roman Catholics in York, Birmingham, Norwich, and other places, praying for an unrestricted emancipation

---

[1] English Catholics are quite as much in want of this general reminder as English Protestants.

from all civil and military disqualifications oppressing them. He then moved for the reading of several entries in the journals of the House, of the proceedings relative to the Roman Catholics; which being done, he began a speech on the subject. He assumed as a principle, that Parliament had admitted the expediency of a legislative measure, for the removal of the disqualifications under which the Roman Catholics laboured; and that the question then was, how such a plan was to be carried into operation? The only obstacle, he said, now existing in the way of Catholic emancipation, was the claim to give the Crown a control over the future appointment of bishops, which had been set up on one side, and objected to on the other. He proceeded to show that the Pope's influence over the Irish Church was then not such as to excite apprehension; and he concluded his speech by moving 'that the House will resolve itself into a committee of the whole House, to take into its consideration the laws affecting his Majesty's Roman Catholic subjects.'[1] On this motion there was a long debate. When the House divided, the votes were—For going into committee, 147; against it, 228; the majority against the motion being 81.

Mr. James Daly, one of the Irish members, was accidentally shut out of the division. But on the following day (May 31) he took advantage of having a petition to present from the Catholics of Galway, to say a very few words; which words, even after seventy years, afford matter for reflection. After expressing his regret that the decision of the night before had been so unfavourable to the wishes of the petitioners, he said, " Having been so unfortunate as to have been shut out of the division last night, I take this opportunity of stating my entire concurrence with the motion of the honourable baronet, being fully convinced

[1] " Annual Register " for 1815, pp. 28, 29.

that without putting the Catholics of this empire on a footing of equality with their Protestant fellow-subjects, we shall want that cordiality which is so necessary to the prosperity of the two countries."[1]

These are the words of an Irish Protestant spoken in the House of Commons fourteen years before emancipation. It is now exactly fifty-six years since the Act of emancipation was supposed to put the Catholics of this empire on a footing of equality with their Protestant fellow-subjects. And yet we still want that cordiality which Mr. Daly so truly said was necessary to the prosperity of the two countries. England has, indeed, been prosperous enough, she has had enough prosperity, and over and above what would have been necessary to prove to the most desponding pagan in pagan days that his country was the greatest in the world. But it cannot be said that Ireland has been prosperous. Why has it not been so? So far as England is concerned, it has been because, with intermittent fits of fair-dealing, with a good amount of tinkering legislation, with fifty-six years of that kind of government, the greatest praise of which is to apply to it the old saying, 'Half a loaf is better than no bread;' England has been trying all along to rule an Irish and a Catholic people on English and Protestant principles. Ireland has suffered from the action of England, and therefore she has not been prosperous. One country has been prosperous; but the two

[1] Supplement to the *Orthodox Journal* for 1815, p. 30. Quoting the *Orthodox Journal*, affords an opportunity for a remark. Some years ago, it used to be the fashion with some literary, but nevertheless thoughtless, individuals amongst us English Catholics, to laugh at the *Orthodox Journal*. The fact is, that the first series of that periodical, extending from the year 1813 to the year 1820, both inclusive, is, from more than one point of view, extremely valuable, and those who have that series complete are lucky possessors. It may be enough to say here that the modern history of the Church in England could not be satisfactorily written without it.

have not. The continued prosperity of England is a matter of speculation. Looking at the state of affairs in general, some may be inclined to think that England's first great trouble will come either directly or indirectly from Ireland. If so, it will be from the want of that cordiality which is so necessary to the prosperity of the two countries; in which case England will have only herself to blame.

A few extracts from the speeches in the House of Commons during the debates on the Catholic question in the year 1815, and some remarks suggested by what was said, will be useful as showing the temper of the House, and as offering matter for practical consideration in our own days.[1] In his speech on the 18th of May, Sir Henry Parnell read a number of resolutions which he had intended to propose; but which it was decided on a point of form he could not then bring forward. It appears that these resolutions were drawn up by O'Connell, as was also the draft of a bill founded upon them, and which draft had been circulated amongst the members. I gather this from a passage in the speech of Mr. Peel.[2] Speaking of O'Connell as "a gentleman who possessed the confidence of the Irish Catholics in a greater degree than any other person," and to whom, "at every meeting of the Catholics of Ireland, the thanks of the body were amongst the resolutions;" Mr. Peel went on to say that "the opinion of a person who seemed thus to represent the opinions of the Catholic body was of some importance, and the more so because he had drawn up the present resolutions and the bill, which to save the Parliament the trouble of legislation had been drawn up and previously circulated, and which

---

[1] This account of the debate is taken from the full report of the debate in the supplement to the *Orthodox Journal* of 1815.

[2] Afterwards the great Sir Robert.

the Catholics presented as the only measure they would have."

The draft bill above mentioned embodied in the form of an Act the resolution which Sir H. Parnell had read to the House. The proposed bill was certainly a good one. The object of it, as stated in the preamble, was in short this—to put Catholics in every respect on a footing of equality with Protestants. It provided a short oath to be taken instead of the oaths and declaration which had hitherto excluded Catholics from Parliament and various offices and privileges. This oath, prepared as we have seen by O'Connell, was, like the oath now taken, one which would have suited in the case of every person whether Catholic or Protestant. One clause of the bill provided that marriage between two Catholics according to the forms of the Catholic Church, should be legal. This clause was necessary as it appears to have been doubtful whether such marriages were not included in an Act of George II. for preventing clandestine marriages. Another clause put Catholics on a par with Dissenters in the matter of charitable bequests, and did away with the absurd law about 'superstitious uses.' Why on a par with Dissenters, and not with all his Majesty's subjects, I am not aware. Clause 8 was for the protection of Catholic worship against malicious disturbance. Clause 9 related to the marriage by a Catholic priest of persons both of whom should be Protestant. It changed the punishment of a priest for marrying such Protestants, from that enacted in one of the "ferocious laws" of Queen Anne, to a fine of £50. The tenth clause was for the protection of Catholic soldiers and sailors against those commanders who should compel them to assist at Protestant worship.

This bill drawn up, according to Sir R. Peel, by O'Connell is, of course, free from that foul blot upon the Emancipation Act caused by the clauses against Religious Orders. It is true that there is in this bill no special repeal of the clauses against Religious Orders contained in the Act of 1791. But the words of the bill are so general that, with deference to authorities learned in the law, I think it might be argued that "Jesuits and members of other Religious Orders, Communities, or Societies of the Church of Rome, bound by monastic or religious vows,"[1] would have been included in the benefit, if the bill had passed into an Act. But if the bill could not have been construed to include Religious Orders, the reader will remember that the members of such orders were in a better position under the Act of 1791 than they are under the great Act of 1829. As we are, in this history, still fourteen years previous to the Emancipation Act, this is not the time to mark with the infamy they deserve the hateful clauses against Religious Orders. Suffice it here to say that they are a standing disgrace to the Statute Book of a country which boasts of its liberality and independence; and that they are the shame of every Catholic in the land so long as we do not continually protest against them.

In his speech in the House of Commons on May 30, 1815, Sir H. Parnell laid it down that in the Parliament immediately preceding the one then sitting, and also in that present Parliament by the proceedings on the bill of 1813, the principle of the Catholic question had been carried, and that all that remained was to consider the best mode of carrying that principle into effect. He spoke of Grattan as the man "to whom was due all the merit of having virtually carried this great question; and to whom every Catholic would always look up as to his great deliverer from the most persecuting system that ever disgraced a Government or aggrieved a people."

[1] The words of the Act of 1829.

Considering that it was through Grattan's eloquent and persevering advocacy of our claims that the principle of emancipation was admitted by the House of Commons, Sir H. Parnell's words in 1815 were not more than the great Irishman deserved. But the years which followed up to 1829 showed that there was a vast difference between admitting the principle and acting upon it; as much difference perhaps as there is between admitting the rules of morality and putting them in practice. Grattan obtained an admission of the principle. O'Connell forced the Act. Sir Henry Parnell declared himself an anti-vetoist. He spoke of that security as altogether unnecessary, and that it was absolutely impossible for the opponents of Catholic emancipation to prove a case of necessity sufficiently strong to justify their anxious adherence to the argument, that it was indispensable the Crown should possess the control over the appointment of Catholic bishops. Sir Henry having explained the nature of the resolutions which he proposed to ask the House to adopt in committee, then moved the resolution which the reader has seen in the preceding chapter. Sir John Cox Hippisley, whom Canning had effectually crushed two years before, ventured to reply to Sir Henry Parnell. He announced himself a vetoist at starting. True to the character of a meddler and mischief-maker, he had the dishonesty to tell the House that the power of imposing restrictions had even been conceded in the rescript of Monsignore Quarantotti, at the time vested by the Court of Rome with ample powers for that purpose. This assertion was not honest; for it is impossible to suppose that Sir John Hippisley, who notoriously busied himself with Catholic affairs, was not aware that Pope Pius VII. had a year before declared that Monsignore Quarantotti had no authority to write the rescript.[1] He harped upon the want of that information which would be obtained if the House would grant him the committee which Canning had ridiculed two years ago; and he concluded, as a weak but opiniated man might have been expected to conclude, by saying that he should vote neither one way nor the other.

A long speech was made in the debate on the 30th of May by Mr. C. Yorke. It was a strong anti-Catholic speech; but not quite stretching to the Eldon sticking point. With all sorts of securities, Mr. Yorke would probably have voted for the motion for going into committee. The mind of the hon. member seems to have been greatly exercised because he was not "perfectly aware of what the See of Rome meant to do." And he spoke one of those sentences in which the confusion of ideas and words is so amusing to Catholics when Protestants talk about Catholic affairs. He said, "he did expect that his Holiness would, before this, *sui juris*, have made some disclosure, *ex cathedrâ*, on these subjects, to his flock in Great Britain and Ireland. Up to that moment, however, he was convinced nothing had been done; and such were the differences between the Catholics of England and Ireland, that intrigues, he believed, were being carried on at Rome, by the missionaries of the respective bodies, with a view to prevent the present Pope from coming to any opinion on the disputed points." The fact was, as the reader will remember, that the Holy Father had well considered the matter, and that Cardinal Litta had sent the decision of the Holy See to Dr. Poynter more than a month before Mr. Yorke made his speech. Mr. Yorke, of course, voted against the motion. He was followed by a

---

[1] Mr. Yorke, who follows Sir John in the debate, showed that he (Mr. Yorke) was aware of what the Pope had done. Sir J. Hippisley had the same means of knowing it.

gentleman of the name of Knox, who fell into the same error as did Sir John Hippisley, and, alluding to the Quarantotti rescript, said it was proved that the Pope had agreed to the veto. So much for the knowledge which Protestants profess to have of Catholic affairs. After Mr. Knox, Mr. Maurice Fitzgerald rose and made a very sensible speech in support of Sir H. Parnell's motion. His remarks on the veto are especially worthy of notice. He said—

"With respect to a veto, his opinion remained totally unchanged. As to the feelings of the Catholics on this point, which was so nearly connected with their Church, he should say nothing. It was a pure matter of conscience. But, as a Protestant, he disliked a veto—which, if effectual, would give to a Protestant Government a most dangerous and mischievous power. It would be the means of lending the patronage of the Catholic Church to the purposes of Protestant politicians; and this, he conceived, would be exceedingly dangerous. It would also have the effect of introducing sectaries amongst the Catholic clergy, who would endeavour to entice the people over to them, in the same way as similar causes had operated in the Protestant Church."

Mr. Peel made a speech which in one respect is extremely curious. He did not enter into the merits of the Catholic question; but the whole of his address was an attack upon the various organizations which had been formed in Ireland for obtaining redress. He voted against the motion. His speech is curious, because Mr. Peel, as Sir Robert in the year 1829, proposed and carried the great Act on the sole ground, as both he and the Duke of Wellington admitted, that, in face of O'Connell's Catholic Association, the choice of English statesmen lay between emancipation and civil war. Sir John Newport, a good friend of the Catholics, spoke after Mr. Peel, and made a remark which it would be well for those English Catholics to take special note of who are constantly shocked, or pretend to be shocked, at what they call the intemperate language of the Irish.

"He could not," he said, "persuade himself to believe that the House would repel the case of the petitioners unheard, merely because some of those aggrieved individuals had given expression to their honest minds in rather an intemperate manner. For it might be that if any set of gentlemen in that House were equally aggrieved they would vent their dissatisfaction in terms even more intemperate. . . . According to the last speaker," continued Sir John, "the House should decline to concede to, or even abstain from, the consideration of the Catholic claims until the Catholics should altogether suppress the declaration of any angry feeling; but in his" (Sir John Newport's) "view, it would be the better policy at once to remove the cause of such angry feeling."

Sir John also gave Mr. Peel a very wholesome lecture on the line he had taken in his speech. Mr. Bathurst, who next rose, made one of those speeches which present the melancholy exhibition which we so often witness, of an Englishman losing all his good sense when he is speaking of Irish and Catholic affairs. "He would never concur," he said, "in any measure of this description, until the respectable class of the Roman Catholics stept forward to sever themselves from the thraldom of those who were meeting, with an avowal of ingratitude, the interposition of the legislature in the adjustment of their claims." This avowal of ingratitude was O'Connell's declaration that he would not accept of emancipation if accompanied by the veto.[1] One honourable gentleman of the name of Bankes said he could not think of voting for the Catholic claims

[1] Some of the members seem to have been especially annoyed because O'Connell, at an aggregate meeting, alluding to the cheer with which the rejection of the principal clause of the bill of 1813 was received in the House, called it a "ruffian shout." This description of a cheer in which no doubt he who became afterwards the great Sir Robert joined, seems to have considerably affected the sensitive nerves of Mr. Peel and some smaller men.

"until the Church of Rome should entertain different opinions of those whom it called heretical." And another gentleman, who ought to have known better, Serjeant Best, said that before he could agree even to deliberate, he must know several things; one of which was whether Dr. Milner "had laid it down as a maxim that 'the arm of power might be lawfully raised against a heretic king.'" Another thing he wanted to know was whether his Holiness Pope Pius VII. held an opinion alleged to have come from the Court of Rome "that oaths taken against the Church were null and void."[1] Lord Castlereagh, who was foreign secretary, made the kind of speech that might have been expected from him. Having been, along with William Pitt, one of the originators of the security or veto question, he, of course, announced himself a vetoist, and he thought that a bill should be passed containing a security clause, whether the Irish Catholics liked it or not, "even," he said, "though it were met, on the part of the people of Ireland, by the most extensive dissatisfaction." This speech was only one symptom of the spirit which guided him in everything connected with Ireland; and it was his general conduct, acting under this spirit, which has made the name of Castlereagh one of the most hateful sounds in the ears of an Irishman.[2] Mr. Whitbread, who followed Castlereagh, made a good hit at the noble lord's intolerance, observing that "the conduct of Mr. O'Connell in Ireland had been exactly the same as that of the right honourable secretary, who by all kinds of exaggeration endeavoured to aggra-

---

[1] There are many Protestants, and amongst them no doubt some good lawyers like Serjeant Best, who are quite capable, even in these days, of uttering such *stuff* as this. It requires some one who has the wit of Sydney Smith to apply the proper whip to such people.

[2] Castlereagh became secretary for Ireland in 1798; and he continued to hold that office all through the arrangements for the union of Great Britain and Ireland and for a few years after.

vate the Protestants, as Mr. O'Connell, by exaggeration, thought to inflame the Catholics." Mr. Wellesley Pole[1] made a short speech in which he showed very clearly that he was in complete ignorance of the state of feeling amongst Irish Catholics. Mr. Huskisson, who held the office which was then called the "Woods and Forests," said he should vote for the committee; but when in committee, he hoped the House would not allow itself to be dictated to. When Huskisson sat down, the great orator (and with the exception of his being a vetoist, the best, as he was one of the two most eloquent and persevering advocates of the Catholic claims) Henry Grattan rose to make the concluding speech. However disappointed he must have felt at having been rejected by the Catholics of Dublin for the presentation of their petition, he must have been gratified at the manner in which he was spoken of in the House. One-half of the speakers expressed their great regret that the petition and resolution had been entrusted to other hands than his; and he received continued compliments on his fidelity to the Catholic cause. In fact, on reading the debate, it is evident there was a great disappointment, and even a general soreness, felt in the House at the rejection of Grattan by the Irish Catholics. The great patriot's speech was on this occasion not a long one; but it was very vetoistical. He said, amongst other things, "I have no hesitation in saying that I condemn (I am sorry if I give offence to persons who are of a different opinion), but I condemn the application for unqualified concession. The knowledge I have of the sentiments of this House convinces me that such a proposition will not pass. When the petitioners desire emancipation without

---

[1] This is the gentleman who was afterwards known as Mr. Long Tilney Wellesley Long Pole, and subsequently as Earl of Mornington. He was nephew to the Duke of Wellington.

any conditions, they desire two things—they desire emancipation, and then they desire that it may not be granted, because the annexation of no conditions must render the grant in this House impossible. . . . I mean to support the Catholic question with a desperate fidelity—if I may so express myself. I use the word 'desperate,' not with reference to any disposition on my part to sacrifice a single principle of good government or a single necessary security on that question, but because to my fidelity I cannot promise success. . . . Sir, I have an ardent love for the Catholic body. I do not ascribe the errors of some individuals to the body at large; but I say once more that unless they adopt the spirit of conciliation, they have not the smallest chance of success." By a spirit of conciliation, Grattan meant a willingness to give the securities required, amongst them the veto. But Grattan was not a prophet. Emancipation was delayed for nine years after his death in 1820; but when it did come, it came, not indeed without some ugly features, but without any one of the securities for which he and so many others, Catholics as well as Protestants, had contended. Such is a short account of the debate in the House of Commons on the Catholic claims on the 30th of May, 1815, within less than three weeks of the day on which hundreds of those to whom the House refused the rights of British subjects, laid down their lives, for the security and the honour and glory of Britain, on the field of Waterloo.

On the 19th of May, 1815, the old and trusty champion of the Catholics, the Earl of Donoughmore, presented the Irish petition in the House of Lords. The 1st of June was appointed for its consideration, and for that day the House was ordered to be summoned. Chiefly in consequence of the illness of Lord Donoughmore, the Catholic question had to be postponed until the 8th of June. On that day the Duke of Sussex, one of the King's sons presented a petition from certain Roman Catholics in the county of Lancaster, praying for the complete abolition of all disabilities, without any condition or restriction. His Royal Highness said that as the petition was couched in respectful language, he thought it his duty to present it, though he did not by any means pledge himself to support the prayer of it to the full extent. The Duke was followed by Earl Stanhope, who said that he should vote that the petition be laid on the table, not only because it was couched in respectful language, but because he completely concurred in the prayer of it, being of opinion that everything necessary for the enjoyment of the fullest religious liberty was a matter of right and justice, and not of grace and favour. Lord Donoughmore then presented several petitions from Ireland ; and also two from England, one of them being from the town and neighbourhood of Sheffield, and the other a more general one signed by five thousand names. His lordship then proceeded to address the House on the subject. His speech was a long one. It may be read in its entirety either in Hansard or in the *Orthodox Journal*. A few extracts from the speech will be useful in this history, as they will afford both interesting information and occasions for remarks which may be practical for those who choose to make them so. One of his observations is on the different state of the law in the three great divisions of the United Kingdom.

"If," he says, " this system " (that is, the penal laws) " (supposing it to be deserving of such a name) is indeed capable of justification, on the plea of necessity, it ought surely to be at least uniform in its operation against the proscribed class—wheresoever found within the precincts of the State. Is such, however, the state of the case? or is it not, on the contrary, directly the reverse of this ? In Scotland, the Catholic has the capacity to hold every office, civil or military, without any toleration of his religion; in England, a very limited admission into the State, under the Statute of 1791; in Ireland the elective franchise, and all the important acquisitions of 1793. Is not this existing anomaly alone a sufficient reason for prompt consideration? And ought it not to be considered, almost as an axiom, in every well regulated Government, that the civil and military capacities of all the subjects of the same class and description should be similar and uniform within the same state."

This difference, alluded to by Lord Donoughmore, arose from the fact that the greater part of the penal laws were enacted before the formation of the United Kingdom, by the legislative union of England with Scotland in the year 1707, and by the union of Great Britain with Ireland, the act establishing which was passed in the year 1800, and took effect on the 1st of January, 1801.

On the question of "securities" Lord Donoughmore said—

"That from what he had already so fully stated as his opinion upon that subject, the House must be already aware that he looked for none, because he was convinced in his conscience that none were wanted. It was, therefore, scarcely necessary for him to say that he had disapproved altogether of the additional clauses which had been added in committee to the bill which was so much debated in 1813, in another place. In addition to the Pope, they had now two new personages brought forward upon the stage as objects of great apprehension, and against whom, for the protection of the Protestant establishment, these additional barriers had been raised. These objects of alarm were no other than the Catholic bishops and the Catholic deans."

"Will any noble lord," exclaimed Lord Donoughmore —and his words are worthy of record, not only as honourable to himself, but as applicable to our affairs now, when there may be some Catholics both in Church and State who are not so loyal to the Catholic cause as his lordship was, though a Protestant—

"Will any noble lord conscientiously declare that he has himself known, or has heard repeated to him by any other person whatever, one solitary circumstance, on which the slightest suspicion could attach of disloyal conduct towards the State, against any of these calumniated ministers of religion. Rummage the dark and dismal records of the eighty years of proscription, pursue the inquiry through the more auspicious period of the last forty years—and will there be found a single instance of criminality—nay, even of suspicion? He, therefore, objected to these clauses, to all that measure of security, because it was in the first place unnecessary, and in the next place, because it tended to throw on the character of blameless and meritorious individuals an unjust and cruel aspersion."

Thus we see two other reasons given by a Protestant statesman against a veto, in addition to those we have seen given by Edmund Burke. Burke said it would be unjust and an intolerable hardship, adding that the members of one religious sect were not fit to appoint the pastors to another. Lord Donoughmore said it would be unnecessary and insulting. Lord Donoughmore went on to make some remarks which are so excellent, the reading of which is so profitable even now, so likely perhaps to be more profitable in the future, that it would be a careless thing to leave them shut up in books which so few can open. I therefore give his words; and let the reader remember that Lord Donoughmore is not speaking of a proposition to give the English Government a right to *appoint* a Catholic bishop, but merely a right to *veto* an appointment. Immediately following the last words quoted from Lord Donoughmore's speech he goes on to say:

"It was repugnant to his feelings in another point of view, inasmuch as it offered privileges to the Catholic laity, at the price of the degradation of the character of their Church. But these securities have been rejected *una voce* by the whole Catholic community, lay and ecclesiastical.[1] Whether they were or were not

[1] Lord Donoughmore was alluding only to Ireland when he expressed the

inconsistent with the religious feelings of that persuasion, the noble earl said that it was not his province to argue. Those whose province it was to consider and decide had determined that question in the negative and had set it at rest."[1]

We must admire here the strong common sense, the fairness, and the great political prudence of Lord Donoughmore's words. There was evidently in his mind a just discrimination between the authority of the Church and the authority of the State. His principle was clearly this : let the Catholic Church mind its own business, and let us mind ours. That is certainly a fair principle ; and it has strong common sense in it. It is also politically prudent. The last power in the world which would be likely to interfere, or which would wish to interfere, with the temporal power and prosperity of the British nation is the power of the Catholic Church. It would perhaps be not too much to say, that the strongest foundation on which the integrity of the United Kingdom has rested since the Act of Union has been and, it may be added, still is the Catholic Church. Many Englishmen know this well : the *Times* newspaper knows it when periodically, after having heaped every kind of abuse upon the Irish clergy for a dozen years, it calls out to the priests, like a woman crying for protection, to help England out of some Irish trouble. There are many Englishmen who would no doubt laugh at the notion that the power of the Catholic Church is

unanimity of the Catholic community on the subject of the veto. And in Ireland the unanimity was amongst the Bishops and priests and those laymen who were actively engaged in the agitation for emancipation. The vetoists, numerically a small minority, had seceded and were for the time doing nothing.

[1] As the question is put by Lord Donoughmore, the Irish Catholics had decided in the affirmative, namely, that the securities were inconsistent, etc. The question decided in the negative was whether or not they would accept the veto.

a surer base of union and prosperity than the power of the British Grenadiers. And in their merriment they might utter some vulgar blasphemy, worthy of being the complement of Napoleon's too famous exclamation when he heard that he had been excommunicated by the Pope. But if they care not to be affected by the terrible punishment of the great Emperor, they may at least learn the lesson which has been constantly before their eyes, in our home affairs. What has England profited by impeding the action of the Church in the British Isles? What did it profit in the days when it was a principle of Government not only that the Protestant majority should lord it over the Catholic minority in England, but that the Protestant minority should tyrannize over and trample upon the Catholic majority in Ireland? What was the end of such folly in political action? The end was, and it cannot be denied, Protestant England had to go down on her knees before an Irishman and a Catholic who stood facing her at the head of six million unarmed Irish Catholics, and ask him what he would take to leave the State in peace. And in more modern days what has England profited by interfering in the action of the Church? What has been the result of trespassing upon ground not their own? The foolish conduct of the English people in meddling with the arrangement of the Church regarding the purely ecclesiastical Government of English Catholics, and in questions concerning the superintendence of convents and religious education, has been keeping up a continual irritation, an abiding sense amongst us that at any moment we may be subjected to impertinent interference in our religious concerns. The Catholic Church will never hurt a hair of England's head; and yet a vast number of Englishmen are only too happy to seize any silly pretext for abusing her and insulting her members. Notwithstanding all he has done for Ireland, Catholics cannot trust the late prime minister of England (Mr. Gladstone). And why? It is chiefly because when his education scheme for Ireland had been rejected by the bishops, he wrote his Vatican pamphlets. How much better both for him and for us it would have been if, instead of being angry and writing against us, he had said what Lord Donoughmore said fifty years before: "those whose province it was to consider and decide, had determined the question in the negative, and had set it at rest." We may find out, unfortunately when it will be too late, that the best policy would have been to let the Catholic Church mind her own business while Englishmen were minding theirs. Having said the words I have just quoted, Lord Donoughmore continued as follows:—

"His own objections were derived from another source. He rejected them" (that is, the securities), "because they affected to improve the constitution of an important class of individuals, which, in his opinion, did not stand in need of any amendment. He said he knew the Catholic clergy well; that a more meritorious and valuable body of men existed not in the Protestant State—they passed their exemplary lives in the faithful discharge of a laborious duty. The magistrates themselves were not more effectual in the preservation of the peace; they desired no rewards but the voluntary offerings of their own flocks; to them, to their ecclesiastical superiors, and to their fellow-labourers in the same vineyard, and to no other quarter, they looked for approbation, countenance, and support. I will never consent," said the noble earl, "to an arrangement, the tendency of which would be to give these thoughts another direction, and to turn their eyes to some inferior agent of a Provincial Government in the Irish castle-yard. In short, these security clauses are a piece of cumbrous machinery, as little necessary as they would be likely to be effectual to any beneficial purposes."

Thus we have now two further reasons against Government interference in the affairs of the Catholic Church: it would tend to give another direction to the thoughts of the clergy; and it would be ineffectual; that is, it would not produce the effect intended by the Government. No doubt this last reason is a perfectly sound one. In all probability if the Government were to veto the choice of those appointed by the Church to elect a bishop, it would find that its own choice would not be so good a one, even for its own purposes. The State is no better judge of a man fit to be a bishop, than the Church is of a man fit to be commander-in-chief. When the Pope shall meddle in the affairs of the English army, then the English Government may interfere in the affairs of the Church. Lord Donoughmore concluded his speech by moving, " That this House will immediately take into consideration the state of his Majesty's Roman Catholic subjects of Great Britain and Ireland, with reference to the laws by which they still continue to be respectively affected."

When the question was put from the Woolsack, several speakers addressed the House. Lord Liverpool, the prime minister, opposed the motion chiefly on the ground that no inquiry as to the state of Roman Catholics in the United Kingdom was necessary, as that state was perfectly well known. He, however, enunciated the principle that "a Protestant Dynasty and a Protestant ecclesiastical Establishment should be supported by a Protestant Parliament and a Protestant Administration." It is nearly seventy years since Lord Liverpool said this; during fifty-five of those years, the Parliament has not been Protestant except in the sense that there are more Protestants than Catholics who are members of it; but as yet there has been no Catholic in the Cabinet. Nor is it likely that a Catholic will be in the Cabinet, until a Catholic shall arise who will make it necessary that he should not be excluded. Lord Melville opposed the motion, but admitted that things could not remain as they were. The Duke of Sussex supported the motion, and so did Lord Mulgrave who dissented entirely from Lord Liverpool's Protestant principle alluded to above. Lord Boringdon told the Peers not to lay the flattering unction to their souls, that the question could rest as it was, and said he should vote for the motion. Lord Donoughmore in reply said that seeing the temper in the House, he would not persist in his present motion, but change it; so that instead of being worded as at present, to "go *immediately* into a Committee," it should be altered to "*an early period* in the next session." Lord Aberdeen then said he should vote for it. The motion was then put in the amended form, and the House divided, the result being: contents, 60; non-contents, 86; the majority against us being 26.[1]

There was no vulgar abuse of Catholics in this debate. Several of their lordships were ultra-Protestant in their remarks, but avoided what was personally offensive. It must, however, always be more or less offensive to Catholics to whose ancestors England is indebted for the strong foundation on which her liberties rest, to be told that they are not fit to have a share in making new laws. If a first-rate architect had been employed to lay the foundations of a palace, and if he had done his work well, he would reasonably feel an injured man if he were excluded, and another man were brought in to raise the superstructure. But seventy years ago a Catholic of the United Kingdom was by some Protestants supposed to look upon himself as a lucky man if the rope were only round his hands, and not round his neck.

[1] The Duke of Norfolk, who at the end of the last century had, as the expression was, "taken the oaths," voted for the motion. He was the cousin and immediate predecessor of the great-grandfather of the present duke.

CHAPTER XXVI.

THE CATHOLIC CAUSE IN 1816.

Emancipation an open question in the Cabinet—Petitions of English Catholics—The "Seceders"—Petitions of Irish Catholics—State of the question in Ireland—State of parties in Ireland—State of Catholic parties in England—Proceedings in Parliament—Petitions from Ireland—Proceedings in the House of Lords—Lord Donoughmore's speech—The bugbear of "Popery"—Loyalty of Catholics—Attacks on Catholics—Proceedings in the House of Lords—Speech of the Bishop of Norwich.

EARLY in the year 1816, Mr. Canning, having accepted the office of president of the Board of Control, joined the Cabinet of Lord Liverpool. This event is a notable one in the history of emancipation, for with the entry of Mr. Canning into the Ministry the Catholic claims became practically an open question in the Cabinet. The reader has already seen that when Lord Castlereagh joined Lord Liverpool's Ministry in 1812, it was necessary that on his account the Catholic claims should be an open question. But it was only nominally an open question. It remained an understood thing that all the ministers were to oppose it; and it was for this reason that Canning would not join Lord Liverpool. But when he entered the Ministry in 1816, it was understood that he might speak and vote in favour of emancipation. This, of course, was a great step in advance, and is one of the claims which Canning, though a vetoist, has upon our gratitude.

But still it appears that the voice of Canning in favour

of emancipation was to be nothing but a voice. Lord Campbell, in his "Life of Lord Eldon," says, " He " (that is, Lord Eldon) " was annoyed by the return to office of Mr. Canning, whom he regarded as little better than a Whig. Although Catholic emancipation henceforth became an open question, he had the full assurance of Lord Liverpool and of the Regent that it should not be granted. On this understanding alone would he have consented to remain in the Cabinet."[1]

The first proceeding of the English Catholics towards bringing forward the question of emancipation was taken by the Catholic Board. At a meeting held on the 15th of January, 1816, it was agreed to present an address to the Prince Regent, and a petition to both Houses of Parliament. The address to the Prince brought prominently forward the services of the Catholic soldiers and sailors in the armies and fleets of England, as a reason for repealing the penal laws.[2] The petitions to Parliament were what in these days would be called "mild." English Catholics as a political body then stood at zero, or rather at some degrees below zero. They were obliged to adopt the tone of humble suppliants, not to say slaves. It is, therefore, not surprising that our grandfathers should have meekly reminded the House of Peers that their petitioners "had at different times presented petitions to their right honourable House for relief from the laws remaining in force against them, and that they were truly grateful for the full and benign discussions which their petitions had received." The petition then concludes in these words : " They now again approach your right honourable House, and with the most perfect reliance on its wisdom and humanity, and

[1] Page 324.
[2] I do not see, either in Butler's " Historical Memoirs," or in the *Orthodox Journal*, any account of the presentation of this address.

most humbly pray that your lordships will again take their case into consideration, and grant them such relief as your lordships shall deem proper, for extending to them the enjoyment, in common with their fellow-subjects, of the blessings of the Constitution."[1] The House of Lords was, at the time this petition was signed, under the influence of Lord Eldon, and it was well known that his lordship never deemed it proper to give any relief whatever to Catholics, whom he would gladly have seen extirpated from the land. Our ancestors are not to be blamed for the tone of their petitions. They had not emerged from those days in which they were only too glad to be able to petition at all.

The petition to the House of Commons was presented on the 21st of May by the Right Honourable William Elliot. He introduced the petition, says the "Annual Register," "by an energetic speech that drew loud cheers from all parts of the House." The petition was read, but Mr. Elliot did not found any motion upon it. Describing the petition, the "Annual Register" says it "was expressed with all the temper and decorum which had characterized every application to the Legislature from that respectable body." The English Catholics were the "respectable body," and surely they did not require the offensive patronizing of any Protestant in England to feel sure that they were so. But what chiefly induced the Protestant writer in the "Annual Register" to call them respectable was the quietness with which, from the smallness of their numbers, they were obliged to submit to oppression. The meekness of their utterance was "temper and decorum." Whereas, when Irish Catholics, who were a strong political power, knocked loudly at the doors of Parliament, it was thought, simply because the Irish were

[1] *Orthodox Journal* for February, 1816, p. 31.

Catholics, that it was neither temperate nor decorous to disturb the proceedings of the Protestants of the United Kingdom. The petition of the English Catholics was presented to the House of Lords on the 11th of June by Earl Grey; it was read and laid upon the table.[1]

To understand the proceedings in Parliament on the presentation of the petitions from Ireland in the year 1816, it is necessary to describe the state of things in Ireland. Amongst the Irish Catholics there was, as has been already mentioned, a party called the "Seceders." They are thus spoken of by John O'Connell:

"In January of that year (1815), the 'Seceders,' as the *soi-disant* aristocratic party of the Catholics were generally designated, showed some activity in giving trouble; and in that and the following month the strange and discouraging spectacle was more than once presented to the Irish public, of two distinct meetings of Catholics in the metropolis—the seceders at Lord Trimleston's house; and the 'Catholic Association' at Fitzpatrick's, in Capel Street: the first resolving to entrust their '*emancipation with securities*' petition to Mr. Grattan in the Commons; the other equally resolving to entrust their '*unconditional emancipation*' to Sir H. Parnell. Both chose the same person in the Lords, Lord Donoughmore, to present their respective petitions in the Upper House."[2]

The same divisions amongst the Irish Catholics continued to prevent vigorous action, and the two parties had each their own advocate in the House of Commons, as the reader will presently see.

"O'Connell," says his son John, "always spoke of this period as the most trying of his eventful life. By no kind of means, by no manner of exertion—and he *did* look about for means, and *did* use a thousand exertions—could he arouse the Catholics to action,

---

[1] "Annual Register," 1816, p. 53.
[2] "Select Speeches of O'Connell," by John O'Connell, vol. ii. p. 34.

or even to a defensive position. For more than two years a moral lethargy, a faint-hearted and hopeless apathy, hung over the country, and, with the exception of himself, scarce any one was in the field for Ireland."[1]

Speaking of this time, Mr. Wyse, in his "History of the Catholic Association," after remarking that a "nice and judicious management" of the national character "has always been one of the most difficult tasks in the province of the Irish popular leader," makes the following remarks:—

"To excite has never been difficult, but to keep the steam up to its original pressure, without risking an explosion on the one side, and on the other avoiding that tendency to relapse into former coolness, incidental to natures so singularly excitable,— has been indeed a problem which, in almost every instance of Irish politics, has eluded the intellect and defied the exertion of the most zealous and sagacious patriots. Nor could there be a stronger illustration of this position than the period which is actually before us. It was quite extraordinary, the thick obstruction, the flat and utter lethargy, which in a moment replaced the former menace and tumult, the high-crested defiance, the unchangeable resolve, the bold action of the body. The component parts of their assembly had flown back to their original situations; the aristocracy, the clergy, the merchant, had all resolved into their respective classes. The very action of their opposite and balanced forces had produced rest: they crouched, and slept; their very friends sickened at the unavailing attempt to raise to a level with other citizens a caste essentially inferior; they gave the task up in despair; a pact of eternal silence was struck; the Whig was to enjoy the cheap reputation of liberality, and the Catholic was not to mar with injudicious complaint the political views or influence of the Whig. The Catholic spirit had totally passed away; the dead body only was left behind."[2]

This condition of things appears to have lasted for some years, for immediately after the above words, Mr.

[1] "Select Speeches of O'Connell," vol. ii. p. 38.
[2] Vol. i. pp. 190, 191.

Wyse says, "From this disgraceful state of lethargy the Catholics were momentarily aroused by a very remarkable event." This remarkable event was the visit which George IV. paid to Ireland in the year 1821.

The Catholics both of England and Ireland were, however, not altogether so inactive as Mr. Wyse's words would lead us to suppose. They continued to petition, and the Catholic claims were in each year brought before Parliament; O'Connell wrote letters and addresses, and a few aggregate meetings were held.

Amongst the English Catholics also there were differences. The Catholic Board represented by its more active members the party who would have accepted emancipation with securities. The Board consisted chiefly of the aristocracy. Many of the members were, however, men who had too much Catholic faith and public spirit to advocate a policy opposed to the liberty of the Church; they belonged to the Board because it was the only organization of the English Catholics for the purpose of obtaining their rights. The other party amongst English Catholics consisted of a few of the aristocracy and the greater part of the middle class, at the head of whom Bishop Milner was always ready to appear whenever his services were required. This party was represented in the press by the *Orthodox Journal*, conducted by William Eusebius Andrews.

Having given the reader a notion of the state of things in Ireland and England, it is now time to return to what passed in Parliament. On the 26th of April, 1816, Sir Henry Parnell presented the petition from the party of which O'Connell was now the undisputed leader. Knowing, as Sir Henry did, that Grattan had another petition for relief from the seceders, he was obliged to apologize to the House for the fact of there being two petitions from two different parties; and he had to explain, which he did in a very lame way, that honourable members needed not to be puzzled under the circumstances, as between the two parties in Ireland there was a distinction without a difference. The idea of a Protestant member of Parliament, a true and thorough friend of Catholics, endeavouring in the most amiable manner to explain away in the House the differences among us is amusing, though lamentable.

The petition from the seceders was presented by Grattan on the 15th of May.[1] On the 21st of May, after Mr. Elliot had presented the petition from the English Catholics, Grattan rose to make the motion of which he had given notice, relative to the petition from Ireland which he had presented a few days before. He said, amongst other things, that the petition was signed by nine hundred persons, among whom was a large portion of the Irish nobility. He produced the letter of Cardinal Litta to Dr. Poynter, and, taking his stand upon it, argued that, in consequence of the terms which that letter proposed, there was no longer any excuse for withholding emancipation. He concluded with the following motion: "That this House will, early in the next session of Parliament, take into its most serious consideration the state of the laws affecting his Majesty's Roman Catholic subjects in Great Britain and Ireland, with a view to such a final and conciliatory adjustment as may be conducive to the peace and strength of the United Kingdom, to the stability of the Protestant establishment, and to the general satisfaction and concord of all classes of his Majesty's subjects." Sir Henry Parnell seconded Mr. Grattan's motion, though he thought it was not that which the circumstances required. He considered the penal code the principal cause of the discontent with

[1] For the proceedings in Parliament, see Hansard or the "Annual Register" for the year 1816.

which Ireland was then agitated. The motion was supported by Lord Castlereagh, and opposed by Mr. Peel; and on a division it was lost by a majority of 31, the numbers being—for the motion, 141; against it, 172. The reader will not have failed to notice that Mr. Grattan's motion which was lost in this year 1816 by a majority of 31, was word for word the same as the motion proposed and carried by Canning with a majority of 129 in the year 1812. Thus after four years the Catholic question in Parliament, instead of making progress, had lost ground. But in the mean time the battle of Waterloo had been fought and won. Irish soldiers were no longer wanted to crush the Emperor; and so it was the old story—fear ceased to be a motive, and the Catholics remained in chains.

But Sir Henry Parnell was determined to keep the Catholic claims before Parliament. On the 30th of May, he presented a petition from twenty-three Catholic bishops and 1052 priests of Ireland. He said that "the petition which they had placed in his hands contained their unanimous opinion on those ecclesiastical arrangements which some persons had thought necessary to be connected with the measure of Catholic emancipation, and it comprised a very able argument to show that no alteration was necessary in the present mode of appointing bishops."[1] He concluded his speech with saying he should give notice that evening of a motion for that day sen'night, for the House to resolve itself into a committee to take the petitions into consideration. This petition of the Irish bishops and clergy shows their continued determination to resist any interference of the English Government in Irish-Catholic affairs. On the 6th of June, according to the "Annual Register," "Sir H. Parnell, pursuant to notice, called the attention of the House to the petition which he had presented, and which,

[1] "Annual Register," 1816.

he said, contained the prayer of nine-tenths of the Irish
Roman Catholics, including all the clergy." Either the
petition just alluded to was a petition separate from the
one which Sir H. Parnell had presented on the 30th of
May from the bishops and clergy, or the petition of the
30th of May must have included the names of the laity
as well as of the clergy ; but that such was the case is
not mentioned either in the " Annual Register " or in the
Orthodox Journal, which latter publication has a long
report of Sir Henry's speeches. At any rate, it would
appear that something was done in Ireland, and that there
was a good deal of talking in Ireland in the year 1816, on
the Catholic question. Sir H. Parnell made a long speech,
and brought before the House several resolutions tending
to better the state of Catholics. As I shall have to refer
to this speech when we come to the next year, 1817, no
more need be said about it now. Mr. Peel raised a point
of order with a view to prevent Sir H. Parnell from putting his resolutions ; but the decision of the speaker was
practically in favour of Sir Henry. Lord Castlereagh,
however, strongly objected to the course pursued by Sir
Henry, and the latter then withdrew his motion. On the
28th of May in this year, an episode in Catholic affairs
occurred in the House of Commons. The reader will
remember that, in the year 1813, Sir John Cox Hippisley
had been effectually overwhelmed in the torrent of Mr.
Canning's ridicule. But the meddlesome and persevering
baronet had gradually worked his way back to his old
position. As the House of Commons had refused the returns
which he asked for in 1813, he set to work on his own
account, and collected a mass of papers relating, according
to the terms of his motion, to the " laws and ordinances
existing in foreign states, respecting the regulation of their
Roman Catholic subjects in ecclesiastical matters, and their

intercourse with the See of Rome or any other foreign jurisdiction." Having most industriously made his collection of returns, Sir John laid them upon the table of the House, and on the 28th of May, 1816, he moved for a select committee to report upon them. Mr. Canning, who in 1813 had ridiculed such a proposition, did not on this occasion oppose it. On the contrary, he allowed his name to be placed on the committee along with the names, amongst others, of Lord Castlereagh, Grattan, Peel, and William Wilberforce. Canning did not speak in the debate, which ended by the motion being agreed to without a division. It may be asked how it was that Canning submitted to what he thought the absurd motion of Sir John Hippisley. In human affairs, persevering impudence and persevering absurdity, if carried on with calmness and determination, very often gain their ends at last. But Canning very probably thought that, in the position in which he then stood, it would be more prudent on his part, as the avowed advocate of Catholics, not to put himself too prominently forward on a question which was substantially immaterial. He no doubt saw that the result of the committee would be nothing. The committee drew up "their report, which with its supplement filled 595 folio pages." It was brought up to the House "on the 25th of June, 1816; it was ordered to lie on the table, and to be printed; but it was never heard of afterwards."[1]

---

[1] Husenbeth's "Life of Milner," pp. 313-316. The debate on Sir John Hippisley's motion may be read in Hansard, or in the *Orthodox Journal* for June, 1816. The "Annual Register" has no mention of it. Dr. Lingard wrote, in the year 1817, a very learned and closely argued pamphlet on this report. He showed that many of the regulations existing in foreign states with respect to the concerns of the Roman Catholic Church, are of such a nature that Roman Catholics cannot conscientiously assent to them; that the regulations contained in the report and accompanying documents are of such a nature as not to be applicable to the Catholic Church in this kingdom, because they all, with one or two trifling exceptions, relate to Churches placed

In the conversation in the House which followed the bringing up of the report, Canning spoke. He complimented Sir John on his labours, and he avowed himself to be in favour of "securities." With all his brilliant advocacy of our claims, Canning remained to the end a decided vetoist. If he had lived, we should probably have had to surrender something as the price of justice. But Canning's compliments to Sir John were on this occasion no doubt meant to heal the wounds which his severe castigation of the honourable baronet in 1813 had inflicted.

It has been already stated that both the Catholic parties in Ireland entrusted their petitions to the House of Lords to the Earl of Donoughmore. He presented them on the 11th of June, 1816, at the same time moving that they should be taken into consideration on the 21st of that month. Accordingly, on the last-mentioned day, he proposed a resolution, of which he had given notice; but before doing so, he presented a petition in favour of the Catholic claims from certain of the Protestant nobility, gentry, and freeholders of the county of Galway, which

in very different circumstances from those of the Catholic Church in the British Islands. There is an excellent chapter "On the origin and object of the 'Placet'; " and the pamphlet concludes with some observations which it would be well for both Protestants and Catholics to keep fresh in their memory. They are these : " In conclusion, he " (that is, Lingard) " would wish to point the attention of the reader to ordinances of foreign states which do not appear in the report and appendix—to the ordinances which have restored the Protestants in Catholic kingdoms to the full enjoyment of civil rights. In every Catholic country in which Protestants exist in any number, all disqualifications on account of religion have been abolished. Now, on what condition have these concessions been made? On no conditions whatever. None were ever required. It never occurred to Catholic legislators, when they emancipated their Protestant brethren, that it was necessary to make men purchase the extension of their civil liberties with additional restrictions on the exercise of their religion." This pamphlet was reprinted in the year 1851. It has an advertisement prefixed to it signed " M. A. T." The occasion of its reproduction was an order of the House of Commons requiring the above-mentioned report originally drawn up in 1816 to be laid on the table of the House. This little work of the great historian should never be forgotten.

petition, his lordship observed, claimed particular attention, on account of the number and respectability of those by whom it was signed. The petition having been read and laid upon the table, Lord Donoughmore, as well as Sir Henry Parnell, had to explain the reason why two petitions were presented. The earl seems to have made short work of the explanation—

> He said "it had been conceived that the Catholics themselves were not agreed on the subject of their claims. This, however, was an obvious misapprehension. All of them agreed in petitioning for the removal of their disabilities, and there was no substantial difference in any point of view. They all said, 'We are under heavy disabilities: restore us, we beseech you, to our constitutional privileges and rank in the State.' The petition of the Catholics at large said nothing about securities, but prayed generally for the removal of disabilities, without giving a negative to what might be proper securities; so that there was no contradiction between this and the other petitions. The petition of those noblemen and gentlemen who met at Lord Trimleston's house, stated that the petitioners were willing to agree to such arrangements as might be consistent with the spirit and practice of their religion; and further expressed their opinion that such an arrangement might easily be made."[1]

It is interesting and somewhat amusing to notice how differently the question of the veto was treated in Ireland and in Parliament. The split amongst the Catholics was a difference on a vital question. The bishops and clergy, with O'Connell and the bulk of the Irish people, were determined to resist the veto at all risks; but they said nothing about this in the petition they entrusted to Lord Donoughmore. He therefore took advantage of the omission to make the difference appear a mere trifle. "There was no substantial difference in the petitions in

---

[1] The report of this debate in the "Annual Register" is very short. I have taken the extracts from the speeches from the *Orthodox Journal*, which probably reprinted them from one of the newspapers of the day.

any point of view," said his lordship. But from the point of view at which the word "arrangements" could be seen in the petition of the noblemen and gentlemen, and also from the total omission of all reference to arrangements in the other petition, the suppression of the truth in the latter, combined with the hint of a veto in the former, must have suggested to any but the most careless observer a very substantial difference indeed.

Lord Donoughmore then alluded to a portion of the petition which he had presented from "the bishops and clergy professing the Roman Catholic religion in Ireland." As this portion of the petition contained a proposal on the part of the bishop and clergy of an expedient for satisfying the English vetoists without conceding the veto, the mention of it will be interesting to the reader. The passage was as follows :—

"Though the mode which exists at present of filling the higher offices of our Church should afford no just ground of jealousy to the State, since a reference to the past conduct of Roman Catholic bishops in Ireland must prove to every unprejudiced mind that pure, disinterested, conscientious loyalty is a prominent feature in the character of that body; though it must appear strange that, when every temptation to disaffection shall have been removed, new pledges should be required to secure that loyalty which has withstood unshaken the severest trials; though we ourselves, when placed in other circumstances, have at various times deprecated any change in this part of our discipline, and even the very measure which we now propose ;— yet, with a view to satisfy as far as possible even prejudice itself, and to evince our readiness to give every proof of a conciliating spirit which a due regard for the purity of our religion would permit, we would, in the event of Catholic emancipation, cheerfully concur in obtaining from the spiritual head of our Church, for the future appointment of Roman Catholic bishops in Ireland, that mode of election which is called 'Domestic nomination.' This domestic nomination (that is, election to the vacant sees by a certain number of Irish clergy, already bound by a solemn oath of allegiance to his Majesty, and afterwards swearing anew that they would not elect any individual of whose loyalty they were not convinced) appears to us a test of loyal principles and peaceable conduct quite above the reach of the most jealous suspicion; and is, moreover, in our opinion, the only new security which could be exacted without spreading unutterable terror and discontent through the Roman Catholic population of Ireland."

The petition concludes with an earnest entreaty that the House will not sanction any interference on the part of the Crown with the appointment of the Catholic bishops.[1] Lord Donoughmore held out this offer of the Irish bishops as an inducement to the vetoists to vote for his motion; but, at the same time, he said that he thought no securities were really wanted. If any were anxious for further securities, he said he thought the offer of domestic nomination "was the best that could well be devised against that bugbear, foreign influence."[2]

Even though we are reading what was said nearly seventy years ago, it is cheering to find that a Protestant nobleman, speaking in the House of Lords, characterized the English delusion about foreign influence in Catholic affairs as a bugbear. His lordship's words were nothing more than the words of common sense, speaking under the influence of reason unaffected by the requirements of party, or by bigotry, or by human respect. The common sense of the English people has got rid of many bugbears; but that old and antiquated bugbear, "Popery," that terrible spectre of foreign influence, the creation of the Anglican mind, still exerts its influence wherever it suits the purpose of the enemy of mankind to remind our Protestant fellow-subjects of their temporarily forgotten horror. The absurd idea seized upon all English Protes-

[1] *Orthodox Journal* for 1816, pp. 198, 199.
[2] Ibid., p. 242.

tants in the year 1850, and made them an object of astonishment and ridicule to the whole world. And there is something mysterious and unexplainable in the effect the bugbear has in this country, as there is something unexplainable in the effect which what is called the gadfly has upon a herd of cattle quietly grazing in a Leicestershire meadow.[1] In the year 1874, the conversion of the grand master of the Freemasons, and the refusal of the Irish bishops in the previous year to be dictated to by a Protestant in the matter of education, so irritated an ex-prime minister that he raised up the spectre, frightened a few Protestants, and disgusted all her Majesty's Catholic subjects. But on this occasion St. George scotched the dragon, and things remained tranquil.[2]

Only last year (1884) the *Times*, which I believe is still called the "leading journal," took advantage of what it called the "ceremonial opening of the magnificent Roman Catholic Church attached to the oratory at South Kensington," to remind us that the old bugbear is still somewhere in existence, and ready to be evoked. "Though the old animosities are happily abated," said the journal, "it would be a great mistake to suppose that they are incapable of ever being revived." That is, the bugbear is being kept somewhere till it shall be wanted. But what are these old animosities, so far as they have any reality? They are entirely on the side of English and Irish Protestants. The old animosities are the diabolical hatred

---

[1] There were, however, some Englishmen in 1850 who took a very practical view of what their highly intellectual political leaders chose to call "papal aggression." A Shropshire Protestant farmer, on an estate belonging to, I think, Mr. Howard, of Corby, was twitted by a Catholic agent with the Pope coming to govern the country. The farmer replied, "I wouldn't care, if he would do it a little cheaper." I had this anecdote from the agent himself.

[2] The dragon here alluded to is, of course, *the* dragon, the one who is at the bottom of all mischief, and not the then ex-prime minister.

of the Catholic Church always existing, and ready to be brought into action whenever it shall suit the spite or the policy of any person or thing possessing sufficient influence to set the mischief afloat. It is clear that the animosities here alluded to are religious animosities, not political or national animosities ; and their revival simply means that the religion which is physically strong is about to persecute the religion which is physically weak. The same journal in the same article has also the following words :—" Roman Catholics well know that they have nothing to fear from England, so long as England has nothing to fear from them." But why should Catholics fear England, or why should England fear Catholics? So far as English Catholics are concerned, certainly not on account of either politics or nationality. Protestant England will not merely condescend to allow, but will no doubt admit the right of Catholics to be either Whigs or Tories, and to act up to their political principles without molestation. And with regard to nationality there can be no question between English Protestants and English Catholics. English Catholics are, to say the very least, quite as national as English Protestants. Indeed, the English Catholics as a body would not be content with that amount of loyalty to the throne and love of mother country which a vast and increasing number of English Protestants consider quite sufficient. It is, therefore, the meaning of the leading journal that it is simply because we are Catholics that we can have anything to fear from them, or they anything to fear from us.

And with regard to Irish Catholics, the common sense of the English will admit their right, in the matter of politics, to choose their own line within the limits of the Constitution. So too in respect of nationality, if the leading journal had intended to say that the Irish, as Irish, had

nothing to fear from England so long as England had
nothing to fear from them, it would have said so; it would
have limited its words to its meaning; it would not have
said, in words applicable to all her Majesty's Catholic
subjects, that they have nothing to fear from England so
long as England has nothing to fear from them. It is,
therefore, clear that what was meant, is that it is only
because we are Catholics that England need fear us, or
we fear England. And this is precisely where the mischief
of the sentence lies: it separates us as having something
to fear, and as objects of fear, from the rest of our fellow-
countrymen simply because we are Catholics. The motive
for publishing such a mischievous sentence can be no other
than religious rancour. To speak of Catholics having
anything to fear from England, or of England having
anything to fear from Catholics, would be merely a gross
impertinence, if it were not really intended to keep alive
those old animosities in the breasts of Protestants, which,
their principal organ in the press says, "it is sometimes
politic to abate, but never expedient to extinguish."

Lord Donoughmore concluded his speech by moving
that in the next session the House would "take into its
early and serious consideration" the "disabling statutes"
against Catholics. The preamble to his resolution is
worthy of being recorded, as showing that some at least
appreciated the services of the Irish soldiers in the French
war. It is as follows:—

"Resolved, that at the termination of a long and arduous
contest—glorious beyond any former example to the British
nation, and effectuated by the concurrent energies of all denomi-
nations of men in this United Kingdom—it has become the
bounden duty of Parliament to endeavour, by a confiding policy
and measures of just conciliation, to bind together in grateful
loyalty to the King, and assured attachment to each other, our

fellow-subjects, of whatever religious persuasion and of whatever class and degree."

The Earl of Aberdeen declared himself in favour of the motion, and made a good speech, except for one remark at its commencement. He said, "he thought the noble earl who moved the resolution had not sufficiently disclaimed the principle of the Catholics prosecuting their claims as matter of right." Here again is the influence of the "bugbear." In the mind of Lord Aberdeen, Catholics had no *right* to sit in Parliament, because in spiritual matters they owned the supremacy of the Pope, which was a foreign influence acting on British subjects. It is difficult to understand how any one, not to say a legislator, but any one who had read the history of England, however cursorily, could come to any other conclusion than that Catholics had at least an equal right with others to make laws for England. Lord Bathurst, who was opposed to the motion, made a remark about Lord Grenville, which the reader should know. He said that "a noble baron (Lord Grenville) was, he believed, the first to suggest this measure" (that is, the veto) "in a letter which had appeared in public; but now he understood that the noble lord, as well as other supporters of it, had altered their opinions on this head." If Lord Bathurst was right in what he said, as Lord Grenville had been a most decided vetoist, his lordship's change of opinion was another consequence of the firm stand made by Milner and the Irish bishops against securities. Lord Redesdale made a very bigoted and foolish speech against the motion, for which he received a severe castigation from Earl Stanhope. Lord Eldon, of course, opposed the motion. He said one sensible thing, namely, that he thought the veto of little consequence.[1] But he said that

---

[1] That is, as a security.

the petition acknowledged the "situation of bishops," which was against both the constitution and the oath of allegiance; and if it were granted he did not know what might be asked for next. Comment on the speeches of Eldon and of the Eldon school is useless. It is as unnecessary to do so, as to comment on the speeches of lunatics. This debate was chiefly remarkable for the support given to our claims by a member of the royal family and by a bishop —the Duke of Sussex and Bathurst, Bishop of Norwich. This was, I believe, the first time that a bishop had advocated emancipation. There was nothing very remarkable in the speech of the duke. It may be gathered from what he said that he was a vetoist; but no doubt he would have consented to any terms agreed to by his Majesty's ministers.

The speech of the Bishop of Norwich, coming from a person in his position, was certainly remarkable. As this speech was much spoken of at the time, and called forth the gratitude of Catholics, the reader will no doubt be glad to see some of the principal sentences.[1] Lord Eldon had said in the course of his speech that it was the particular duty of the bishops to resist the resolution.

"I do not know," said the bishop, "what the opinion of the noble and learned lord may be as to the duty of bishops; but I beg leave to say, that it is their duty, as it is the criterion of an English bishop, to conciliate, not to divide; to allay, not to exasperate, religious differences. The only way to secure permanently the existence of any establishment, civil or ecclesiastical, is to evince liberal and conciliatory conduct to those who differ from us, and to lay its foundation in the love, affection, and esteem of all within its influence. To use the words of my

[1] The extract from this speech is taken from Mr. Butler's "Historical Memoirs," vol. iv. pp. 275, 276, edition of 1822. All that Mr. Butler quotes is word for word the same as in the *Orthodox Journal*, but in the *Orthodox Journal* the speech is given at somewhat greater length.

favourite author, '*Carum esse principem, bene de republica mereri, laudari, coli, diligi, gloriosum est: metui vero et in odio esse, invidiosum, detestabile.*' The most enlarged principles of toleration, while they tend in their operation to reconcile all sects, to bring all dissents of faith within the pale of charity, and to smooth the asperity of religious differences, never yet disturbed the tranquillity of any state, or shook the security of any Church. A Christian spirit can never endanger a Christian establishment. I will trouble the House no longer; but I hope I may be pardoned for saying that the sentiments which I have delivered deserve the serious consideration of his Majesty's ministers. Having obstinately persisted in opposing the claims of four millions of his Majesty's subjects, and having raised the dangerous cry of 'No Popery,' when concessions to them were proposed, they may, unless they adopt a more conciliating conduct, be compelled to hear from the other side of the water the more dangerous cry of, 'No Union.'"

Thirteen years after this speech was delivered the Emancipation Bill was passed, and became an Act. But for some years after 1829 there was an extreme reluctance to act up to the spirit of emancipation. And up to this day, it is not Irish and Catholic, but English and Protestant opinion which has governed Ireland. For many years, the cry from "the other side of the water" was, "Justice to Ireland;" now it is, "No Union."

At the conclusion of Bishop Bathurst's speech, the House divided, with the following result: For Lord Donoughmore's motion, 69; against it, 73; the majority was, therefore, only 4. The number of peers, spiritual and lay, at that time was about 350, so that not more than between a third and a half of the members voted.

Mr. Butler says, speaking of the Bishop of Norwich's speech, that " no words can express the gratitude and veneration which, from this time, every Catholic of the United Empire has felt for the prelate who thus advocated our cause." For many years after Mr. Butler's time the services of the Bishop of Norwich were remembered. In proportion as Catholics were pleased, the Lord Chancellor was annoyed. Lord Campbell says that Lord Eldon was exceedingly distressed to find Lord Donoughmore's motion supported by a bishop.[1]

[1] "Life of Eldon," p. 324.

CHAPTER XXVII.

THE ACT OF 1817.

The Test Act—Declaration of Indulgence—Pretended conspiracy—The Test Act—The Act of Indemnity—The dispensing power—Catholics under William and Mary—The Annual Act of Indemnity—A Catholic refused a commission—The case of Captain Whyte.

IN the year 1817 an Act was passed which was a short step in advance towards emancipation. The Act, as cited by Butler, is "for regulating the administration of oaths, in certain cases, to officers in his Majesty's land and sea forces."[1] As the history of this Act is interesting, the reader will no doubt be glad to have it. In the month of March, 1673, the twenty-fifth year of the reign of Charles II., an Act was passed, entitled "An Act for preventing dangers that may happen by Popish Recusants."[2] This Act has always been known by the name of the Test Act. Just one year previously, Charles II. published what was commonly called the "Declaration of Indulgence." The Declaration stated that—

"The experience of twelve years had proved the inefficacy of coercive measures in matters of religion; that the King found himself 'obliged to make use of that supreme power in ecclesiastical matters which was not only inherent in him, but had been declared and recognized to be so by several Statutes and Acts

[1] "Historical Memoirs," vol. iv. p. 259, second edition of 1822.
[2] "Parliamentary History," vol. iv. p. 564.

of Parliament;' that it was his intention and resolution to maintain the Church of England in all her rights, possessions, doctrine, and government; that it was, moreover, his will and pleasure that 'all manner of penal laws in matters ecclesiastical, against whatever sort of nonconformists or recusants, should be from that day suspended;' and that to take away all pretence for illegal or seditious conventicles, he would license a sufficient number of places and teachers for the exercise of religion among the Dissenters, which places and teachers so licensed should be under the protection of the civil magistrate; but that this benefit of public worship should not be extended to the Catholics, who, if they sought to avoid molestation, must confine their religious assemblies to private houses."[1]

At the opening of the session of Parliament on the 5th of February, 1673, Charles, in his speech, amongst other things, justified the Declaration of Indulgence. But the country party—that is, the Church of England party—"directed," says Lingard, "all their efforts to procure the recall of the declaration. . . . They were willing to extend relief to Protestant Dissenters, but it must be done in a Parliamentary way; . . . the King might remit the penalties of the offence, but he could not suspend the execution of the law."[2] The Commons passed a resolution embodying this doctrine; and Charles, without waiving his right to suspend the law, said he would give his consent "to any bill better calculated than his declaration to effect the object which he had in view."[3] The House, however, was not satisfied with this answer, and asked for a further reply. Charles then acted in the most disgraceful manner. He wanted money to carry on the war against the States of Holland; he could not get it from the Commons unless he revoked the Declaration of Indulgence. Louis XIV. of

[1] Lingard, vol. ix. p. 206, edition of 1849, quoting " Parliamentary History," vol. iv. p. 515.
[2] Ibid., pp. 221, 222.
[3] Ibid.

France was afraid that Charles would yield, so he made a promise of money to the King of England to be paid at the termination of the war. Charles then immediately cancelled the Declaration. The Church of England party having got the revocation, wanted further securities without delay. They wished to include the Dissenters in penal law; but at the same time they contrived to persuade the Dissenters that the securities demanded were intended to be enforced practically only against Catholics. In order, therefore, to delude the Dissenters, and to prevent opposition on their part, the Church of England party, which was then the popular party, invented a conspiracy on the part of Catholics against the reformed churches. Their proofs were that the Duchess of York had died a Catholic; that they suspected the Duke of York himself of being a Catholic; that Charles was in "alliance with France, a Catholic power, against the Dutch, a Protestant State;" that Major-General Fitzgerald and some other officers of the army were Catholics; and that "Schomberg, the commander-in-chief, though a Calvinist, was not only a foreigner, but also held high rank in the French army."[1] The reader may be struck with the absurd notion of the conspiracy and with the extreme absurdity of some of the proofs. But the English Protestants were at that time hurrying on, as if driven by some infernal power, to that abyss of absurdity, bigotry, and cruelty, which they reached five years afterwards, when they fell headlong into "Oates' Plot." These are the men whom we English Catholics, who have always been loyal to the Church and loyal to the Crown, have to excuse as far as we possibly can, for very shame, simply because they were Englishmen. On the strength of the above ridiculous proofs, the King was asked to discharge all Catholics from the

[1] Vide Lingard, vol. ix. pp. 225, 226.

army, and exclude Catholics in future from all offices both civil and military. The monarch who never said a foolish thing and never did a wise one, was in want of money, and of course consented to the demands of his Protestant subjects. The question, then, was how were the Protestants to be sure that no Catholic should be appointed to an office. A test was invented, which was to be applied to every one demanding to serve his country in an honourable position. "The House of Commons resolved that every individual 'refusing to take the oath of allegiance and supremacy, and to receive the sacrament according to the rites of the Church of England, should be incapable of public employment, military or civil;' and a bill was introduced requiring, not only that the oaths should be taken and the sacrament received, but also that a declaration against transubstantiation should be subscribed by all persons holding office, under a penalty of a fine of five hundred pounds, and of being disabled to sue in any court of law or equity, to be guardian to any child, or executor to any person, or to take any legacy or deed of gift, or to bear any public office."[1] The bill passed through Parliament, and received the royal assent. With one of the tests every Catholic would only have been too happy to be tried, that is the oath of allegiance. Our Catholic ancestors would have taken that oath with greater pleasure, and kept it with a truer faith, than any other set of men in the land. But the three other tests no Catholic could take without disloyalty to his God and his Church. He could not take the oath of supremacy; he could not take the bread and wine from a Protestant minister; he could not make the declaration against transubstantiation. A Dissenter was quite willing to take the oaths of allegiance and supremacy, and would have declared against tran-

[1] Lingard, *ut supra*, pp. 227, 228.

substantiation; but he could not take what he called the "Sacrament" according to the rite of the Church of England. Nothing was done to relieve the Dissenters, and thus they were, as Lingard observes, "duped by the artifice of their pretended friends;" ... the Act "was so framed as to comprehend them, though its avowed object was the exclusion of others."[1] The Dissenters may tell their own tale of their exclusions in consequence of this Act. The consequence to Catholics was, that until the year 1817 no Catholic could rise in the army or navy above the rank of lieutenant.[2] Partly because they had no chance of promotion, partly because they were looked upon with suspicion whenever they mixed in public affairs, very few, indeed hardly any, Catholics entered the army or navy for several generations except during the short reign of James II. And this is the reason why many young Catholic men of the best families who did not wish or were not allowed to lead idle lives in their father's house embarked in trade; some of them, because they could get nothing else to do, becoming retail shopkeepers. Many young Catholics who were fired with the military spirit entered some foreign service, the Austrian army being the one generally chosen. Even so late as fifty years ago entering the Austrian army was one of the employments held out to a young Catholic Englishman, when he had to choose his state of life. When the country began, towards the end of the last century, to realize the value of the good old Catholic stock, a few young Catholics entered the army. Some of them were with Wellington through the Peninsular War, and others fought under him in Belgium; but they could not rise higher than a subaltern officer until two years after the battle of Waterloo.

---

[1] Lingard, vol. ix. p. 229.
[2] The test was not put until a man was ready for promotion to the rank of commander in the navy and captain in the army.

Such, then, was the original "Test Act." Mr. Butler mentions that "by 1 George I. and subsequent Acts, all persons holding offices, civil or military, are enjoined to take the oath of supremacy within six months."[1] These acts were additional Test Acts. Mr. Butler also mentions a provision contained in the original Test Act which led to important consequences. This provision was that the oaths were to be taken and the "Sacrament" to be received within six months after appointment to office. "It is observable," he says, "that neither of these Acts" (that is, the original Test Act and the Act 1 George I. and subsequent Acts) "authorizes the tendering of the prescribed oaths to any person *before* he enters into office, to qualify him to hold it."[2] The important consequence to which this proviso led was that some few men, having entered the army or the navy, did not take the prescribed oaths and receive the "Sacrament" within the prescribed time.

In the course of years it became notorious that there were officers in the two services who had not complied with the conditions. Whether it was because these few officers were Dissenters, whose animus against the Church was as strong as that of the members of the Establishment, or whether it was because the State did not wish to be deprived of valuable men, or whether it was for both of these reasons combined, the Government was determined not to disturb them. The Government also went a step further, and in order to legalize the position of those who had not taken the oaths, it passed, in their favour, a Bill of Indemnity. This Act was passed in the year 1727, and was one of the first measures decided upon after the accession of George II.[3] The Act, however, was only

---

[1] "Historical Memoirs," vol. iv. p. 258, second edition of 1822.
[2] Ibid. Lingard has omitted to mention this provision.
[3] George I. died June 10, 1727.

retrospective. But other men continued to get commissions and take rank in the army and navy without having taken the oaths. In consequence of this, an Act of Indemnity was passed in every succeeding year until the year 1828, when, as we shall see, it was no longer necessary. This Act was commonly called "the Annual Act of Indemnity." Mr. Butler gives the following account of the Act:—

"The very small number of those who comply with the requisitions of these acts, gave rise to *the Annual Act of Indemnity*, which provides that persons who, before the passing of it, have omitted to qualify, in the manner prescribed by the Acts which have been mentioned, and who shall properly qualify before the 25th of the ensuing December, shall be indemnified against all penalties and disabilities; and that their elections and all acts done by them shall be good."[1]

It would be difficult, and perhaps impossible, to ascertain whether there were any Catholics who entered the army and had the benefit of this Act of Indemnity. It seems probable that no Catholics, and even no Dissenters, would have been allowed to enter the army and navy immediately after the passing of the Test Act.

On the accession of James II., several Catholics got commissions in the army. The Test Act remained on the Statute book; but James came to the assistance of the officers with his dispensing power. The conduct of the King in this matter was one of the chief causes of that dissatisfaction with his policy which made the English Protestants prefer to be governed by a Dutch Protestant rather than by a British Catholic. As it is an interesting passage of history, and as it will throw light on the relief given by the Act of 1817, I will give a somewhat lengthy quotation from Lingard.

[1] "Historical Memoirs," vol. iv. p. 258, edition of 1822.

"At home," writes the historian of England, "the King pursued with ardour his project in favour of the Catholic officers in the army, and at first had the satisfaction to find himself successful. Patents under the great seal were issued, discharging them from the penalties to which they were liable by the Statute 25 Charles II., and enabling them to hold their commission, 'any clause in any Act of Parliament notwithstanding.' This kind of expedient had first been suggested to James in the reign of his brother by Herbert, chief justice of Chester, who waited on the duke on his return from Scotland, and informed him, that if he sought to resume his office of lord high admiral, the Test Act could oppose no effectual bar to his desire, because it was in the power of the King to dispense with that Statute. The opinion of Herbert was confirmed by that of Jeffreys after his elevation to the bench; and it is not improbable that such a dispensation was secretly obtained by the duke, before he entered on the duties of privy counsellor and lord high admiral towards the close of the last reign. He now asked for the opinions of the several judges separately and in private; those who doubted, he desired to argue the question with the lord chancellor; and the indocility of four was punished by their removal, and the vacancy filled by others of more courtly principles or less scrupulous ambition. The result was now certain, and Godden, coachman to Sir Edward Hales, received instructions to bring an action for the penalty of five hundred pounds to which his master was subject, for holding the commission of a colonel in the army without having previously qualified according to the provisions of the Test Act. Hales pleaded a dispensation under the great seal; and the cause was heard in the Court of King's Bench before the same Herbert, now lord chief justice, and a lawyer whose upright and blameless conduct was calculated to give weight to his judicial decision. He openly professed to entertain no doubt; but the question was of the first importance, and before the court gave judgment, he would consult the rest of his brethren. Nine concurred with him in opinion: of the two dissentients, Powel, after some delay, came over to the majority, and the only one who persisted was Street, a judge of a very indifferent reputation. Fortified in this manner, Herbert delivered judgment in favour of the defendant, on the ground that the King of England was a sovereign prince, and that the laws were his laws; whence it followed that it was part of his prerogative to dispense with penal laws in particular cases and upon necessary reasons, of which necessities and reasons he was the sole judge; and that this was not a trust committed to him by the people, 'but the ancient remains of the sovereign prerogative which never yet was taken, nor can be taken, from the Kings of this realm.'"[1]

When William of Orange and his wife Mary had seized the English throne, there was, of course, a cessation of any suspension in favour of Catholics, of the penalties imposed by the Test Act. Severe and active persecution again began. In the first year of the reign of William and Mary, an Act was passed, providing that "all persons, who should be put into employment, as a commission officer, or non-commission or warrant officer, by sea or land, should, before the delivery of such commission or warrant, take the oaths of allegiance and supremacy."[2] But taking the "Sacrament" before appointment was not by this Act enjoined. This Act would seem to exclude Catholics effectually unless any should, by chance or favour, be admitted without having first taken the oaths. If a Catholic should have been admitted he would, after the year 1727, have taken the benefit of the "Annual Act of Indemnity." But it is not likely that any one known to be a Catholic would have been admitted as an officer into either the army or the navy. For during the reign of William and Mary, the laws against Catholics were so stringent, that it was not safe for any man to be known as a Catholic in public, or even in private life. The Act which immediately follows 1 William and Mary, just quoted, is an Act for requiring the declaration against transubstantiation to be put to all reputed Papists in London and Westminster,

---

[1] "History of England," vol. x. pp. 227, 228, where the reader will also see Lingard's opinion on the judgment of the court.
[2] 1 William and Mary, cap. 8.

and within ten miles of those cities.[1] But the Act 1 William and Mary, cap. 8, would not exclude Dissenters, as they had no objection to take the oath of supremacy. During the reigns of Anne and the first two Georges, it is probable that no Catholic ventured to enter the army or navy unless as a common soldier or a blue-jacket. Catholics were looked upon with as much suspicion during those reigns, as during the reign of William and Mary.

Towards the end of the last century, it would seem that the Act of 1 William and Mary was not enforced, for Catholic gentlemen used to enter the army, as we have seen, though the words "commission officer, non-commission or warrant officer" appear to extend to lieutenants as well as to captains. And, as we shall presently see, some Catholics also entered the navy.

The Annual Act of Indemnity, as Mr. Butler observes, contained nothing which excluded Catholics from the benefit of its provisions.

"Upon this Act," continues Mr. Butler, "it was concluded that Catholics were virtually eligible to civil and military offices, as much as his Majesty's Protestant subjects. It was admitted that, by accepting the offices, they were equally subject with Protestants to the penalties of not qualifying for them; but it was contended that their appointment to such offices would be good, and that, like his Majesty's Protestant subjects, they would be relieved against the penalties by the Annual Act of Indemnity. This certainly was the opinion of Sir James Mansfield and Mr. Sergeant Hill, when, in the year 1796, Lord Petre, raised and equipped, at his own expense, a body of two hundred and fifty men, and requested the command of them for his son. His request was refused; and Mr. Petre served in the ranks."[2]

[1] 1 William and Mary, cap. 9.
[2] "Historical Memoirs," vol. iv. pp. 258, 259, second edition of 1822. The Lord Petre who raised the men was Robert Edward, 9th Lord, who died in 1801.

This refusal was a shameful instance of what Lord Brougham called the "proverbial unreasonableness of tyranny." A Catholic could not become a captain in the army, because he was supposed to be a disloyal subject. A Catholic raises at great expense a company of two hundred and fifty men in order to defend his King and country; his son wishes to command the men that he may lead them against threatened invasion; he is refused the appointment because he is supposed to be disloyal. The unreasonableness of the persecution of Catholics in Great Britain and Ireland, has been as great as the unreasonableness of the persecution of Christians by the Roman emperors. But such always has been, and perhaps always will be, the fate of the Catholic Church. Even in our own days it has more than once happened that when a minister has wanted to strengthen his position or pour out his vexation at a failure, he has turned upon Catholics, raised up the bugbear of temporal power, aggression, and disloyalty, exciting the majority against the minority with as much of the spirit of Titus Oates as the temper of the times would admit of. And all the while the Catholics are as loyal to Queen and country, as the first Christians were told by St. Paul to be, and actually were, to the Roman emperors. An instance of gross injustice to a Catholic lieutenant in the navy led to a change in the law. The case was as follows:[1]—

Early in the year 1796, an Irish Catholic young gentleman named Edward Whyte entered the naval service

---

[1] This account is taken, for the most part *verbatim*, from a pamphlet published by Coyne, of Dublin, in the year 1834. It is entitled "Correspondence with the Admiralty, and Petition to His Royal Highness the Prince Regent, of Captain Edward Whyte, R.N., in 1816 and 1817, which led to the repeal of so much of the penal code as excluded Catholics from rank in the Army and Navy of England." Captain Whyte was the father of Admiral Whyte, now (1884) second in command of the Channel Squadron, under the Duke of Edinburgh, and of the Rev. Edward Whyte, S.J.

of this country. From that time until the close of the war in 1814, Mr. Whyte was constantly employed upon active service, and in almost every climate. During that period he bore a part in one general action with the fleet of the enemy, and in several of those desperate and brilliant minor actions which so materially contributed to establish the naval renown of this country. In the year 1804, Mr. Whyte was promoted to the rank of lieutenant. At the time of his promotion, no oath was proposed to him, which, to use his own words, "could lead him to imagine that the same rank was not open in the naval as in the military service."[1]

On the 6th of December, 1813, a letter was addressed to Lieutenant Whyte, informing him, by Lord Melville's desire, that he had been promoted to the rank of commander. Shortly after this promotion the first peace of Paris was signed. Mr. Whyte then went to reside in Ireland. In August, 1815, Mr. Whyte received a letter from the Admiralty, directing him to take the earliest opportunity of applying for his commission promoting him to the rank of commander. At the same time he was told to present himself to the admiral stationed at Cork, in order to qualify for the appointment. Upon application at Cork for the commission, Lieutenant (now Captain) Whyte found that part of the oaths which the service deemed necessary for qualifying for the rank he had attained was of a nature that he could not take it consistently with the dictates of his conscience. He accordingly refused to take the oaths, and in consequence of his refusal, his commission was withheld and his half-pay as commander was stopped. Captain Whyte then applied to his

[1] It is not quite easy to explain this now. As lieutenants in the navy rank with captains in the army, it would seem that Captain Whyte's words apply to a captain in the army. But the year 1804 was only eight years after the time when Mr. Petre had been refused a commission.

old and intimate friend, Lord Henry Paulet, who was one of the lords of the Admiralty, and asked his advice how to proceed.

The following extract from the captain's letter, dated February 22, 1815, to Lord Henry, will help the reader to realize the condition in which Catholics who had proved their devotion to their country in the surest possible way, were condemned to live even in the second decade of this nineteenth century:—

"Born of an old and respectable Catholic family, I could not, my lord, hesitate in declining to take an oath that at once not only abjures that religion, but stamps as idolaters all those who profess it. From a conviction that your lordship cannot hold an uninterested feeling for a man for whom you have done so much, I am induced to solicit your kind interest, that if it is possible for a Catholic to hold the rank to which, through your protection, I have been raised (and which rank *my own heart* tells me, I have not undeservedly attained), I may be enabled to get my commission; but, should my religion prove a bar to my arriving at that station in the service to which it has ever been my fondest ambition to aspire, may I, my lord, venture to implore your advice how to act, in order to obtain some remuneration for my past services? as my half-pay has now been under an impress since June last, which circumstance, to a man with but little else to rely upon, has proved no trifling inconvenience."

As the oaths which Captain Whyte refused to take were ordered to be tendered by an Act of Parliament, the Board of Admiralty had no power, after the refusal, to redress the grievance. The Board might indeed have never tendered the oaths to Captain Whyte, in which case he would have been saved by the Annual Act of Indemnity. Lord Henry Paulet might himself have consented to such a course; but most probably some of the other lords, or all of them, including Lord Melville, would not have acted in so liberal a manner. In his answer to Captain Whyte, Lord Henry seems to hint at a change either in the law or in the practice of the navy, when he says, " I am very sorry for your situation, but know of no means by which it can be remedied at present."

Captain Whyte then went to London, and memorialized the chief lord of the admiralty, Lord Melville. In this memorial the captain alludes to circumstances which, in a preface to the pamphlet I am quoting from, he speaks of as follows : —

"The officer whose very peculiar case forms the subject of the following correspondence is a member of a family whose sacrifices have been, he believes, unequalled in the empire, he and another (a lieutenant in the royal navy) being the only survivors of eight brothers—six having lost their lives either in battle or by casualty in the service of their country, viz. three captains, one lieutenant, one vice-consul, and one midshipman."

A stronger example of the power of religious bigotry could hardly be conceived than all the circumstances of this case of Captain Whyte. The persecution unto death of Catholics in the United Kingdom ceased with the martyrdom of Oliver Plunket, Archbishop of Armagh, in the year 1681. With the exception of the three years of the reign of James II., during a long course of years, extending even into the reign of George III., penal laws were continually passed in order to render the life of a Catholic as unbearable as possible. During the reign of Queen Anne, these laws attained the degree of unnatural severity which is called by Edmund Burke "ferocious."[1] The better times began for us English Catholics in the year 1778, the eighteenth of George III., when the first Relief Act was passed. We were again further relieved in the year 1791. The loyalty of Catholics to the

---

[1] "Letter to a Peer of Ireland," etc. See Burke's works.

House of Hanover had been for a long time undoubted. Any charge of disloyalty to the reigning House might have been answered in the words so familiar to all who can read English: "'Tis sixty years since."[1] Catholics had fought and bled for their country, and given every other sign of their devotion to England which the laws would allow them to give; and yet in the year 1816, the whole world rejoicing in the peace which Englishmen and Irishmen, shoulder to shoulder, had been mainly instrumental in bringing about, the hatred of the religion of their forefathers during a thousand years was still so bitter in the hearts of our countrymen, that it impelled them to stop a Catholic officer in the midst of a brave and honourable career, not for any act, but merely because he held what Protestants look upon as a mere opinion, the doctrine of transubstantiation.

Captain Whyte's memorial to the Chief Lord produced no favourable result, and religious bigotry against a Catholic caused the authorities acting for the nation, to do an act of meanness which would have disgraced the most vulgar-minded person. Captain Whyte's name was struck off the list of commanders, and he was reduced to the rank of lieutenant. But he was determined to persevere in obtaining some recognition of his services. He sought an interview with Lord Melville; but that nobleman, no doubt feeling his relations with the gallant captain whom he had degraded somewhat uncomfortable, declined to see him. Captain Whyte was not daunted, and sent in another memorial to his lordship, in which amongst other things, he submitted that had the oaths been proposed to him at the time he was appointed lieutenant, his

---

[1] But I must here notice again what has been already observed in the introduction, that Catholics cannot be accused of disloyalty on account of their loyalty to the House of Stuart, so long as the title of the House of Hanover was only a title *de facto*.

rejection of them, and consequently of his lieutenancy, would not have been of so material a consequence, as he was then at an age at which he might, without much detriment, have chosen some other profession or pursuit. Lord Melville then consented to see Captain Whyte: but at the interview the chief lord only expressed his regret at the state of the law; promised, as far as lay in his power, to assist Captain Whyte in obtaining the remuneration he sought ; and assured him that, on the repeal of the laws against the Catholics, his name should be replaced on the list of commanders. As the captain had no idea of being put off to the Greek Kalends, he made up his mind, after consulting Lord Henry Paulet and Captain William Parker, to petition the Prince Regent for redress. He did so, and the result was that he was restored to the rank of commander, his commission was given to him, all arrears of what should have been his pay from his first appointment were paid up, and Lord Melville introduced a Bill into the House of Lords to place Catholics on a footing of equality with Dissenters in regard to navy and army appointments. The bill passed the Upper House without opposition ; it was brought in in the Commons by Mr. Wilson Croker, secretary to the admiralty, and having passed through the House without opposition, it finally received the royal assent. It was not, however, in consequence of the passing of the bill that Captain Whyte was restored to his well and hard-earned rank. Mr. Croker's letter, informing the captain that he had been restored, is dated March 4, 1817 ; it was not until towards the close of the session that the bill was passed.[1] As it is not often that a good word is said for George IV., I may say one here. In the case of Captain Whyte, "the first gentleman in Europe" did an act of justice to another gentleman, in not

---

[1] *Catholicon* for July, 1817, p. 36.

allowing him to be persecuted and degraded because he would not deny the truth of a doctrine held by the vast majority of all the gentlemen in Christendom. To put before the reader a clear statement of the more legal as well as the practical effect of this Act of 1817, I cannot do better than quote Mr. Butler's remarks upon it.

"The Act of the 57th of his Majesty, 'for regulating the administration of oaths, in certain cases, to officers in his Majesty's land and sea forces,' authorizes the delivery of commissions or warrants to officers in the army and navy, without requiring them, before their commissions or warrants are delivered to them, to take the oaths or subscribe the declarations in question. This Act, however, does not dispense with their obligation of taking or subscribing them subsequently to their appointments; but from the consequences of this omission they are relieved by the annual Acts of Indemnity. Thus, his Majesty may now appoint a Catholic to any office in the land and sea service, and his commission or warrant may now be delivered to him, without previously requiring him to take the oaths or subscribe the declarations required by the qualifying Acts. This is the whole benefit conferred on the Catholics by the Act in question; for the oaths and declaration may be previously required, if the person authorized to receive them insist upon it. Neither does the Act extend to civil offices. Small, therefore, in this point of view is the boon conferred on the Catholics by this Act, but its effects are likely to be considerable. It is something gained upon the remaining penal code; this alone makes it of consequence. Public opinion gives it a much greater operation than it really has; this, too, is of consequence. It completely removes the objection to the appointment of Catholics to offices from the supposed unconstitutionality of such appointments. This was its most salutary effect, and made the Act invaluable." [1]

This act, therefore, did not repeal the Test Act; on the contrary, it contained a proviso expressly leaving Catholics, as well as others, bound by the clauses of that and other

[1] "Historical Memoirs," vol. iv. pp. 259-260, second edition of 1822.

Acts which required the oaths and declaration to be taken and signed *after* appointment to office. But this Act of 1817 did virtually, though not in words, repeal the Act 1st of William and Mary, requiring the taking of the oaths and subscription to the declaration against transubstantiation *before* receiving a commission in the army or navy.

The passing of this Act was certainly considered by the Catholics of the day as a great boon. As regarded both the army and the navy, it removed a stigma to which practically only Catholics were subjected ; it opened the navy, which, though not absolutely shut to Catholics, had been much more closely guarded against " Popery " than the army ; and, though it left a discretionary power with the authorities to put the test or not, it was not meant to be exercised, unless, perhaps, in some extreme case ; and, as a matter of fact, I believe it never was used until the Act of 1829 set it aside for ever.

With regard to Captain Whyte, the influence of the Prince Regent seems to have extended no further than has been already mentioned. He was anxious for employment; but he could not obtain employment. The ambition of his life had been to be a post-captain. In the preface already quoted from, he says that his name was struck off from the list of commanders " at a time when he had hope (almost amounting to a certainty) of an early advancement to the post rank, as his friend Vice-Admiral Lord Henry Paulet, under whose auspices he had entered the navy, and with whom he had served better than twelve years, and who was then one of the lords of the admiralty, had informed him he was one of the first commanders noted for employment. The circumstances herein " (that is, in the pamphlet) "detailed, of course proved a bar to his appointment ; and previous to the termination of this correspondence, his lordship had, from ill health, been obliged to retire from the Board. Since that period Captain Whyte has never had the honour of being employed, though his applications had been frequent."

There can be little doubt that the refusal of the Lords to employ Captain Whyte, and so enable him to become a post-captain, arose from their vexation at having been obliged, by the interference of the Prince Regent, to eat their own words and undo their own work. For having dared to petition the Prince Regent, the captain incurred the displeasure of Lord Melville and Mr. Wilson Croker, and they made him feel it.[1] The conduct pursued towards Captain Whyte is only one of the countless instances in which the administrators of the law defeat at pleasure the very object of the law itself.[2]

---

[1] This is pretty evident from the ill-natured remarks of the *Courier* newspaper on the passing of the Act of 1817 (*vide Orthodox Journal* for August, 1817). The *Courier* was the organ of Wilson Croker. This right honourable gentleman, besides being secretary to the admiralty, was the political agent of the too-notorious Marquis of Hertford. Readers of Lord Macaulay's essays know Mr. Croker well as the editor of an edition of Boswell's "Life of Johnson." He was also said, at the time of the publication of "Coningsby," to be the original of the character of "Mr. Rigby" in that novel.

[2] Lord Campbell, as it appears to me, in his "Life of Lord Eldon," alludes to the passing of the Act of 1817 under the year 1813, in which year, as the reader will remember, the bill for general relief to Catholics was abandoned. Lord Campbell makes some remarks on the passing of the Act which are of interest, and which will apply to the year 1817, especially as the same Ministry was in power. "One liberal measure," he says, "passed without meeting the smallest opposition, and without exciting any notice in or out of Parliament ; the very identical measure, which, in the year 1807, had turned out 'all the Talents' and set the whole country in a flame ;—the bill to allow Roman Catholics to hold commissions in the army as field officers ! It was introduced into the House of Lords by the Duke of Norfolk ; and Lord Liverpool, the prime minister, in a short speech, said that he entirely approved of it. Nevertheless," adds Lord Campbell, "there are indiscriminate admirers of George III. who still applaud his policy, when he not only refused his assent to this measure, but required a written pledge from his ministers that they never again would propose it to him." Lord Campbell has confused two Acts of Parliament. Mr. Butler, in his "Historical Memoirs," after mentioning the different Test Acts, has the following paragraph :—"All these Acts were repealed, *to a certain extent*, in favour of the Irish Catholics, by the Act of 1793 ; but, by a strange inconsistency, the Irish were subject to them in all places within their

operation, except Ireland. For their relief in this respect, an Act was passed on the motion of the late Duke of Norfolk."* One of the clauses of limited relief in the Irish Act of 1793 was, that Catholics could hold commissions in the army up to the rank of colonel. In his " Life of Lord Eldon," Lord Campbell has no mention of any Act in favour of Catholics during the year 1817. His remark that the Act passed, as he states, in 1813 was "the very identical measure which in 1807 turned out 'all the Talents,' answers to the Act passed in 1817 for the general relief of the Catholic officers in the United Kingdom, and does not answer to the Act introduced by the Duke of Norfolk, which was a mere extension as to place of a very limited relief to gentlemen of one portion of the kingdom. The Duke of Norfolk's bill was introduced in the year 1813 (*vide* Hansard for 1813); so I think it is clear that Lord Campbell supposed that to be the Act which was passed in 1817.

* " Historical Memoirs," vol. iv. p. 259.

CHAPTER XXVIII.

PROCEEDINGS IN IRELAND, AND DEBATES IN PARLIAMENT.

"Friends of reform in Parliament"—Catholic and Protestant co-operation—Principle of Catholic action—O'Connell and the Vetoists—The "Conciliating Committee"—Speech of O'Connell—Intrigues of the Irish Vetoists—Grand resolution of the Irish Catholics—Debates in the Houses of Parliament—Motion and division in the Commons—Motion and division in the Lords—Dr. Milner on the debates—The threat of a second Board—The Tralee dinner.

ALTHOUGH the state of affairs amongst Irish Catholics may have been as apathetic and dreary in the year 1817 as Mr. Wyse has described it, yet something was done both in Parliament and outside. We have already seen that a step towards emancipation was taken in passing the Act for the benefit of Catholic Officers in the Army and Navy. There were also long debates in Parliament on the general question. But before alluding to them, I must mention two incidents which occurred in Dublin in the early part of the year.

"In January, 1817," says Mr. John O'Connell, "Mr. O'Connell gave every assistance in his power to an abortive attempt made in Dublin to get up a society of 'Friends of Reform in Parliament.' It was composed of Protestants and Catholics, and, though its numbers were very limited, and its duration did not extend beyond a few meetings and dinners, it was so far valuable as being the first occasion since the Union when Irishmen of different creeds had associated on something like terms of equality in one body."[1]

[1] "Select Speeches of Daniel O'Connell," vol. ii. p. 38.

To Catholics of the present day it may seem curious that the fact of both Catholics and Protestants being found in the same political association should be a noticeable event. Yet, such it was in the year 1817. O'Connell was undoubtedly right in being willing and anxious to work along with Protestants for an end in which all Irishmen had an equal interest. In O'Connell there was nothing bigoted or exclusive. His greatness consists chiefly in the successful war which he carried on for years against Irish and English Protestants to obtain emancipation. But he also showed his greatness in the way in which he encouraged the Catholics of the United Kingdom to enter into the battle of general politics, and not to keep away from the fight from a sense that, because they were Catholics, they were an inferior class who were not entitled even to pretend to win their spurs. As in Ireland the vast majority were Catholics, it was easy for them, when once the effort was made, to place themselves on an equality with others in all matters where the law put no absolute bar to their advance. In Great Britain it was not so easy; and it has only been during the last very few years that there has not been a remarkable tendency amongst English Catholics to keep aloof from Protestants in almost all those matters in which, for various objects, people join together in united action. To such an extent was this spirit of retirement carried, that it is only about forty years ago since a Catholic Insurance Company was started. It must, however, in justice be said that it was not every Catholic, even forty years ago, who saw the special connection between his religion and the security for the payment of money when his house might have been burned down, or after his death. A Catholic association for the defence of Catholic interests is an excellent thing. It was a good thing in 1845, and it would be a good thing in 1885. If there were two societies now in existence, one for the defence of Catholic rights, and the other to insure the houses and the lives of Catholics, and if neither of the two societies were to do much business, it certainly would not be for the same reason. In the one case, separate combination is usual amongst Englishmen; in the other, it is eccentric. To be independent of party where the interests of religion are concerned; to combine together for the protection of civil rights, and especially to prevent oppression of the poor; to welcome help from anyone who will give it; in all matters not connected with religion, to be and to act as Englishmen are, and do act—to make these things a rule of conduct is to act as a Catholic should act, and is the surest way to obtain the respect and esteem of all. A Catholic is not despised now because he is a Catholic; he is despised and contemned when, suffering a wrong, he tries to obtain his right in an un-English way, when there is nothing open, straightforward, and manly in his manner; when he shows by his conduct that he desires secrecy when others would show themselves in public; when he prefers the weakness of private influence to the strength of public pressure; or when he lets "I dare not" wait upon "I would." Catholics are, in many respects, most essentially English. We ask for no eccentric exemptions. We do not insist upon making an affirmation when the law prescribes an oath; we do not make it a matter of conscience to keep our hats on in presence of her gracious Majesty the Queen. It may be said with truth that no institution on the face of the earth, from the beginning of time, has set its face with such determined vigour against such foolish nonsense as the Catholic Church has done. If we are anxious to mix with our fellow-countrymen in all matters which do not touch religion; if we vote with them for or against a Franchise Bill, according to the opinions of each one; if we join in partnership with them in a mercantile speculation, or play cricket with them on a July evening—we expect in return that they will not complain when we make use of our liberties as Englishmen in defence of our religion as Catholics. On the contrary, we have a right to be certain that the more we act as any other body of Englishmen who have separate interests do act, the more they will admire our conduct. We may expect an occasional visitation of the Romaphobia, as we expect an occasional visitation of the cholera morbus. But in cool moments English Protestants will admit that Catholics have as much right to combine for the protection of their religion as ironmasters have to protect their trade.

It appears to me that the rule of conduct for Catholics may be expressed something in this way: In all matters of doctrine, and also in all matters of discipline which the Holy See wishes to be universally observed, we should be as Roman as possible; in all matters of taste, of opinion, of business, of social intercourse, of political action—in short, in all matters where the Church leaves us at liberty to follow our own ideas, we should be as English as we can be. A vast number of English Protestants object to the Catholic Church simply because it is Roman. We can hardly expect our countrymen to see at first glance that the Church is Catholic because it is Roman. But we need not put a veil between them and the truth, by acting so as to make them suppose that all English ideas must be given up on entering the Church. This would be a most un-Catholic way of acting. The Holy Father would heave a sigh at such conduct. Even in ecclesiastical matters, Pope Pius IX., the very Pope who defined the infallibility of the Roman See, had no wish to destroy national customs which were not unreasonable. "They have attributed to me," he said to Father Ravignan, "the wish forcibly to establish the Roman Liturgy in France. I do not insist upon such a thing more than is reasonable; but I do not choose that a bishop should compose, at his pleasure, a missal or a breviary. As for particular usages, I will authorize them willingly."[1] And yet there have been, and perhaps still are, some amongst us who seem to delight in putting the Catholic Church before the eyes of Englishmen in as disagreeable a form as possible. They scare away the children of the north by putting before them an apparition which makes them imagine that the Catholic religion is fit only for the city of Rome.[2]

After this short digression, suggested by the wise conduct of O'Connell, we must now continue the history. The second of the two incidents alluded to at the beginning of this chapter was a collision between O'Connell and the Vetoists. "Early in February," says Mr. John O'Connell, in the edition of his father's speeches,[3] "occurred a collision with the vetoists, or 'seceders.' Profiting by the general apathy we have mentioned as prevailing in the popular

---

[1] "On m'a attribué, de vouloir à toute force en France la liturgie Romaine : je n'y tiens pas plus que de raison ; mais je ne veux pas qu'un évêque puisse faire á son gré un missel, un breviaire. Pour des usages particuliers, je les autoriserai volontiers" ("Vie du Père de Ravignan, par de Ponlevoy," vol. ii. p. 249).

[2] To such an extent do some silly people carry this conduct that, rather more than a quarter of a century ago, there was in the Holy City a coterie of British Catholics, who stigmatized as a *Gallican priest* an English priest who was as good a *Roman* Catholic as themselves, and perhaps better than some of them; merely because, at an evening party, he launched out, as he was quite justified in doing, against the Roman climate and the Roman dogs. It may also be well to mention that the above words in the text were written before the appearance of Mr. St. George Mivart's interesting article in the *Dublin Review* for July, 1884. And, in order to avoid ill-considered criticism, it may be added that these words are meant to apply not to one or two instances, but to a variety of manners and customs.

[3] Vol. ii. pp. 38, 39.

mind, this . . . little coterie had been busy in their small way, meeting, speechifying to each other, resolving and labouring with infinite pains to show the minister how anxious they were to subserve his hostility to Irish ecclesiastical independence, if he would only renew and carry on his attacks with his pristine activity." They announced a meeting to be held on the 4th of February. In the public advertisement there was no reservation limiting the attendance at the meeting to persons who held any special views on the Catholic question. O'Connell and his friends determined to attend the meeting. An unsuccessful attempt was made to prevent the O'Connell party from even entering the room. This attempt was made on the ground that the meeting was only of those gentlemen who had, in the preceding year, entrusted their petition to Mr. Grattan. O'Connell insisted on being heard, and made a very prudent and conciliatory speech, which he concluded " by entreating, at all events, further deliberation, and an adjournment for three or four days, with the appointment of a committee," consisting of persons whom he named, and "who could meet in the mean time from day to day, and consider whether there were any means of reconciling all parties in the Catholic body, and procuring unanimity." A motion founded on this suggestion was accordingly made, but was defeated by a majority of fourteen to four, the chairman (Lord Southwell) refusing to receive the votes of O'Connell and his friends.[1]

O'Connell then withdrew from the meeting. He was satisfied with having done his duty. He knew well, even in 1817, that the Vetoists were not to be feared. He knew the opinion of the clergy and people of Ireland, and he

[1] For a more detailed account of what Mr. John O'Connell calls this "hole-and-corner" meeting, the reader is referred to the "Select Speeches of Daniel O'Connell," as above referred to.

knew his own determination. Before leaving the room, he told the seceders that "their puny efforts for a veto were poor and impotent, and would be blasted by the voice of the Catholic clergy and people of Ireland, whose zealous, honest, and conscientious opposition to that measure only accumulated as the attempt to betray them appeared more manifest. It was ridiculous to expect success for that measure, from such miserable support, against the universal voice of Ireland."

O'Connell was still anxious that the note of discord should not be heard from the Catholics of Ireland, even from the small number of the seceders. He therefore joined in the establishment of what was called the "Conciliating Committee," which, says Mr. John O'Connell, "was formed to endeavour to keep matters in the right channel, and at the same time suggest any concessions compatible with preserving Catholic independence. This body issued a circular, inviting the co-operation of every Catholic. It was drawn up in the spirit of Mr. O'Connell's remarks to the Eccles Street coterie, repudiating the veto, securities, etc., as matters against which the nation had pronounced; and suggesting as follows:—'There is an arrangement which would take away all pretext of argument from our enemies, and which has already been sanctioned by our prelates, and received the full approbation of the people— it is that of domestic nomination.' Under this title," continues Mr. John O'Connell, "was meant the system prevailing at the present day,[1] when the Catholic bishops of Ireland are *selected* by the Pope out of a list or lists forwarded to him from the prelates of the province and the clergy of the vacant diocese. It had come practically into operation in the recent election of as excellent a

---

[1] I cannot give the time when Mr. John O'Connell wrote this, as there is no date to the book.

bishop and as true a patriot as ever lived—the late Right Rev. Dr. Kerman, Bishop of Clogher."[1]

The Conciliating Committee held a few meetings. At one of the first of them, some observations of O'Connell give, as his son says, "a striking view of the difficulties and perils besetting the Catholics at this time."

The occasion of O'Connell's remarks was as follows. On the 24th of February, 1817, Lord Sidmouth introduced into the House of Lords a bill for the suspension of the Habeas Corpus Act in Great Britain. The bill was not to extend to Ireland; but, until that fact became known, O'Connell considered it advisable that no aggregate meeting should be held.

"The suspension of the Habeas Corpus Act," said O'Connell, "which would leave the personal liberty of every individual in the land at the mercy of the minister of the day, whoever he may be, appeared to him an evil of such tremendous magnitude that all lesser evils should give place to it; and, in the contemplation of so monstrous a calamity, they should forget their individual grievances. As long, therefore, as that vital part of the Constitution should remain suspended, he for one would most earnestly recommend the suspension of all meetings, petitions, and applications to the Legislature. There was another point of view," continued O'Connell, "in which he deemed this relaxation from petition necessary. When the Habeas Corpus Act should be suspended, the minister might take up his threatened Veto Bill under the name of an Emancipation Bill. He might seek to enlarge his own influence upon the ruins of the Catholic Church in Ireland, under the name of emancipation. If any man dared to call the people together to remonstrate against the veto, if any attempt were made to resist it by the expression of public indignation, would it not be competent for persons in power to interrupt the organs of the public sentiment, and immure them in prison for as long as they might think fit? Thus, while the opponents of the veto were silenced by the hand of authority,

[1] "Select Speeches of Daniel O'Connell," p. 41.

and sent, perhaps in solitary confinement, to expiate in the long and heavy hours of seclusion their criminal fidelity to the ancient faith of Ireland, the veto might be enacted, *as if in pursuance of their own petition.* To obviate those fearful possibilities, it would be best to withdraw the petition, and officially to inform the Legislature that all we desired for the present was to be left in a state of oblivion."[1]

The reader need not be surprised at the alarm expressed by O'Connell at the idea of a suspension of the Habeas Corpus Act. Judging from the severity of an Act introduced by Lord Castlereagh, and which accompanied the Act for the suspension of the Habeas Corpus in Great Britain, O'Connell's fears that speakers at an anti-vetoist meeting might be arrested were not at all groundless. One clause of the Act for preventing seditious meetings in Great Britain inflicted the pain of death on such persons as should not disperse after being required so to do.[2] If such a clause for the government of Great Britain could be passed, and administered in the spirit of Lord Castlereagh, what might not the Irish expect? But Ireland was not included in the bill.

"In the mean time," says Mr. John O'Connell, "the Irish Vetoists were hard at work. Both Mr. Grattan and Sir Henry Parnell declared openly and unreservedly for the veto; and at the same moment an alarming letter from the Rev. Richard Hayes, agent for the anti-vetoists at Rome, was received, detailing intrigues in support of the measure which threatened to be successful with the authorities there."[3]

We have already seen one example of the kind of

---

[1] Sir John Newport opposed that clause of the bill which enacted that it should not extend to Ireland. He did this not for the purpose of stopping the agitation for unqualified emancipation, but because it would afford the Government an opportunity, if they chose to make use of it, of putting down the Orangemen. Vide "Annual Register" for 1817, p. 33.

[2] Vide "Annual Register" for 1817, p. 31.

[3] "Select Speeches of Daniel O'Connell," vol. ii. p. 42.

information which Rome gets about the Church in the British Isles.[1] As it is well that all Catholics who wish to think correctly, who desire to know the truth, and to act wisely in relation to Catholic affairs, should be well posted in past intrigues, in order to be put upon their guard against present intrigues as far as possible, the reader will find it profitable to peruse the following extract from the work just cited:—

"The following," says Mr. John O'Connell, "is an abstract of this long and interesting letter" (that is, the letter of Mr. Hayes). "It commences with stating that the hopes of the vetoistical party at Rome, with Cardinal Consalvi at their head, had been revived by the coming of 'young Wyse, late of Waterford, and Counsellor Ball;' that 'these youths had repeated to the cardinal, to the Pope, to Cardinal Litta, and other officials that all the property, education, and respectability of the Catholics of Ireland were favourable to the veto; that the clergy were secretly inclined to it, but were overruled by the mob, etc. . . . It is true that Cardinal Litta now abhors the veto more, if possible, than any Catholic in Ireland, and the Pope is resolved to take no step without his advice; yet you may judge of the intrigue, when the miserable farce of these silly boys is given the importance of a regular diplomatic mission.'

"The letter went on to complain of the stoppage and interruption of his correspondence with Ireland, in its passage through different countries. 'What a combination of misfortunes, Italian villainy, French tyranny, British corruption, vetoistical calumny, and, more than all, apparent Irish neglect, have conspired to throw your affairs into the utmost difficulty and danger. Now or never a more powerful effort should be made in Ireland, or the infernal veto, with all its train of evil, religious and political, will sink the wretched country of our birth and dearest affections lower than she has been, even in the periods of bloody persecution.'"[2]

At this meeting of the Conciliating Committee, a resolu-

[1] Page 146.   [2] "Select Speeches of Daniel O'Connell," p. 43.

tion was passed which is worthy of being recorded as a grand expression of a noble determination on the part of the Irish to stand fast by the rights and liberties of the Church, even with the loss of their own. The resolution is the more worthy of note because the Irish Catholics stood by the resolve expressed in it until they obtained emancipation, without paying for it the price of the veto. The resolution was as follows:—"That we should not receive as a boon any portion of civil liberty, accompanied by that which the Catholic prelates and people of Ireland have condemned as essentially injurious, and probably destructive of our religion; and we do solemnly declare that we infinitely prefer our present situation in the State to any emancipation which may be directly or indirectly coupled with the veto."

The debates in the two Houses of Parliament on the Catholic question during this year were long and interesting. Even an analysis of them would be too long to insert in a history. They should be read by every one who wishes to understand the various opinions which were held concerning Catholic affairs and the state of Catholics in this kingdom. There ought to be some amongst us anxious to know well the history of the Church in the British Isles from the time when the Legislature began the relaxation of the penal laws. No legislator, no person pretending to have an opinion on any political question can act or form a judgment with propriety, unless he has a good knowledge of English history. And no Catholic can act in defence of the Church, or form a correct opinion of any matter affecting the interests of the Church in England, unless he knows the ground on which he stands—his rights as a Christian, and his rights as a British subject; his rights under the law, and his right to fair dealing in the administration of the law. That thorough knowledge which makes the opinion of anyone worth having, can only be got by studying well the history of the past.

On the 9th of May, 1817, on the respective motions of Messrs. Grattan and Elliot, the petition from the Catholics of Ireland, presented to the House of Commons on the 26th of April, 1816, and the petition from the Catholics of England, presented to the House on the 21st of May, 1816, were read.

Dr. Milner's account of the debate which ensued cannot fail to be of interest. I will, therefore, give some extracts from his review of the speeches. This review is contained in a letter to the *Orthodox Journal*, dated London, May 17, 1817, and signed "Mentor." "The twofold battle," he says, "has now been fought, and victory has followed her accustomed course." The "two-fold battle" which Milner speaks of was the debate in the Commons and the debate in the Lords. The motion made by Grattan on the 9th of May, after having presented the petitions, was as follows :—

"That this House do resolve itself into a committee of the whole House, to take into its most serious consideration the state of the laws affecting his Majesty's Roman Catholic subjects in Great Britain and Ireland—with a view to such a final and conciliatory adjustment of them as will be conducive to the peace, strength, and security of the United Kingdom, the stability of the Protestant establishment, and the general satisfaction and concord of all classes of his Majesty's subjects."

The motion was seconded by Mr. Elliot, but was lost by a majority of 24, the numbers being 245 to 221.

In the House of Lords, Lord Donoughmore had presented a petition from "the Roman Catholics of Ireland"; and on the 16th of May he moved their lordships to resolve into a committee to consider that petition, and also two other petitions which he had presented the year before. His motion was rejected by a majority of 52, the contents being 90, and the non-contents 142.

Dr. Milner, in the letter above cited, continues his remarks by comparing the general character of the debate in the Commons with that in the Lords.

"On that day," he says (that is, the day on which the motions were defeated in the House of Commons), "the Catholics lost, together with the victory, their former reputation for superior talents; and, what was worse than all, they were led into defiles and ambushes, in which temporary success would have been ultimately more ruinous than the repulse which they suffered. In these respects they were more fortunate in the second engagements" (that is, in the House of Lords), "because, though overpowered by numbers, they were headed by officers of inflexible integrity, no less than of unrivalled courage and skill. There were not wanting an Achilles, a Diomed, an Ajax, and an Ulysses on one side; while there was no Hector on that of the enemy. Still, as numbers alone command success in the species of warfare of which I am speaking, though we have completely recovered our credit, yet we have lost the field. As the battle must and will be renewed without ceasing, till at last we are victorious, it is the part of wisdom to look back on the errors and misconduct which occurred in the late action, in order that we, our leaders and allies, may concur in preventing them on a future occasion. But I shall drop allegory, and speak literal facts.

"By what right, then, sir, or on what ground, did Mr. Grattan assure a Protestant assembly that they might *make whatever terms they pleased* with the Catholic Church as to its religion, provided they granted certain civil privileges to a part of the professors of that religion; likewise that the prelates and clergy of it were secretly favourable to the restrictions which had been proposed, that the Holy See was prepared to sanction them, and lastly, that the people themselves would soon be reconciled to them! Are the Catholics to apostatize? Are the prelates hypocrites? Is the Pope become Protestant? I maintain, then, that neither he nor his supporters had any right or plausible pretension to make any one of these assertions. In fact, they are belied by the

solemn decisions of the bishops, by various documents from
Rome, and by the honest, uninfluenced, unequivocal voice of
ninety-nine in every hundred of the Catholics of our two great
islands. . . . The baronets, Sir H. Parnell and Sir J. Hippisley,
supported their respective characters—the former, that of disinterested benevolence to the dearest interests of the people whose
cause was at issue; the latter, that of narrow selfishness for his
own advancement to office and emolument. The honourable
Charles Yorke showed himself a true, honest, and consistent
patriot. His mistakes are grounded in just and honourable
motives, and require nothing but information to disappear entirely. He wants no religious oppression or domination; nothing
but the safety of the State. With him we can treat, on a future
occasion, without apprehension of deceit or danger of disappointment. The Right Hon. Lord Castlereagh is *qualis ab incepto*, in
the year 1799. His tone and manner of acting is that which
Chesterfield so much recommends, *suaviter in modo, sed fortiter in
re*. To be brief, he inflexibly adheres to the plan traced out by
Mr. Pitt, that of gaining a complete control over the Catholic
Church of Ireland, and making it a political tool. But how often
was Mr. Pitt himself deceived in judging of Catholic affairs! And
was he not in particular, manifestly deceived in applying to the
prelates of Ireland that maxim of his predecessor Walpole, '*Every
man has his price.*' A little cool reflection will, I hope, convince his
lordship that such unbought, conscientious loyalty as these personages, according to his own honourable declaration, have proved
themselves possessed of in the hour of danger,[1] is more solid and
lasting than any which can be procured by money or distinctions.
Finally, his information and experience must convince him how
ill-calculated *vetoistical arrangements* are to restore or secure the
peace of Ireland.

"In the Upper House, Lord Donoughmore has, if possible, increased the veneration and love of his Catholic countrymen
towards him and his family, whilst he and his fellow-advocates
have rendered their best services to our common country. An
equal tribute of praise and gratitude is due to the venerable

[1] Castlereagh said in his speech that he had always found the Irish
bishops, in times of disturbance, disposed to exert themselves to tranquillize
the public mind.

Bishop of Norwich, to the Lords Harrowby, Grenville, Grey, Darnley, etc. But what we are chiefly indebted to these truly noble and liberal personages for is, that they have, one and all, advocated our civil rights without attempting to injure our more important religious immunities. Even those right honourable peers who were most adverse to our claims drew no argument from our refusal of the veto; ridiculed the laboured and erroneous report;[1] and some of them expressly declared that they would *not give a straw for the above-mentioned pretended security.* Such also were the professed sentiments of the head minister of his Majesty's Government, Lord Liverpool, who, moreover, with generous liberality, added that *the selection of our bishops had been as good and unexceptionable hitherto, as it would have been under any other form of discipline which can be proposed.* Hence, I argue that those innovations which our prelates have unanimously proposed in synod to be 'essentially injurious to the Catholic religion, and which may eventually subvert it,' being no longer required or valued by the most illustrious and intelligent of our legislators, it would be worse than idle, it would be criminal in any Catholic to make an offer of them to the State, or any way to support them."

In concluding his remarks upon the debates in Parliament, Milner lets us into the knowledge that there were murmurs amongst many Catholics at the conduct of their affairs by the Catholic Board.

"Another most important observation," he says, "occurs from the late debates, which is this: our most determined opposers, even those on the episcopal bench, have publicly pledged themselves to support any measure of relief to Catholics short of legislative or other very high power. On the other hand, it is an undoubted fact, that many Catholics, both laymen and clergymen, are murmuring at the present day that they should remain deprived of the civil and religious advantages within their reach, merely because our nobility and leading gentry cannot attain to their peculiar object. They begin openly to threaten that, if the existing Board does not attend to their grievances, they will form

---

[1] This was the report of the committee appointed to examine the papers collected by Sir John C. Hippisley.

another Board for the purposes in question. With respect to the peculiar complaints of the Catholic clergy respecting soldiers, marriages, etc., they are convinced that they need but ask for Acts of Parliament to redress them (which Acts are indeed so obviously wanted for the welfare of the State) in order to obtain them. I am," concludes Milner, " far from wishing to divide our body in any way or degree whatever ; and, therefore, I hope that the present Board will act in such a manner as to satisfy the complaints, and to render a second Board totally unnecessary."

" The defiles and ambushes " into which, Milner says, the friends of the Catholics were led during the debate in the Commons, were the various schemes which were being thought over for arranging terms with the Pope and the Irish bishops as the price of emancipation. Milner observes that we were overpowered by numbers in the House of Lords, and that the talent and strength of argument were all on our side. This has very commonly been the case in Parliamentary discussions of Catholic questions. In the annual debates which used to take place on the " Maynooth grant," it was always noticed that the negative side of the division list was swelled into a majority by all the " nobodies " in the House. With a few notable exceptions, bigotry against Catholics, narrow-mindedness, and stupidity have been, and are still, the three *disgraces* of our opponents.

It would no doubt have been a great mistake if the Catholics in 1817 had accepted any act of emancipation which did not include a right to sit in Parliament. Yet it would appear, from what Milner says, that he would have sanctioned a bill containing minor relief. Two separate bills, one legalizing marriages by a Catholic priest, and the other forbidding the compulsory attendance of soldiers and sailors at Protestant worship, might have been introduced with prudence. The two grievances which those bills would have remedied were the two which were most sensibly and most immediately felt at the time, and the separate removal of them would not have injured the prospect of general relief. But the passing of any bill of so-called general relief, which did not give full relief, might have weakened the force of O'Connell's agitation and postponed our emancipation beyond the year 1829.

The reader will have noticed that Milner speaks of Lords Grenville and Grey as having made no mention of the veto. It was the sincere wish of Lord Grenville that England and Ireland should be "united," as he said at the conclusion of his speech in this debate, "in the sacred and indissoluble bonds of law, and unity, and affection." He saw, no doubt, that emancipation could not be carried with a veto, and, therefore, he did not insist upon it; Lord Grey probably thought it best to follow the example of his former chief.

As O'Connell is now a prominent figure in the contest for emancipation, I may conclude this chapter by mentioning a public dinner given to him towards the end of the year at Tralee, "in testimony of the approbation of the gentry of his native county, of his public and private character." Mr. John O'Connell gives an account of this dinner in his edition of his father's speeches.[1] It was certainly a most enthusiastic entertainment. Upwards of fifty toasts were given: Mr. John O'Connell gives the titles of forty-six of them, and says that several others were drunk. The thirty-ninth toast, at which time the company must have been pretty well in their cups, was "Universal Benevolence," a most charitable sentiment, considering that it included in its generalization the Houses of Lords and Commons of the United Kingdom. With this expression of good-will towards our enemies, the history of emancipation in the year 1817, during which our rights were again refused, may, with Christian propriety, be brought to a close.

[1] Vol. ii. pp. 49, *et seq.*

CHAPTER XXIX.

THE CATHOLIC QUESTION IN 1818.

General Thornton's motion—Fox's dictum—Action of the English Catholic Board—Proceedings in Ireland—First remonstrance of the Irish Catholics to Pope Pius—Rev. Mr. Hayes' mission to Rome—Second remonstrance of the Irish Catholics—The Pope's reply to the second remonstrance—Mr. Hayes' remarks on the Pope's reply—Remarks of the affair of Mr. Hayes—Bishops Milner and Collingridge on the bill of 1813—Milner challenged to fight—Milner's portrait—Termination of the Blanchardist schism.

THE year 1818 was almost barren of proceedings in favour of the Catholic cause. In Parliament the discussion of the subject had been exhausted in the long debates of the previous year. The majorities in both Houses against our claims discouraged the idea of any immediate reaction. The majority in the Commons, it is true, was not very large; but, considering the fact that in the year 1812 the House of Commons had decided to consider the Catholic question with a view to its speedy settlement by a majority of 129, it was rather ominous that five years afterwards it should refuse to consider the still unsettled question by a majority of 24.

Amongst English Catholics next to nothing was done to forward the cause. In Ireland the state of apathy was so great, that it was as much as O'Connell could do to keep alive any active interest in the question. The divisions of opinion on the veto and matters arising out of it were damping the ardour of Catholics and puzzling and irritating our Protestant friends. There were, however, some proceedings in this year which the historian cannot pass over.

And first with regard to what was done in Parliament. On the 7th of May, General Thornton "rose for leave to bring in a bill for the repeal of the Acts 25 and 30 Charles II., requiring a declaration against transubstantiation, and asserting the worship of the Church of Rome to be idolatrous."[1]

The general said that he should have brought in the question earlier, if he had not "understood that the Catholic question would be brought on in the present session, and he feared that his motion would have interfered with that question." His main argument against the declaration was that "the Legislature had no right to ask any man to state his opinion on doctrinal points of this kind which did not interfere with the safety of the State." He maintained that the safety of the State was not in danger. I may interrupt for a moment the account of this debate, to note that the principle on which General Thornton argued was the one most emphatically laid down by Charles James Fox. In the year 1806, only a few months before he died, Fox sent for Charles Butler, and asked him what he thought was the best ground on which Catholic emancipation could be advocated. Butler answered that he thought the best ground was that it is both unjust and detrimental to the State to deprive any portion of its subjects of their civil rights on account of their religious principles, if these principles should not be inconsistent with moral or civil duty. "No, sir!" replied Fox, with great animation, "that is not the best ground. The best

[1] This account of General Thornton's motion is taken from the *Globe* newspaper of the 8th of May, 1818, as quoted in the *Orthodox Journal* for the year 1818, p. 199.

ground, and the only ground to be defended in all parts, is that *action*, not *principle*, is the object of law and legislation. With a person's principles no Government has a right to interfere." Butler, wishing to bring the matter at once to issue, by supposing an extreme case, said to Fox, "Am I, then, to understand that, in 1713,[1] when the Houses of Brunswick and Stuart were equally balanced, if a person published a book in which he attempted to prove that the House of Hanover unlawfully possessed the British throne, and that all who obeyed the prince on it were morally criminal, he ought not to be punished by law?" "Government," said Fox, "should answer the book, but should not set its officers upon its author." And then, rising from his seat, the great Whig leader exclaimed, "No; the more I think of it, the more I am convinced of the truth of my position : *action*, not *principle*, is the true object of government."[2]

General Thornton's bill would have been of no avail to Catholics; for, while he proposed to get rid of the declaration against transubstantiation, he would have retained the oath of supremacy. Besides his chief argument, which has been already mentioned, General Thornton relied very strongly on the fact that many who were not Roman Catholics, and who denied the supremacy of the Pope—such as members of the Greek and Russian Churches, and many Protestants also—believed in transubstantiation, and that to them, as well as to Catholics, the oath was most objectionable. The general's motion was seconded by Mr. William Smith, one of the chief Whig members of Parliament. Lord Castlereagh opposed the

[1] This date must be a mistake for 1714; Queen Anne did not die until August, 1714.
[2] Butler's "Memoirs of the English Catholics," vol. ii. p. 205, edition of 1819.

motion. He said that the Test Act was evidently of a political, not of a religious nature; that a bill for its repeal should come sanctioned by the resolution of a committee of the whole House; and that it was prematurely introducing the general question of the "Catholic claims," which would be incidentally discussed, "contrary, perhaps, to the wishes of those who were most intimately connected with it." He therefore moved the previous question, which was put and carried; and the motion was lost.

The last words of Lord Castlereagh, just quoted above, may, no doubt, be accounted for by the action of the English Catholic Board. Under the head of the year 1818, Mr. Butler, in his "Historical Memoirs," begins by saying, "Still the Catholics persisted in their determination not to relax their efforts for obtaining the repeal of the laws which remained in force against them. Their spirits were revived by the discussions which took place in May, 1818, upon General Thornton's motion, 'for the repeal of the Acts 25 and 30 Charles II., requiring a declaration against transubstantiation, and asserting the worship of the Church of Rome to be idolatrous.'"

"The general," continues Mr. Butler, "had proceeded without consulting the Catholics, and so far against their wishes that a deputation from the Board had waited on Lord Liverpool, expressing that there was no concert between them and the general; admitting, however, that the repeal of both Acts was earnestly desired by them. The deputation was received by his lordship in the most obliging manner. He discussed with the gentlemen who waited upon him the comparative situation of the English Catholics in respect to the nation at large, the Protestant Dissenters, and the Irish Catholics; he appeared," adds Mr. Butler, "to be extremely well informed on these subjects, and intimated, in a clear but not an unfriendly manner, the nature of the difficulties in the way of their relief. These circumstances, and some things which took place while General Thornton's motion was in agitation, were of a nature to raise the hopes of the Catholics, and stimulate them to new exertions."

The above notice of General Thornton's motion is all the information which Mr. Butler gives his readers of the proceedings of English Catholics in the year 1818.

With regard to the proceedings in Ireland in relation to emancipation during this year, it will be necessary to commence with an account of the mission of the Rev. Mr. Hayes to Rome. On the 29th of August, 1815, at an aggregate meeting of the Catholics of Ireland, Sir Thomas Esmonde, Mr. Owen O'Connor, and the Rev. Richard Hayes, a Franciscan friar, were appointed as a deputation to Rome, to present to Pope Pius VII. a remonstrance on the part of the Catholic laity of Ireland. It was ordered that the remonstrance should state "an entire concurrence with our venerable and revered prelates, in perpetual and unremitting opposition to any measure which would directly or indirectly authorize the Crown, or the servants of the Crown, to interfere with the appointment of our bishops; and praying his Holiness not to countenance, directly or indirectly, the plans of the bitter and unrelenting enemies of our religion."[1] Sir Thomas Esmonde and Mr. O'Connor declined to form part of the deputation; upon which the Irish Catholics "invested Mr. Hayes with the whole weight of the mission."[2] Mr. Hayes accordingly went to Rome, and presented himself to Cardinal Litta, the cardinal prefect of the propaganda. This seems to have displeased Cardinal Consalvi, the political minister of his Holiness. His Eminence thought that the matter

[1] *Orthodox Journal* for 1815, p. 361.
[2] Ibid. for 1818, p. 209.

which Mr. Hayes had in hand ought to have been mentioned to him in the first instance. Mr. Hayes remained in Rome until the month of July, 1817—that is, nearly two years. The history of his diplomacy may be described in a general way as a contest between himself and Cardinal Consalvi, in which the cardinal was successful as against his opponent personally, but unsuccessful in the matter in dispute. Mr. Hayes was not a first-rate diplomatist. He was honest, well informed in the case he had to manage, devoted to his cause, bold, laborious, and persevering. But he wanted the cool, calculating caution which was necessary when he had to contend with a diplomatist like Consalvi; he was too impetuous, and asserted his independence in too decided a manner, even on his own showing, when treating with the Pope in person. He was imprudent in the way in which he denounced Consalvi both by words and by writing. Consalvi was the political minister of Pope Pius VII., and the most powerful man in Rome. He had represented his Holiness in the previous year, 1814, at the Congress of Vienna, and he had there made the acquaintance of all the great statesmen of Europe, and in particular of the statesman who represented England, Lord Castlereagh. This nobleman was especially civil to the cardinal, and treated him with marked respect.[1] Such conduct on the part of Castlereagh was no doubt prompted, in the first instance, by the natural instincts of a well-bred man. But the people of England generally had a great and sincere regard for Pope Pius VII. on account of the sufferings which he had endured from the French Emperor, chiefly because his Holiness would not join the Emperor against England. This was, no doubt, a strong motive of the

[1] Cardinal Consalvi used to say that Lord Castlereagh was the only one of the members of the Congress who treated him in the manner due to the representative of the Pope.

courtesy of Lord Castlereagh to the representative of the
Pontiff. But there was another powerful motive which
induced the English minister to conciliate Cardinal Consalvi. Castlereagh was strongly in favour of Catholic
emancipation ; but he advocated emancipation on the
lines laid down by his friend and former chief, William
Pitt. With Castlereagh, the *sine qua non* of emancipation
was an effective veto on the appointment of bishops, and
a State provision for the Irish clergy. The English
minister, no doubt, had great hopes that Cardinal Consalvi
would help him to carry out his scheme of emancipation.
When the allied sovereigns visited London in June, 1814—
that is, between the signing of the first treaty of Paris and
the Congress of Vienna—Cardinal Consalvi also " crossed
the Straits and appeared in London. He was the bearer
of a brief or letter to the Prince Regent from the Pope."[1]
He was exceedingly well received in England. From
what was universally said of him for many years after 1814,
it would appear that he was looked upon by the English
not only as a great diplomatist, but as a man of a conciliating disposition. This sentiment towards Consalvi
may be formulated by a very common and very English
expression : "This is a man we can deal with." The
reception here of the cardinal was so cordial and respectful
that Pope Pius gave an account of it in an allocution to the
Consistory of the 4th of September, 1815. Though the
words which his Holiness used have been recorded by
Cardinal Wiseman, they may well find a place in this
history. They are as follows :—

"The cardinal, having quickly reached Paris, and having
discharged those duties which we had confided to him towards his
most Christian Majesty, and having been received with that

[1] Cardinal Wiseman's "Recollections of the last Four Popes," Pius VII., chap. vi. p. 111 of the first edition.

interest and affection for us which it was natural to expect from his piety and religion, proceeded to London without delay; whither the other sovereigns, with the exception of our beloved son in Christ, Francis, Emperor of Austria, had gone. And here we cannot sufficiently express to you what feelings of joy and gratitude filled us, on learning what occurred on that occasion, in that most splendid city, capital of so mighty a kingdom. For the first time since more than two hundred years, a cardinal of the Holy Roman Church, and, moreover, a legate of this Apostolic See, appeared publicly in that city, by the kind and generous permission of the Government, adorned with the distinctive badge of his dignity in the same way as if he had been in this, our own city.

"And further, when he proceeded to an audience of his Royal Highness the Prince Regent of England to present our brief, and express the sentiments of admiration, friendship, and attachment which we entertain towards him, as well as towards that valiant and in so many ways illustrious nation, he was received at the palace with such marks of benevolence and kindness for us whom he represented as could with difficulty have been exceeded. On which account, professing ourselves deeply obliged to that Prince, and to the different orders that compose that generous nation, towards which we always entertained great good-will, we most gladly seize such an occasion to attest thus publicly our esteem and our lively gratitude."[1]

When Cardinal Consalvi was in England, he took advantage of the occasion to speak about emancipation. It is probable that it was during this visit to London that he first made the acquaintance of Lord Castlereagh, and it is not unlikely that he spoke to several statesmen on the subject of the Catholic claims. A few days before he died, in a long conversation which he had with Pope Leo XII., he said, amongst other things, "Live, and Catholic emancipation will take place in England, under your pontificate. I have worked hard for it, having begun when in London."[2]

[1] "Recollections of the last Four Popes," Pius VII., chap. vi. pp. 111, 112 (first edition).
[2] Ibid., p. 125.

Cardinal Wiseman attributes to Consalvi ability, perseverance, and admirable tact, and says that his Eminence "seems to have been quite in his place among the most acute diplomatists of the" Congress of Vienna.[1] We learn also, on the authority of Cardinal Wiseman, that Consalvi, in his political career, always manifested partiality towards England.[2]

Such, then, was the man with whom Mr. Hayes had to contend. The Franciscan friar was an Irish patriot with a grievance against England ; the cardinal was a first-rate Italian diplomatist, determined to oblige England as much as he conscientiously could. Mr. Hayes had to fight his battles alone ; Consalvi was assisted by Baron Ompteida, the Hanoverian ambassador at Rome,[3] and by British and Irish vetoist meddlers working in the Holy City in the interest, and perhaps also in the pay, of the English ministers.

A man like Consalvi, with his English propensities, should have been met by a diplomatist of tact and experience. Mr. Hayes, on the contrary, set about his attack on a politician much in the same spirit in which one of Lord Clare's dragoons would have charged at Ramillies.

The reader will, therefore, not be much surprised to hear that the battle ended by Mr. Hayes being ordered by the

---

[1] "Recollections of the last Four Popes," p. 113.   [2] Ibid., p. 100.

[3] As any minister of England who should have held political communication with the Vatican would thereby have incurred the dreadful penalties of a *præmunire*, the English Government, until the death of King William IV., used to transact business with the Roman Court through the Hanoverian ambassador at Rome, the King of England having been, since the accession of George I., the King of Hanover as well. So that England stood, in this respect, in a very absurd position. She had been assisting the Pope with troops and ships against Napoleon, and paying court to his ambassador to Paris ; but when there was a question of diplomatic communications, she drew herself up and assumed the ridiculously pompous position of the Grand Master of the Templars, in Sir Walter Scott's "Ivanhoe," when Isaac of York presented his petition. The words of Beaumanoir to Conrad may be slightly changed as follows :—" Back, sir ! I touch not Papists, save with the rope. Ompteida ; take thou the letter from the Pope."

authorities to leave Rome within twenty-four hours, and the States of the Church within three days; that Mr. Hayes refused to retire, unless he knew the reason why; that, having found no one who would tell him the reason why, he was captured at his lodgings, and conveyed with a military escort to the Tuscan frontier, where the Pope's dragoons left him and trotted back to Rome, leaving the reverend deputy from the Irish people to make the best of his way to Dublin. When Mr. Hayes arrived in Dublin, he drew up a long report of his negotiations in Rome. He read this report to the Catholic Board at a meeting held on the 18th of December, 1817.[1]

On the 1st of June, 1818, a meeting of the Irish Catholic Board was held, at which a second remonstrance to his Holiness Pope Pius VII. was read, and which had been sent to Cardinal Litta in the July of the preceding year. The ground of the remonstrance was twofold: the Irish Catholics were disappointed because the Pope had never answered their first remonstrance, sent, as we have seen, in the year 1815; and they were also dissatisfied with the reception their delegate had received in Rome, and indignant at the treatment he had received from Cardinal Consalvi and the Hanoverian ambassador. The remonstrance forcibly alludes to both these causes of complaints. It is very respectful towards the Head of the Church; it is strong in its denunciation of lay interference in the affairs of the Irish Church; and it also protests against the interference of "the political minister."[2] Under the circumstances, this remonstrance was worded in proper but very spirited terms: it was sent to Rome.[3]

---

[1] A copy of this report may be seen in the *Orthodox Journal* for the year 1817, pp. 471, *et seq*.

[2] This was an allusion to the interference of Consalvi.

[3] This remonstrance, as well as the answer of the Holy Father, may be seen in the *Orthodox Journal* for the year 1818, pp. 231, *et seq*.

At the same meeting on the 1st of June, 1818, the answer of Pope Pius to the second remonstrance was read. It was dated from St. Mary Major's, the 21st day of February, 1818. It may be divided into three parts. In the first part, his Holiness gives his reasons for not having answered the first remonstrance ; in the second part, he speaks of the conditions on which terms might be made with the English Government if emancipation were granted ; and in the third part, he alludes to the conduct of Mr. Hayes. Pope Pius tells the Irish Catholics that his reasons for not having answered their former letter were, in the first place, that he was not pleased with the tone of the remonstrance ; and secondly, that his letter to the bishops of the 1st of February, 1816, was a sufficient answer to the matters contained in the remonstrance, and that their lordships could have communicated that answer to the laity. Pope Pius then proceeds to explain to the Irish Catholics the spirit in which any concession would be made to the Government as the price of emancipation. All that his Holiness says is in complete accordance with the letter of Cardinal Litta to Dr. Poynter, and with what he himself had written to the Irish prelates. It is not necessary, therefore, to enter more particularly into this portion of the letter. The whole tone of what has been called the two first parts of the letter is very paternal, and, though it contains a slight rebuke, the admonition is given in such a way that no offence could be taken in Ireland. The condescension with which the Pope enters into the question of the veto shows that his Holiness appreciated the anxiety which the Irish laity showed on that subject. But in the third part of the letter the tone is completely changed, and Mr. Hayes is denounced in the strongest terms. He is accused of abusing "the hospitality which he enjoyed in the city," that is, in Rome ; he is charged with conducting himself in a manner "altogether unbecoming a man professing a religious institute;" he is censured for his "arrogance and audacity;" his expulsion from Rome is justified; and the letter concludes by saying, "That same man of whom we speak, since his return to his own country, has not changed his line of conduct; for, in the public journals of the 17th day of last December, printed in Dublin, we have seen a report delivered by him to you, of his proceedings in this city. Like his former writings, it is full of falsehood and calumnies, to which report, therefore, we most unreservedly declare to you that no credit should be attached."[1]

After the reading of this letter at the meeting, Mr. Hayes made a few remarks which were highly creditable to him, as showing his entire submission to the Pope, and expressing his intention to implore the forgiveness of the Holy Father. He, however, made some other observations to the effect that Pope Pius had been induced to sign the letter by representations which were not true; and that those who advised his Holiness and had to carry out his intentions, especially in the matter of Mr. Hayes' expulsion from Rome, had behaved to him in an arbitrary manner. Under all the circumstances, these remarks seem to have been justified.

It is well known that official letters, like the answer to the Irish remonstrance, are prepared in the offices which have the management of the affairs to which the letters relate. The remonstrance in question related to the appointment of bishops, a thing which in itself is a purely spiritual act, and only accidentally connected with the civil authority. The office, therefore, which would properly

---

[1] The Latin words of the letter referring to Mr. Hayes' report are, "calumniis refertam, cui propterea nullam esse adhibendam fidem, vobis apertissime declaramus."

take cognizance of the remonstrance would be that of the congregation *de propaganda fide*, of which Cardinal Litta was the prefect. I presume that the first remonstrance was in fact sent from Ireland direct to his Eminence, for Pope Pius, at the commencement of his answer, mentions that the remonstrance was delivered to him by "our venerable brother, Laurence, Cardinal Litta." But, as the appointment of bishops does, in the majority of cases, carry with it civil consequences, it becomes a matter of interest, and sometimes of the highest interest, to the Government of the country in which any particular appointment has to be made. It is, indeed, this accidental circumstance which has caused many, and perhaps most, of the disputes and difficulties which, in the history of the Church and of nations, have arisen between various Governments and the Holy See. That the appointment of bishops is a matter of interest to the civil power is fully recognized by the authorities in Rome; this is clearly acknowledged in Cardinal Litta's letter to Dr. Poynter of the 26th of April, 1815, which has already been mentioned in this history.[1] As the appointment of bishops is therefore generally a matter also of civil interest, it may sometimes involve serious political questions. In the instance we have now before us, the civil aspect of the affair was important. Under great pressure to join Napoleon against England, the Pope had steadily refused to do so. His Holiness had suffered severely in consequence of his friendly attitude towards this country. The English Government had helped in preserving the temporal dominions of the Pope; it had sent ships and troops to Civita Vecchia. There was a large party in the British Parliament, including the most distinguished statesmen and orators, determined to carry emancipation, but with

[1] *Vide* Chap. xxiii.

concessions by the Pope in the matter of the veto. To obtain the Act was one of the favourite projects of Cardinal Consalvi, and was an object very dear to the heart of the Pope. So that the mutual friendly relations which existed between England and Rome, the strong wish in Rome, and the desire of a large party in the United Kingdom, were circumstances which combined to induce Consalvi to make sacrifices to which, under other circumstances, he might not have advised the Pope to consent. It would have been impossible—indeed, if possible, it would not have been advisable—to settle the affair in Rome without consulting the political minister. And though the matter belonged properly and in the first instance to the cardinal prefect of the propaganda, it was one which was also closely connected with the department of the cardinal secretary of state.

When, therefore, Cardinal Consalvi saw that the Irish, through their deputy in Rome, were strongly opposing any interference whatever on the part of the English Government in the choice of bishops—even that limited interference which had been sanctioned by Pope Pius—his Eminence was naturally extremely annoyed, and was afraid his negotiations with England might be injured. The indiscreet conduct of Mr. Hayes afforded Consalvi a plea for demanding the expulsion of his opponent from Rome. The Hanoverian ambassador supported the cardinal, and the result followed which the reader has already seen. It was remarked above that the cardinal was successful against his opponent personally; of this there can be no question. It was also observed that the cardinal was unsuccessful in the matter in dispute. This is proved by the fact that neither Cardinal Consalvi nor any other cardinal, nor any English minister, nor any meddling intriguer, English or Irish, Protestant or

Catholic, has from that time to this been able to effect any arrangement whereby the Pope would have conceded to the English Government any right whatever to interfere in the appointment of bishops in the United Kingdom.[1]

There were some Catholics in England who thought that the Irish laity were wrong in sending any remonstrance to the Pope on the subject of the veto. I judge such to be the case from the perusal of a long article written by Andrews in the *Orthodox Journal*. The ground which Andrews takes is, that the appointment of bishops being a purely ecclesiastical matter, the Irish bishops having addressed the Pope on the subject, and his Holiness having written to them a final reply, it was no business of the laity to interfere. We have seen that Pope Pius tells the Irish laity that they might have been content with the answer he had sent to their bishops. But still, there is nothing in the Pope's words which can be described as anything approaching to severe blame. Nor, indeed, could any impartial person, calmly and sensibly viewing all the circumstances, impute positive blame to the action taken by the Irish Catholic Board. Cardinal Consalvi, looking at the veto question chiefly from a political point of view, may have blamed, and no doubt did in private blame, the conduct of the laity. But in objecting to the remonstrance, his action in this particular would seem to justify the proceedings of those of whom he complained. The interference of his Eminence in the question can only be justified on the ground that it was one which involved civil and political matter. But if the question of the veto concerned politics in Rome, it was because it concerned

---

[1] In the letter of his Holiness to the Irish Catholics, there is a marked difference in the tone of that part in which Mr. Hayes is denounced and of all that precedes it, rather conveying the idea that Cardinal Litta prepared the first two parts of the letter, and that Cardinal Consalvi prepared the third part. The calumnies which his Holiness speaks of were, no doubt, the statements which Mr. Hayes publicly made respecting the action of Consalvi.

politics in Ireland. Cardinal Litta also may have been a little annoyed that the affair had not been allowed to rest after his last letter to the Irish bishops; but he could hardly have blamed the remonstrants when he saw the action of the political minister, the Hanoverian ambassador, and the English and Irish intriguers who were then in Rome. It is not a matter of surprise, therefore, that the letter of Pope Pius should have contained only mild terms in speaking of the interference of the Irish board. The appointment of bishops, though a purely ecclesiastical affair, is one of the greatest political importance to the Irish. It is a vital matter that no right of interference should be conceded to the English Government which would prevent the supreme Pontiff from appointing prelates acceptable to the Irish nation. The Holy Father should not be made in the smallest degree the means of enabling English statesmen to govern Ireland on British and Protestant principles. Without any concordat, the prime minister or the foreign secretary may make what communication he pleases to the Pope. And, if this communication be made in a regular manner, no one could complain, though many would prefer that there should be no communication at all, rather than run any risk of undue pressure being put upon the action of Rome. At the time of which I am writing the history, the English Government was interfering in the question of the veto; it was interfering purely and simply because the appointment of bishops carries with it civil consequences. Cardinal Consalvi, anxious to conciliate England, was negotiating in the question as the adviser of the Pope, not in spiritual, but in temporal matters. The Irish Catholic laity, who were vetoists, had their lay agents in Rome, urging the temporal advantages which would follow from giving the minister a voice in the choice of prelates. When the chief question in Rome was about the political or civil part of the affair, when everybody else was allowed to talk and intrigue as they pleased, could it have been said that the staunch Irish Catholics, who stood up for the freedom of the Pope, even at the sacrifice of their own liberties, were not to interfere, and that they alone were to remain silent and inactive when their opponents were at work? Pope Pius VII. would never have consented to such a proposition. He wished only to chide the Irish Board for a little over-zeal in the cause of the liberties of the Church and of their own.

During this year Dr. Milner was busily employed in finishing his great work, so well known as "The End of Religious Controversy." But his pen was not idle in general Catholic affairs. He wrote several letters in the *Orthodox Journal*, in order to keep his fellow-Catholics alive to the dangers which might result from the activity of those, who based all action upon the principles of the Fifth Resolution and the penal clauses of the schismatical bill of 1813. But the valiant bishop had, during this year, great cause for consolation. The other Catholic prelates of England joined with Milner in denouncing the principles of the bill of 1813, and the persevering efforts of Sir John Cox Hippisley to carry out what Milner calls his "projected reformation of our religion." Dr. Collingridge wrote a very spirited pastoral against the provisions of the obnoxious measure; and Dr. Milner expressed his joy on the occasion in a letter to the *Orthodox Journal*, signed "A Catholic Divine."[1] In this letter he mentions a circumstance which shows the length to which a Catholic gentleman was prepared to go, in his eager animosity towards Bishop Milner. Writing of himself in the third person, Milner, addressing the editor, says—

"You have repeatedly mentioned his" (that is, Milner's)

[1] *Orthodox Journal* for the year 1818, p. 59.

"persecutions at Board meetings and in public advertisements, but it is within my knowledge that he only laughs at these, and is better pleased with the votes of censure than he could be with the thanks and commendatory testimonials of our degenerate aristocracy, as long as they show themselves disposed to barter spiritual things for things temporal. He has even laughed, to my certain knowledge, at those threats of personal violence which some consistent Catholics have exhibited against him, in the discharge of his professional duty; one of whom, the same who moved his expulsion at one Catholic meeting, jumped out of his seat on the floor at another, in the attitude of Mendoza, to challenge him to battle. Brave northern hero, to box with his bishop!"[1]

There is also, in regard to Dr. Milner, another instance of the absurdity into which ungoverned hatred and spite will fall, and which occurred during this year. It is related in a letter written by the Rev. Edward Peach to the *Orthodox Journal*.[2] A good portrait of Milner had been painted by a Mr. Radclyffe, and it had been determined that an engraving from it should be published. Mr. Peach, writing from Birmingham on the 12th of May, 1818, says, amongst other things—

"When the engraving had been determined upon, and the engagement with Mr. Radclyffe, the artist, had been settled, in order to excite an interest amongst the lovers of learning and of the arts, the original painting was sent to London, and presented at Somerset House, to be admitted into the exhibition. It was refused admittance; and the cause of the refusal was not because it was the representation of a Catholic bishop, nor because it was deficient in point of execution—for the portrait of Dr. Poynter was not objected against, although in execution it was not superior— but because it was the portrait of Dr. Milner, whose very likeness was more than the jury of Somerset House could endure! It was afterwards received into a private museum of great note in London,

---

[1] Mendoza was a celebrated member of the "Ring" in those prize-fighting days.

[2] Vol. vi. p. 173.

and hung up in a place sufficiently conspicuous for the friends of genius and of virtue to see the *original* from which the engraving was to be taken. It had not been there four-and-twenty hours before such hints were given to the worthy proprietor by one or two members of the Ministry, and by many who are ranked amongst the highest classes of Catholics, that he found himself necessitated to remove it, or run the risk of losing a considerable portion of the patronage on which his prosperity depended."

So far Mr. Peach. I may just mention, in passing, that the men who could behave in so mean and disgraceful a manner were the men to whom Cardinal Consalvi was listening in Rome, while his Eminence was discouraging the representations of those who were fighting for the liberties of the Church in these islands. There are, unfortunately, many things which show the degradation of the human race in consequence of original sin; and one of those things is, that the secret whisperings of those who speak falsely have generally more influence over men who have the direction of affairs than have the outspoken words of those who tell the truth.

As Bishop Milner's efforts to extinguish Blanchardism have been mentioned in the course of this history, I will conclude this chapter with an account of the final end of that disgraceful schism. And I cannot do better than give the history in the words of Bishop Milner. In a letter to the editor of the *Orthodox Journal*, written in the third person, and signed " A Midland Pastor," his lordship writes as follows :—

" It is fitting that your valuable register of the passing transactions of British Catholics should record and celebrate the termination of the ostensible causes of disunion among our chief pastors. The first of these regarded the *test*, unanimously resolved upon by them in their synod of February, 1810, against the French schismatics resident in this country who refused to communicate with the Church of France, as restored by his

Holiness in 1802, and who thereby separated themselves from the whole Catholic Church. The said test excluded from all priestly functions, and even from saying Mass, those priests who refused to acknowledge *that Pope Pius VII. is not the author or supporter of heresy or schism*, which is the same thing as to say that the Church of France, restored by the Pope, is not heretical or schismatical. This test *our bishop* has ever supported in practice and by his printed pastoral letters; while his brethren in the south and west thought it prudent to cushion it, and to indulge the French clergy in the possession of their prejudices. Just now, however, a pastoral injunction has appeared in the London District, no doubt with the concurrence of the Western District, containing the whole meaning of the above-mentioned test, namely, that *no French priest shall henceforward exercise his functions, or even say Mass, who refuses to acknowledge his subjection to the Pope, and that he is in connection with all those Christians who are in the Pope's communion*, and, of course, with the Established Church of France. To this injunction some of the French clergy in London have submitted, and others have refused to submit. In the mean time, this great cause of disunion between the superior of the Midland District, supported by the decrees of all the Catholic bishops of Ireland, in synod assembled, and the superiors of the London and Western Districts, is taken away, and our only remaining anxiety is about the everlasting lot of those French bishops and priests who have died during a course of years in and about London, openly professing those principles which now are *universally allowed to be schismatical*."[1]

Thus the reader will see that Milner was right in both divisions of his contest with his right reverend brethren in the question of the Blanchardist schism and in that of the schismatical clauses of the bill of 1813. But before two years shall have passed, it will be seen that Milner's enemies in England, so far from being generous enough to admit his title to reward for having been substantially

[1] *Orthodox Journal* for 1818, p. 22. As there is no mention of the Northern District in this letter, I conclude that none of the schismatical priests resided in that part of England.

in the right, contrived to obtain from Pope Pius a severe rebuke to the gallant bishop for not having been sufficiently polite in the *manner* in which he had "fought a good fight and kept the faith." With the men of the "Fifth Resolution" St. Paul himself would not have been safe.

CHAPTER XXX.

THE CATHOLIC QUESTION IN 1819.

English Catholic meetings and petitions—Meeting of Protestants in Dublin in favour of emancipation—Meetings in Ireland—Speech of O'Connell—Aggregate Catholic meeting—O'Connell's speech and letter—Proceedings in the House of Commons—Grattan's speech—Remarks on Grattan's speech—The debate in the Commons—The debate in the Lords—Lord Grey's bill—Butler's remarks on the state of the Catholic question.

ON the 13th of January, 1819, there was a meeting of the Board of British Catholics. The Duke of Norfolk presided. It was resolved that a petition to both Houses of Parliament should be immediately drawn up, and that Lord Grey should be requested to present it to the House of Lords, and Lord Nugent to the House of Commons. A petition was accordingly prepared and numerously signed.[1] There were two expressions in these petitions which gave great offence to some of the anti-vetoists. The objections of these gentlemen found expression in a letter which the editor of the *Orthodox Journal* addressed to the Duke of Norfolk in the February number of his magazine. The obnoxious phrases were in the prayer of the petition. The words were: "That your honourable House will take their" (that is, the Catholics') "case into consideration, and grant them SUCH RELIEF as your honourable House SHALL DEEM PROPER for extending to them the enjoyment, in common with their fellow-subjects, of the blessings of the

[1] Vide "Butler's Historical Memoirs," vol. iv. p. 280, edition of 1822; and the *Orthodox Journal* for January, 1819, p. 46.

Constitution,"[1] Many Catholics took alarm at the expressions "such relief" and "shall deem proper." They maintained that the relief asked for by the Board was only the relief which up to that time the House of Commons had consented to give ; that is, a partial repeal of the penal laws, accompanied with the veto and other restrictions on the free action of the Church. The Board, it was said, ought to have asked for unconditional relief, and the fact that it did not do so, but only asked for what the respective Houses might think proper, showed a continual adherence to the principles of the Fifth Resolution and the schismatical clauses of the bill of 1813. When the secretary to the Board, Mr. Edward Jerningham, was informed that the words used in the petition were deterring many from signing it, he caused the following words to be written on several of the placards :—" These are *mere* words of courtesy, and bear no reference whatever to any specific concession on the part of the British Catholics, and still less to the particular measure termed *veto*, with which the British Catholics *have no concern whatever*." These words seem to have still further irritated the ultra anti-vetoists. That Mr. Jerningham really meant what he wrote, I have no doubt ; but if the words were dictated to him, it is not improbable that the persons who suggested them had some *arrière pensée* in the matter. Though Andrews, the editor of the *Orthodox Journal*, was quite right to be on the alert against any proceeding of the Board, it may be thought that he exaggerated the meaning and importance of the words of the petition, in the very strong letter which he wrote to the Duke of Norfolk. The assertion that the British Catholics had no concern whatever with the question of the veto may have been, and probably was, an allusion

---

[1] Vide "Butler's Historical Memoirs," vol. iv. p. 280, edition of 1822 ; and the *Orthodox Journal* for January, 1819, p. 46.

to the letter of Cardinal Litta to Dr. Poynter, in which case the expressions used by Mr. Jerningham would have been very proper. I do not find that Dr. Milner made any public objection to the wording of the petition. Had he seen anything very mischievous in it, he would certainly have written a characteristic letter to Andrews on the subject. We have seen that Milner told Pope Pius that there would be no emancipation so long as Lord Liverpool should be prime minister. The bishop may therefore have thought it was unnecessary to quarrel with a petition about expressions which were at most of doubtful meaning.

The words of the underlings of a party and of the editors of newspapers are always very much stronger than the expressions of those who are the responsible leaders. I suspect that Andrews's letter to the Duke of Norfolk is only an example of this tendency in the management of human affairs.

In Ireland, the most notable event in the history of emancipation which occurred this year was a large meeting of Protestants held on the 11th of February in the Rotunda at Dublin to petition Parliament for relief in favour of their Catholic fellow-countrymen. The *Orthodox Journal* says that it was the most numerous assemblage of Protestant rank, wealth, and talent ever known in Ireland. A requisition to the lord mayor was signed, requesting him to call the meeting. This requisition was presented to the Lord Mayor by the Duke of Leinster and the Earls of Claremont and Meath, accompanied by several of the Dublin merchants.[1] The resolutions passed at the meeting were excellent; the form of petition adopted prayed for relief to "the persons professing the Roman Catholic religion, from all civil and political disabilities," and there was not the

---

[1] A long list of the names of the requisitionists may be found in the *Orthodox Journal* for February, 1819.

slightest allusion to the veto or to any other securities. The principal speakers were the Duke of Leinster; Mr. William Humphreys; Mr. Grattan and his son; Mr. Curran, son of the celebrated advocate, John Philpot Curran; Lord Charlemont; and Lord Cloncurry. At the commencement of the proceedings several Catholic gentlemen left the hall at the request of the lord mayor, in order that it might not be said that the resolutions were not carried exclusively by Protestants. An Orange amendment was proposed to the first resolution. Only a few persons voted for it; and having been defeated, they retired from the meeting, leaving no perceptible difference in the number of those present. The Dublin Orangemen afterwards got up a private petition of their own against emancipation.

It might have been thought that when the Catholics of Ireland were supported to so great an extent by the wealth and intelligence of their Protestant fellow-countrymen, some impression would have been made upon the Legislature of the United Kingdom. But the bigotry of the Protestants of Great Britain was not to be softened by the display of Irish Protestant liberality which had taken place in Dublin. We had to wait ten more years for emancipation. The help of our Protestant friends, however great, was of no practical use. Irish Catholics had to learn, after a fierce struggle, the truth of the great principle sung by Lord Byron, and so often sounded in their ears by O'Connell:

> "Hereditary bondsmen, know ye not,
> Who would be free, themselves must strike the blow?"

There were several other meetings in various parts of Ireland, at which petitions for unqualified emancipation were voted. On the 27th of January, a Catholic meeting was held in Dublin, in the first place, to thank the Protestants for the help they had given ; and, in the second place, to agree upon a form of petition to Parliament. O'Connell made a short, but admirable speech.

"He hailed the dawn of friendship and affection which had at length broken in upon Irishmen. He gave Earl Talbot's administration the praise of NEUTRALITY at least, upon the present momentous and memorable occasion. The slightest interference upon the part of his Excellency's Government to check the course of generous feeling then so happily flowing through the country, was not, he said, to be traced. The propriety of petitioning he conceived to be unquestionable. Much benefit always resulted from discussion ; it assisted to enlighten the English people upon the subject of the belief, morality, and condition of the Irish Catholics, and this was all that was necessary to the success of emancipation. . . . He spoke of the expediency of trying to procure the co-operation of the Catholic peers, peers' eldest sons, and baronets, in the application to the Legislature; mentioned the Earl of Fingall in the most respectful terms; and said it was the strongly-expressed desire of the committee of gentlemen who had revised the petition that no topics should be introduced, no words made use of, which could by possibility give offence or create division."[1]

O'Connell showed in this speech how anxious he was for union and cordial action, not only amongst Catholics themselves, but amongst Catholics and their Protestant fellow-countrymen.

But this meeting was not thought sufficient to express the gratitude of Catholics. Accordingly, an aggregate meeting was held on the 1st of March, in the old chapel in Mary's Lane. Mr. John O'Connell calls it "the largest and most respectable meeting of Catholics which ever took place in Ireland." The meeting had no other purpose but that "of expressing," as Mr. John O'Connell says, "in the most marked manner, the gratitude of the Catholic body to the Protestants who have lately come forward to petition

[1] "Select Speeches of Daniel O'Connell," vol. ii. p. 59.

Parliament in their behalf."[1] The Earl of Fingall took the chair. The vote of thanks for which the meeting had been called was passed. A second resolution contained a special vote of thanks to the Right Hon. Thomas M'Kenny, the Lord Mayor, for his "justice and liberality" in calling the Protestant meeting. O'Connell also spoke at this meeting, and it would be impossible to speak in more conciliatory terms than those which the great agitator employed on this occasion. The fact of so many influential Protestants having petitioned for emancipation and the presence at the meeting of so many of the Catholic aristocracy appear to have filled O'Connell with enthusiasm. He seems to have thought for a moment that the union of all Irishmen had commenced, and was to continue. His words were those of a true and disinterested patriot. Englishmen are, no doubt, gradually ceasing to hate and calumniate O'Connell. After the lapse of a few more years, when those whom he conquered shall all have passed away, their descendants will think of him as he expected his fellow-countrymen to think of him, when, in the autumn of this year (1819), addressing by letter the Catholics of Ireland, he wrote as follows:—"The part I have taken in Catholic affairs induces me to expect that you will believe me to be actuated by no other motives than those of an honest and an ardent zeal to promote your interests and to attain your freedom."

On the 3rd of May, Mr. Grattan presented thirteen petitions in the House of Commons in favour of Catholic emancipation, eight of them being from Catholics, and five from Protestants. He then proposed the following resolution:—"That this House do resolve itself into a committee of the whole House, to consider the state of the laws by which the oaths or declarations are required

[1] "Select Speeches of Daniel O'Connell," vol. ii. p. 59.

to be taken or made as qualifications for the enjoyment of offices and the exercise of civil functions, so far as the same affect his Majesty's Roman Catholic subjects, and whether it would be expedient in any or what manner to alter or modify the same, and subject to what provisions and regulations." The orator made a good speech on the occasion. In one part of it he ridiculed the arguments on the other side. "This argument," he said, "is not only not according to human nature, but the reverse. It is supposed that Dr. Poynter, an excellent subject, will, upon the emancipation of his flock, say to the Duke of Norfolk, 'Your Grace is now possessed of the privileges of the Constitution, and will now of course try to subvert the Government—that is to say, lose your head by a fruitless attempt to get me made Archbishop of Canterbury.'"[1] In another part of his speech, he speaks of the charges brought against Catholics as follows:—

"When we say that the Roman Catholic is incapable of moral obligation or political allegiance, we affirm that Christianity does not extend to France, to Italy, to Spain, to a great part of Germany, and of course we deprive it of one great proof of its divinity. You answer this by charges against the Roman Catholics. I have stated those charges to be unfounded. You did not believe in them in the 17th of the King,[2] when you declared the Roman Catholics to be good and loyal subjects; you did not believe in them when you gave them the right of bearing arms; when you gave them, in Ireland, the elective franchise; when you gave them the army and navy; when you restored the Popedom; when you helped to restore the House of Bourbon, and, with them, to give new strength to the Roman religion in France. You saw that a Roman Catholic establishment was better than philosophy, and that Christianity with seven sacraments was better than infidelity."

[1] "Annual Register" for 1819, p. 56].
[2] This must be a mistake for the 14th of the King, as it seems to refer to the Act of 1774.

These last words of Grattan have not lost their significance. The kind of philosophy which the orator alluded to and infidelity have been on the increase since his words were spoken. Englishmen have had the choice constantly put before them, and sometimes in a very evident and prominent manner, between Christianity and the Catholic Church on the one hand, and philosophy and infidelity on the other. Some—only a few, in comparison with the great bulk of the people—have made the right choice; others, chiefly of the upper and upper middle class, have made that choice of Christianity which is represented by what is called Ritualism.[1] There are, no doubt, many others also who, without borrowing the clothes of the Church in order to look like her, still hold some of the fundamental doctrines which she teaches. But the literature of the day, the talk of the day, the instruction given to the youth of our times, the manners and customs of the English people towards the end of the nineteenth century, all go to show that philosophy, in Grattan's sense, and infidelity are now far more widely diffused than they were at the end of the second decade of the century. It is not only religion which is affected by this philosophy and infidelity. Their effects are perceptible in politics, in social life, in the loosening of those traditional principles of conduct, both in the governors and the governed, which like useful props have steadied the life of Englishmen, while old institutions in other countries have tottered to the ground. What is called modern philosophy and infidelity have induced a more universal love of comfort and of pleasure. The making and amassing of money,

---

[1] So far as Ritualists believe in the doctrines of the Church, the increase of that sect certainly adds to the Christianity of the country. But if we look upon Ritualists as a power moving the English people towards the Spouse of Jesus Christ, it remains yet to be seen whether the old saying does not apply to them: " The nearer the Church, the farther from God."

though always the prime end with people in general, is now with us a much more exclusive object than it was. The power of England in the world, her commanding influence, her prestige, her honour, are not the objects of interest to the present generation that they were to our fathers. In domestic affairs a degeneration is perceptible. One of the greatest political changes ever made in this country has just been brought about by the influence of a few men, the great bulk of the people remaining in a state of almost apathetic indifference. Even one opposed to the late change might, as an Englishman, have sighed as he noticed the little interest, the weakened spirit, which the nation as a whole showed during an agitation—if, indeed, it is worthy of that name—which was a mere paltry and vulgar counterfeit of the great and spirited movements which brought about the first Reform Bill and the repeal of the Corn Laws. The wholesome bands of religion are no impediment to political and social progress which is worth anything; on the contrary, they brace up the strength of the soul to resist those lawless rovings of the intellect which are always followed by enervating reaction. In an age when education is becoming universal, a new system can be more easily diffused than in bygone days. We may soon see thousands, and perhaps millions, caught by the sophistries of so-called philosophers, whose ideas are certainly not more sublime, and not much more methodized, than the ideas which enter into the mind of a Catholic school-boy of sixteen or seventeen years of age, who is thinking how nice it would be to invent a new religion, in order to escape going to confession. And this is the philosophy which is gradually sapping the strength of religious feeling, the healthy vigour of political life, and the morality of social intercourse amongst the English people. Could Grattan in these days, addressing the

House of Commons, say, "You see and acknowledge that a Roman Catholic establishment is better than philosophy, and that Christianity with seven sacraments is better than infidelity?"

Mr. Grattan's motion was seconded by Mr. Croker, and, as a matter of course, opposed by Mr. Leslie Foster, an Orangeman. Lord Normanby supported the motion, and other members spoke for and against it. The motion was defeated, but by a majority of only two, the numbers being—Ayes, 241 ; Noes, 243.[1] Alluding to Mr. Croker's speech, Mr. Butler says that he was particularly distinguished by one of the most argumentative speeches ever heard in the House.[2]

On the 17th of May, Lord Donoughmore presented a number of petitions to the House of Lords in favour of emancipation. He then made a motion similar to that which Grattan had made in the House of Commons. He was supported by the Bishop of Norwich and by Earl Grey; but was opposed by the Bishops of Worcester and Peterborough, the Lord Chancellor Eldon, and the prime minister, the Earl of Liverpool. Mr. Butler, commenting on this debate, says that "Dr. Marsh, who had been advanced to the bishopric of Llandaff, and thence translated to that of Peterborough, opposed the motion in an ingenious speech, the object of which was to show that the Catholics were not excluded from the blessings of the Constitution for their belief respecting transubstantiation, the invocation of the saints, or their other speculative opinions, but because they divided their allegiance, giving *part* of it to their own Sovereign, and *part* to a foreigner; and that they ought not, therefore, to be placed on the same rank with those who gave *all* their allegiance to their native

---

[1] "Annual Register" for 1819, p. 60].
[2] "Historical Memoirs," vol. iv. p. 281, edition of 1822.

King. In this notion the right reverend prelate was triumphantly refuted by Earl Grey."[1] Dr. Bathurst, the Bishop of Norwich, spoke very plainly to their lordships, and his words may with profit be kept in memory both by Catholics and Protestants. He said, "It is the duty of the House to let England cease from this day forward to be the only country in Europe where intolerance was established by law, where religious opinions excluded from civil office, and where men were obliged to surrender their rights for the sake of their conscience."[2] Lord Grey concluded his address with some strong remarks about Ireland, which are worthy of notice, as showing an inconsistency between theory and practice, between what he said ought to be done and what he did, or rather what he did not do, when shortly after the passing of the Emancipation Act, he was in office. "He ended his speech," says the "Annual Register," "with noticing the present dangers which threatened our security; and he asked, 'Why is Ireland to be left a continued prey to that system of proscription from whence so much alarm and danger has been felt through the empire? Was it anything less than madness to suffer such dangers to accumulate, and not, when the opportunity presented itself, to take the certain means to allay present discontent and provide future security?'" Lord Grey came into office as prime minister in November, 1830, that is, about a year and a half after the Emancipation Act had passed, and he remained in power until July, 1834, which was rather more than three years and a half; and yet, during the whole of that time, he could not be prevailed upon to appoint a Catholic to any of those offices which were opened to them in 1829. Though he had inveighed against the system of proscrip-

---

[1] "Historical Memoirs," vol. iv. p. 282.
[2] "Annual Register" for 1819, p. 60].

tion, yet when in office he kept it up, and would not carry out in practice the liberal principles which he had advocated during all the best years of his life. A Catholic may speculate upon this difference between Lord Grey's principles and his acts, and he will no doubt find that some practical reflections will be the result. Lord Donoughmore's motion was lost by 41 votes, the numbers being—Ayes, 106; noes, 147.

Lord Donoughmore having been defeated on the general question of relief to Catholics, Lord Grey proceeded to obtain, if possible, some partial relief. Accordingly, on the 25th of May, 1819, his lordship introduced a bill into the House of Lords "to repeal those parts of the Acts 25 and 30 Charles II., which require persons, previous to admission into offices or to either House of Parliament, to subscribe certain declarations against the doctrines of transubstantiation, the invocation of saints, and the sacrifice of the Mass."[1] In the course of his speech, the earl said, "He presumed that no obstacle would be opposed to the passing of this bill, which did not in the least interfere with any securities which some noble lords thought ought to be required of Roman Catholics. It merely affected certain dogmatic opinions, and had no reference whatever to any question of supremacy, political or spiritual."[2] The bill was then read a first time. On the 10th of the following June, the earl moved the second reading of the bill. The reader will have observed that this bill would not have given any practical relief to a conscientious Catholic, for it left the obligation to take the Oath of Supremacy still in force. The relief proposed by this bill would have been a great consolation to Catholics, for it would have effaced a foul and blasphemous

---

[1] Butler's "Historical Memoirs," vol. iv. p. 282.
[2] "Annual Register" for 1819, p. 63].

blot on the statute-book of their country. Lord Grey may have supposed that some Catholics would have taken the Oath of Supremacy, for towards the end of the last century there was a small knot of them who were ready to do so. But it is most probable that Lord Grey would have been mistaken, for when, nine years afterwards, in the year 1828, Lord John Russell carried the repeal of the Test and Corporation Acts, I am not aware that a single Catholic took advantage of it to accept any office. Lord Grey was not, it would seem, singular in thinking that Catholics might take the Oath of Supremacy. During the course of his speech, he read several resolutions which had been passed at a great Protestant meeting called to oppose the bill. The fifth of these resolutions was as follows:—

"That although the said declarations against transubstantiation and popery contain only a renunciation of certain opinions entertained by Roman Catholics, yet they form, in the opinion of this meeting, the principal test by which Roman Catholics are to be ascertained, and without which the oaths of allegiance and supremacy are not sufficient to exclude Roman Catholics from Parliament and from situations of political power."

The bill, however, did not pass the second reading. On the division of the House, the numbers were—Contents, 49; proxies, 33; being 82 for the motion: not contents, 72; proxies, 69; being 141 against the motion, giving a majority of 59 against the bill.[1]

Mr. Butler, in his "Historical Memoirs," after mentioning the division on this bill, has some remarks on the state of the Catholic question. Though the extract is somewhat long, it is of sufficient interest to put before the reader.

"Throughout the whole of this period," he says, "both the Boards[2] were anxious to call the attention of Parliament to the

---

[1] "Annual Register" for 1819, p. 64].
[2] That is, the English and the Irish Boards.

laws in force exclusively against the British Catholics. Their condition seemed entitled to particular notice, as they are liable to several penalties and disabilities from which the Irish members of their communion are exempt. It may be added that the real merits of the Catholic cause were so great that it gained, at least in public opinion, on every discussion; this circumstance was often urged as an argument for multiplying the discussions of it. In these reasons for agitating their case there was weight, but the objections to it were serious. Most of the leading advocates of their cause thought that no application for partial relief would succeed—and that, if it did succeed, it would not materially ameliorate their situation. They also observed that no relief would ever be granted to the English Catholics without granting the same degree of relief to the Irish; and this, it was said, could not be expected, unless the Irish question should be brought fully before the House. It was also observed that the Catholic question, if brought on separately, must either precede or follow the Irish discussion: if it preceded, its discomfiture—which was always too probable—would prejudice the Irish cause; if it followed, then, if the Irish application had succeeded, its success would have rendered an application from the British Catholics unnecessary, and if the Irish had been defeated, it would be impossible to expect that the British should succeed. With respect to the advantages flowing from discussion, it was admitted to be true that the general cause had gained on every discussion; but it was remarked that the repetition must at length weary, and that it would prove fatal to the Catholic cause to bring it before the House so often as to bereave it of its interest, and make it disposed of as a matter of course, without a division. These observations weighed with the Catholic Boards, and withheld their proceeding. Still, they availed themselves of every opportunity which offered, of bringing the cause of their constituents favourably before the public and the Houses of Parliament; and, without intruding themselves on persons in power, they took frequent occasion to wait upon them, to expose their case, and to dispose them favourably towards it. It may be truly said that the conduct of the Boards gained them the approbation both of his Majesty's ministers and the leaders of the opposition. The friends of each frequently mentioned it in the highest terms of approbation. In what light the Board has been considered, and in what terms it has been mentioned by the Supreme Pontiff, will appear in some of the documents inserted in the Appendix." Mr. Butler adds a note to this, in which he says, "The writer feels it honourable to him to have combated in these ranks."[1]

The reader will have noticed that in the last sentence but one of the above extract Mr. Butler says, "The friends of *each*," etc.; and in the second member of the sentence he says, "in what light *the Board*," etc. The transition from the two Boards to the one Board indicates, I presume, that by "the Board" Mr. Butler means the English Board. If the presumption be correct, I must leave the reader to imagine why Mr. Butler should have confined to the English Board the mention of (what I suppose he means) the praises of the Supreme Pontiff. In the "Appendix" referred to by Mr. Butler, I do not find any mention of the Board in the letters written from Rome by his Holiness, or by Monsignore Quarantotti, or by Cardinal Litta.

In the course of this history, the address to Pope Pius VII. has been mentioned which was resolved upon at a meeting of the General Board of British Catholics on the 17th of June, 1814.[2] The answer to that address is directed to "Our dear children, the Catholic inhabitants of Great Britain;" and the praises contained in it are not directed so much to the action of the Board as to the general conduct of English Catholics in preserving their loyalty even under persecution. The opening words of the extract from Mr. Butler are somewhat puzzling. Neither in the printed reports of the proceedings of the two Boards, so far as I have seen them in the *Orthodox Journal*, nor in the speeches of O'Connell, nor in any life of O'Connell, nor in Milner's "Supple-

---

[1] "Historical Memoirs," pp. 282-284.
[2] Vide p. 156.

mentary Memoirs," can I find any mention of what Mr. Butler alludes to when he says, "throughout the whole of this period, both the Boards were anxious to call the attention of Parliament to the laws in force exclusively against the British Catholics." There may be in existence, either in print or in writing, papers which would prove what Mr. Butler says; but, in the absence of such documents, I should be inclined to think that the idea above expressed was only ventilated in conversation between Mr. Butler, or some other member of the English Board, and some member of the Irish Board who might happen to be in London. Nothing could have been more disastrous than that the cause of the English Catholics should have been separated from that of the Irish Catholics, especially if the question in England had been settled before the question in Ireland. We might have had in England an Act resembling the bill of 1813, which Act, having been passed for England, would have served as a model of one for Ireland. From this our good God delivered us.

CHAPTER XXXI.

THE YEAR 1820.

Death of George III.—King George III. and Catholics—George IV.—George IV. and Catholics—Address and petition to George IV.—The death of Grattan—Plunket—Milner receives a rebuke from Rome—Milner's conduct under censure—Reflections on Milner's writings in the *Orthodox Journal*—Proceedings in Ireland—No petition to Parliament this year.

THE first event to be noticed in this year (1820) is the death of King George III. on the 29th of January. Catholics should always remember that it was during the long reign of this monarch that the repeal of the penal laws first began, and that the first great steps toward our emancipation were taken. The refusal of his Majesty to admit Catholics into Parliament was in consequence of a scruple [1] put into his mind by Lords Clare and Loughborough. It was not an original idea of his own, that consenting to put Catholics on a civil and political level with Protestants would be a breach of the coronation oath. But the idea, having been suggested and having been once taken in, became a conscientious difficulty. When it became known that the mere notion of further relief to us endangered the sanity of the King, the Catholics of the United Kingdom entertained no other feelings towards his Majesty than those of respect and pity. In his personal intercourse with Catholics, George III. was always kind and amiable. Catholics were certainly no exception to the general

[1] Vide p. 23.

assertion which is so often repeated, that the "good old King" was universally beloved.

George IV., who since February, 1811, had been "in all but name a king," now succeeded to his father. When he was a young man, he was attached to the Whig party, of which Charles James Fox was the leader. He continued his connection with the Whigs until the year 1810, when, his father's malady becoming permanent, an Act was passed late in the autumn constituting the heir apparent Prince Regent of the United Kingdom. The Prince Regent then transferred his affections from the Whigs to the Tories. There was a corresponding change in his opinions in regard to the "Catholic claims." "Various causes have been assigned," says Lord Campbell, "for this revolution of sentiment.... The more probable solution was the effect of the possession of royal power, which was supposed to have indisposed His Royal Highness to any concession to the Catholics, or any extension of popular rights, and induced him to look with preference to those who were for carrying to the highest pitch the power of the Crown. His Royal Highness certainly did, at a subsequent period, manifest an entire change of opinion on the question of Catholic emancipation, and showed that he became thoroughly reconciled to his father's high prerogative principles of government; but I am inclined to think that as yet he was actuated only by personal motives."[1] Lord Eldon noticed the same change shortly after George became Regent. In a letter to Dr. Swire, in the year 1813, Eldon says, "My young master, who is as eager as his father was upon that" (that is, the Catholic question) "and of the same way of thinking, seems to me to be looking out very sincerely for those who are able and willing to support Church and State as we have had them in times

[1] "Life of Lord Eldon," p. 276.

past."[1] Any scruple that George IV. may have pretended to have after his coronation, on account of the oath he had taken, is not worthy of a moment's consideration. That a man who had broken his marriage vows, and repudiated for political reasons the wife whom he loved as much as he was capable of love; the man who had been guilty of bigamy; who, for the mere selfish motive of having his debts paid by the nation, had authorized his friend to deny in the House of Commons his lawful marriage, and who then told his true and virtuous wife that he had not authorized his friend to do so;—that such a man should object to emancipation on the ground that, if he consented to it, it would be a breach of his coronation oath, is too outrageously absurd to be received with anything but derision. The sentiments of Catholics towards George IV. as King were those of loyal subjects, but for his character as a man they entertained no other feelings than those of contempt and disgust.

But, as in duty bound, the grandfathers of the present generation of Catholics voted and presented a loyal address to the King. This address was agreed upon at a meeting of the British Catholic Board, at which the Duke of Norfolk presided.[2] The address was one of condolence and congratulation. It was proposed by the Earl of Shrewsbury and seconded by Sir Henry Englefield. It received nearly twenty thousand signatures, and was presented at a levee to the King by the Duke of Norfolk, Lord Clifford, Sir Carnaby Haggerston, Sir Richard Acton, Sir Thomas

---

[1] "Life of Lord Eldon," p. 309.
[2] Butler's "Historical Memoirs," vol. iv. p. 287. Authorities differ as to whether this meeting was well or badly attended. Butler calls it "a full meeting of the Board." The *Orthodox Journal* says there were not more than twenty gentlemen present, and adds, "Neither the Arundells, nor the Stourtons, nor the Petres, we believe, listened to the summons of the busy leaders." But many signed the address who were not present at the meeting; and it was certainly not from want of loyalty that any were absent.

Clifford, and Mr. Edward Jerningham. But the Catholics of England were not content with merely presenting a loyal address. At the levee on the 7th of June, a petition was presented to the King, entitled " The humble petition of the undersigned persons, professing the Roman Catholic religion in Great Britain." It was presented by the Duke of Norfolk, and was, of course, numerously signed by the Catholic nobility, clergy, and gentry of Great Britain. The prayer of the petition was in these words : " They humbly pray, if it shall seem meet to your royal judgment so to do, that your Majesty may be graciously pleased to recommend their case to the favourable consideration of Parliament." The reader will observe that in this prayer there is not the slightest allusion to any securities to be given by Catholics as the condition of emancipation. Andrews, in the *Orthodox Journal*, intimates that the petition was got up by the Catholic Board.[1] If so, it is creditable to that body that it did not introduce anything into the address which would have raised again the question which had divided the Catholics for so many years. As the *Orthodox Journal* represented the opinions of a large number of Catholics both of the clergy and of the middle class, it is proper to state here that Mr Andrews, the editor, wrote very strongly in condemnation of the wording of the petition. But it appears to me that his objections were captious, and some of his observations unreasonable, if not ill-natured. Andrews was quite right in keeping a sharp look-out upon the proceedings of the Board, and he would not have been wrong in suspecting any document which it might produce ; but the petition, innocent in itself, would not have been vitiated by the mere fact that it had been got up by the only organized

---

[1] He speaks of it as having been prepared by what he calls the "Stone-buildings' Junto." This means the Board, which used to meet in Mr. Butler's chambers in Stone-buildings, Lincoln's Inn.

body amongst the Catholics of England. It was signed by all the Vicars Apostolic of Great Britain, except the Vicar Apostolic of the Midland District. But the refusal of Dr. Milner to sign the petition does not appear to have been for such weighty and decided reasons as those for which he had opposed the former proceedings of the Board. Mr. Butler says, "From the list of those who signed we must except Dr. Milner. He objected to the language of the petition; but his objections were not distinctly pronounced, and it is probable that they were not considerable, as he permitted the petition to be generally signed both by the clergy and laity within his district."[1] The words of the petition, in which the temporal power of the Pope in this country is rejected, are drawn out with a legal amplitude and exactness which would no doubt have caused Dr. Milner to perceive the odour of Mr. Butler's chambers. Perhaps this may have caused the bishop to throw down the document, when other less sensitive bishops may have detected nothing whatever offensive. There was, indeed, a special reason at this time for asserting our undivided allegiance to the King. Mr. Butler explains the reason in a few words. "By the petition," he says, "the Catholics profess full and *undivided* allegiance to his Majesty. This expression was particularly used to meet the charge which, as we have mentioned in the preceding chapter, was brought against them by the Bishop of Peterborough, of dividing their allegiance between his Majesty and the Pope."[2]

Mr. Butler has also some remarks on the preparation of the petition, which it is necessary to quote, as the facts he mentions may account for some remarks of O'Connell which I shall have to insert. Mr. Butler says—

[1] "Historical Memoirs," vol. iv. p. 289.
[2] Ibid., p. 290.

"It has been asserted that Cardinal Fontana, the prefect of the congregation *De Propagandâ Fide*, expressed a decided disapprobation of this address" (by the "address" Mr. Butler means the petition), "and required the British and Irish prelates to oppose its signature by their respective flocks. It has also been asserted that it was objected to by the present writer. These are great misrepresentations, and render it necessary to state the real fact. We must therefore mention that, previously to the drawing up of the petition which we have transcribed, another had been prepared and submitted to the Board. To this some gentlemen, and among these the present writer, objected, not on account of any substantial impropriety, but because they apprehended it contained some words the import of which was too easily liable to be misrepresented: it was therefore withdrawn. This circumstance, or rather an erroneous notion of it, becoming known and reaching Ireland, a repectable personage too hastily wrote to Cardinal Fontana a letter, which led his Eminence to believe that an oath had been devised by which all authority, both civil and spiritual, was acknowledged to reside in the King. The cardinal, of course, answered that such an oath could not be taken, and that he trusted the bishops would oppose it. This answer was evidently hypothetical. . . . The real petition did not contain any such expression."[1]

As little was done in England during the year 1820 towards forwarding the cause of emancipation, so little was done also in Ireland. But before narrating any of the proceedings which took place in the sister island, a sad and important event has to be told—the death of Grattan.

This illustrious patriot and famous orator died on the 2nd of June. The only thing which prevents absolute

---

[1] In a former chapter it was noticed that it would be worth while to collect together the principal instances in which great mischief has been done by dissensions amongst the Catholics of the United Kingdom. It would be equally profitable to put before Catholics the known cases in which mischief has been created by false, or exaggerated, or over-hasty, or one-sided information given to Rome on the Catholic affairs of this country, not merely by interested diplomatists, or intriguing or unauthorized meddlers, but by those who would come under the class which Mr. Butler would designate as "respectable personages."

praise of Grattan as an advocate for Catholics is that he was a vetoist. But it would appear that he was not a vetoist in the sense in which William Pitt and Castlereagh and Canning were vetoists. These eminent statesmen advocated the securities because they wished to have an effective check upon the action of the Catholic Church in the United Kingdom. Whatever may have been Grattan's private opinion on the subject of the veto, he certainly seems to have advocated it for the first and principal reason, that he felt convinced that the British Parliament would never grant the emancipation of his fellow-countrymen unless the securities should qualify the concession. Grattan was a true lover of his country. The fact that he was a Protestant, and the fact that his countrymen were Catholics, never for a moment lessened the energy with which he fought for the rights of Ireland. He was one of the most eloquent, most faithful, and most persevering advocates of the "Catholic claims:"

" . . . if not first, in the very first line."[1]

The last thoughts of Grattan were for the Catholics of Ireland; and, I may add, for the British Catholics as well, for our emancipation was a necessary consequence of that of the Irish. Grattan may be truly said to have died in the Catholic cause. On the death of George III., the Parliament was dissolved, and the new Parliament was opened on the 27th of February, 1820. Grattan had been returned for the city of Dublin. He was in bad health, but he came to London towards the end of May. The last English Catholic who saw Grattan, and one of the very last of those who could have had any conversation with him, was Mr. Butler. Butler has left us an account of that last interview, and it is an incident which we English Catholics should never forget.

[1] Goldsmith's "Retaliation."

"On the first day of the following June," says Mr. Butler, in his " Historical Memoirs," "the writer of these pages called upon him, and, being informed that he was extremely ill, was retiring without having seen him; but Mr. Grattan, having heard that he was in the house, sent for him. It was evident that he touched the moment of his dissolution; but the ethereal vigour of his mind was unsubdued, and his zeal for the Catholic cause unabated. He pressed the writer by the hand. 'It is,' he said, 'all over—yes, all over; but I will die in the cause. I mean to be carried to the House of Commons to-morrow, to beg leave of the speaker to take the oaths sitting, and then to move two resolutions.' These he mentioned to the writer, but spoke so indistinctly that the writer could only perceive, generally, that they were substantially the same as the clauses which he had prefixed to the bill which, in 1812, he brought into Parliament for the relief of the Catholics. He again pressed the writer by the hand, repeated the intention of being carried to the House, and desired the writer to attend him to it. But he died in the ensuing night."[1]

Grattan was buried in Westminster Abbey. The boys from all the Catholic parochial schools in London attended the funeral.[2]

The question now to be decided by the Irish Catholics was, Who should be chosen to present their petitions and be their advocate in the House of Commons? Grattan had expressed a wish that Plunket should succeed him as the promoter of the Catholic question. The whole body of Catholics in Ireland would have been unanimously in favour of Plunket, except for the fact that he was a decided vetoist, and a more decided vetoist even than Grattan; for Plunket considered that the securities were "not only unobjectionable, but just and necessary."[3]

---

[1] Vol. iv. p. 393. 1812 must be a mistake for 1813.

[2] Butler observes that the boys "behaved with a seriousness which affected every beholder." Surely it was not expected that the boys would behave badly?

[3] Letter to the secretary of the Catholic Board, *Orthodox Journal* for 1820, p. 291.

O'Connell was strongly in favour of choosing an advocate who, like Lord Donoughmore, would ask for unqualified emancipation. O'Connell seems to have thought that the liberties of the Church were in some special and imminent danger at this time. In a letter to the editor of the *Dublin Evening Post*, dated from Merrion Square on the 17th of June, 1820, he says, "I think we are on the eve of another struggle, to preserve from all encroachment the discipline of the Catholic Church in Ireland. I may be mistaken, but it is my firm and decided belief that the greatest peril which that Church has in these latter years encountered now awaits her. I may also be laughed at for raising the cry of 'the Church in danger'; but I am quite content to endure any portion of ridicule, provided I am of any utility in rousing the Catholic people of Ireland from the destructive apathy in which they are now sunk."

I am not able to say what it was that caused the special anxiety which O'Connell expressed at this time. It may be that he attached more importance to the story which reached Ireland about the English petition than the facts warranted.[1] He may also have thought that the English Board was intriguing at Rome with a prospect of success. And O'Connell had reason for so thinking; he had special cause for being afraid of the diplomacy of Cardinal Consalvi. This will be the proper place for telling the reader of the blow which Milner received from Rome. He had been a constant contributor to the *Orthodox Journal*. "In these articles," says Husenbeth, "he spoke out with that plainness and freedom which ever distinguished him, and was often severe and unsparing in his denunciations of those whom he conscientiously considered to be working insidiously and dangerously against the real

[1] *Vide* pp. 328, 29.

interests of religion and the true Catholic cause. . . . Such plain speaking could not fail to give umbrage, particularly to some who fell under the bishop's censures ; and, accordingly, strong representations were made against him to the Holy See, and also against the *Orthodox Journal*, from which certain extracts were sent to Rome, in support of the allegations brought forward. In consequence of these complaints, his Holiness was induced to order the prefect of *Propaganda* to address a letter to Dr. Milner, dated April 29, 1820."[1] Before alluding more particularly to the contents of this letter, the reader should understand that there can be no doubt that the real adviser of Pope Pius in the matter was Cardinal Consalvi. Milner knew well the influences which were at work in Rome, and he unhesitatingly ascribed the letter to Consalvi. Writing to Husenbeth on the 20th of September, 1820, he says, "For my part, if I am dismissed from my apostolic vicarship by Cardinal Consalvi, to gratify Mr. Charles Butler and his ministerial friends, I shall be glad to take the situation of Norwich."[2] The reader must also understand that almost all the letters which Milner wrote in the *Orthodox Journal* were either on the principles of the "Fifth Resolution" and its consequence the schismatical bill of 1813, or on the Blanchardist schism. On both these subjects the other Vicars Apostolic had come round, as we have seen, to Milner's opinion, thereby acknowledging him to have been substantially in the right. Bearing these things in mind, the reader shall have the account of the letter which Husenbeth gives in his "Life" of the illustrious bishop.

"The letter," says Husenbeth, "expresses the uneasiness[3] with which his Holiness and the *Propaganda* have learned the

---

[1] "Life of Milner," p. 420.   [2] Ibid., p. 425.
[3] "Uneasiness, is a rather mild translation of the words "magna molestia" in the original.

circulation in England of a periodical called the *Orthodox Journal*, which is most calculated, it says, to perpetuate dissensions among the Catholics of Great Britain; that the said journal, with the greatest temerity, grievously blackens, by detractions and abuse, and often even by enormous calumnies, the reputation of several Catholics, of the vicars apostolic themselves, and even of ministers of the Holy See; that the said journal contains many articles bearing Dr. Milner's name; and that it is publicly known that he is one of its chief supporters and writers, and supplies the editor with many contributions. The letter expresses surprise that a vicar apostolic should dare to sow discord; trample upon the honour of sacred ministers, eminent for their piety, learning, and dignity; and excite the Catholic people against the nobility, who deserve honour for their generosity in assisting our missions. The reader," continues Husenbeth, "will behold with surprise these most extraordinary charges against Dr. Milner, and be still more astonished at the sentence pronounced upon him in consequence. The document proceeds to declare it to be the will and command of his Holiness that he shall take no part in future in the said journal, directly or indirectly; shall in no way promote or patronize it, nor contribute any matter or arguments to it, much less afford it any assistance; and this he must promptly and fully obey, under pain of being removed from his vicariate."[1]

It does not appear in any document which I have seen that Milner received any notice from the authorities in Rome that specific charges were being made against him with a view to the judgment of the Holy See upon them. If it be true, as I suppose it to be, that he did not receive such a notice, then it follows that he was condemned unheard. It would have been honourable to have informed him that a complaint was pending against him; it would have been fair, it would have been honest, but it would

---

[1] The original Latin of the principal portions of this document may be seen in Husenbeth's "Life of Milner," p. 423. The command to Milner is "in virtute sanctæ obedientiæ;" and the poor old *Orthodox Journal* is called "abominabile istud diarium."

not have been politic. If Milner had been asked for an explanation, a few words from him to Pope Pius would have convinced his Holiness that the substantial good which Milner had done amply compensated for any fault of style in the manner of doing it. This would not have suited the plans of Consalvi; on the contrary, it would have completely upset them. For Milner substantially in the right would have meant Mr. Butler and his party substantially in the wrong; and the English Cisalpines, helped by some of the Irish "seceders," were acting along with Consalvi, and making use of his Eminence's English proclivities to carry out their designs.

Milner himself behaved under the circumstances as a Catholic bishop should behave. He obeyed the Pope. He immediately wrote a private letter to the editor of the *Orthodox Journal*, in which he said, " I am forbidden by Rome, under severe threats, *however unjustly*, from contributing a word or suggestion to the *Orthodox Journal*, though I am still at liberty, as I conceive, to aid Mr. Andrews in a different kind of publication." At the time this order was given to Milner, Husenbeth was about twenty-four years of age, he having been ordained in the February of this year (1820). He was, therefore, quite old enough to know what was thought of the order in England, and he had plenty of opportunities of hearing what was being said. His testimony is therefore valuable. He gives the following extract from a letter, as showing how the "affair was viewed by those who, by their intimate knowledge of Dr. Milner, and of the object and character of his writings, were best qualified to judge. 'Thus by means of *misrepresentation* and *political influence*,'" says the writer of the letter, "' is Dr. Milner, who for near forty years has used the weapon of his pen in defence of truth and waged an honourable war against the enemies of religion, required to throw away his arms and retire from the field of battle, covered with laurels which he had plucked from the brows of his adversaries; but rewarded by those in whose cause he had been exposed with disapprobation and reproof, instead of applause and gratitude.'"[1] The great bishop himself bore his severe trial in patience. "He might," says Husenbeth, "have appealed from his severe sentence to the justice and paternal consideration of the Holy Father, and could have easily vindicated himself from the grievous charges brought against him. He might have published his case, and engaged strong sympathy in his favour, as the victim of false accusation and persecution; but he bore his humiliation in silence, made no complaint, and so completely concealed the treatment which he had experienced that those about him, and in constant intercourse with him, had but a very imperfect knowledge of what had happened."[2]

But the triumph of Cardinal Consalvi and the English vetoists, both Catholic and Protestant, was a barren one. It was certainly a triumph over Milner personally; but it was not a triumph of the cause advocated by his opponents. It did not advance by one step the designs of the vetoists.

It might be an interesting speculation to consider whether Bishop Milner would have effected the good which has made him famous in the Church if he had employed milder terms to express his opinions. There can be no doubt that the strength of his language gave a handle to his enemies. To act upon the rule *suaviter in modo, sed fortiter in re*, is at all times difficult; and there are few persons in whose souls the cardinal virtues are so equally balanced that they can, without extraordinary supernatural

---

[1] "Life of Milner," pp. 424, 425.
[2] Ibid., p. 425.

help, conduct themselves in the manner which theoretically they know to be wise. When the above dictum of prudence is to be practised in a matter where both words and action are combined, it is comparatively easy to make an equitable adjustment of mildness and strength. The lips may distil honey, while the hand will hold its own in an iron grasp. But when the golden maxim has to be applied only to words, whether they be spoken or written words, the difficulty of following the direction in practice is greatly increased. No such evident division of application presents itself, as when a man can give the *suaviter* to his words, and the *fortiter* to his deeds. To speak or write very mildly, and at the same time to speak or write very strongly, is the gift of only a few. St. Francis Xavier could do it; but who ever read any letters like those of St. Francis Xavier? There never was any complaint made against Milner on account of what he did. Every complaint was about what he had said or written. The great and enduring good which Milner effected was all done by what he said and by what he wrote. It required enormous strength to beat those with whom he had to contend. Could he have defended the liberties of the Church with eminent success if, instead of speaking and writing as he did, he had aggravated his voice and pen, so that he should roar "as gently as any sucking dove;" if he had roared "an 't were any nightingale"?[1] I do not believe he could. Milner was naturally good-natured and kind-hearted: he was not of an angry and fiery disposition; he was conscientious and pious, and to the last day of his life he never repented of his words. If his conscience had pricked him in this respect, he would have retracted before his death. If he showed in his writings the imperfection which Dr. Weedall expressed when he

---

[1] Vide "Midsummer Night's Dream," act i. sc. 2.

said that Milner undervalued the little etiquettes of society, it can hardly be imputed to him as a fault deserving censure. If he had polished his sentences too finely, they would not have produced the effect which they did, and the value of his writings would have been lost. In warfare, legitimate weapons are of different kinds. If Richard Plantagenet had ground down his battle-axe to the almost invisible edge of Saladin's scimitar, the redoubtable weapon of Cœur de Lion would have been destroyed on the skull of the first Saracen who would have fallen under its stroke.

The condemnation of Milner's writings in the *Orthodox Journal* was in all probability known to O'Connell, and he would have attributed it to the influence of Cardinal Consalvi. O'Connell might reasonably have supposed that the measure was taken to get Milner out of the way, in order to make easier an attempt to settle the affair of emancipation on vetoist principles. Knowing the great influence of Consalvi, both at Rome and in England, O'Connell may have had great reason to fear the consequences. This may have caused him to say that he had a firm belief that a great peril awaited the Church. This is the only way in which I can account for the anxiety of O'Connell at this time.

Several meetings of the Irish board were held in Essex Street, in order to choose a successor to Grattan for the presentation of petitions for relief. For the reason already mentioned, O'Connell was not in favour of selecting Plunket; and he would have preferred that the Knight of Kerry should be asked. Plunket was quite willing to be the leading advocate of the Catholics, but he positively declined to ask for unqualified emancipation. O'Connell was not as yet the complete lord and master of the agitation. He did not arrive at that pre-eminence until he had established his "Association" in 1823. He was not able to have his own way on this occasion. At any rate, he did not think it prudent to try to force his will upon the Board. The consequence was that a compromise was made. Plunket was chosen to present the petition; but a resolution was passed by the Board, rejecting emancipation accompanied by securities. The petition to Parliament was to be for unqualified emancipation; but it was understood that the advocate was to say that he thought securities both just and necessary. In the state of public affairs, however, it mattered very little what was done by Catholics during this year to forward their cause in Parliament. Almost the whole attention of the two Houses, and indeed of the whole country, was taken up with the "Bill of Pains and Penalties" against the Queen, which is commonly called the "Trial of Queen Caroline," the disgraceful proceedings of the "first gentleman in Europe" against the Princess whom the law of England regarded as his wife. I do not find that any petition for relief was presented during this year from Catholics to either House of Parliament.

Mr. Butler, in his "Historical Memoirs," begins his notice of what was done in this year (1820), in the following words:—"Such as we have described was the situation of the British Catholics when the proceedings for their complete and final relief were begun."[1] These words were published by Mr. Butler in the year 1822. We have seen that nothing was done in the year 1820. In the following year, 1821, a bill, but a very objectionable bill, framed on the lines of the bill of 1813, passed the House of Commons, but was happily rejected by the House of Lords. I can only suppose that when Mr. Butler wrote the words I have quoted above, he was alluding to the preparation of

[1] Vol. iv. p. 287.

Plunket's bill in 1820; to its success in the House of Commons in 1821; and to his hope that that bill would be the model of an Emancipation Act. But in the year following the publication of those words, O'Connell had attained to that high position from which he began as a giant to run his course, and stopped not until he had forced the Legislature of the United Kingdom to yield to his demands.

CHRONOLOGY OF EVENTS IN THE TWO VOLUMES BEARING ON CATHOLIC EMANCIPATION.

REIGN OF GEORGE III.

DATE.		PRIME MINISTER.
1771.	The "Act for the reclaiming of unprofitable bogs" ...	Lord North.
1773.	Commencement of the resistance of the Americans to taxation	,,
1774.	First Act to conciliate the Irish Catholics	,,
1775.	Birth of O'Connell	,,
1778.	February 6. Offensive and defensive alliance between France and the American Colonies	,,
,,	English Catholics address the King	,,
,,	First English Catholic Committee, William Sheldon secretary	,,
,,	First English Relief Act	,,
,,	First Irish Act repealing penal laws	,,
,,	Proposition to extend relief to the Scotch Catholics ...	,,
1779.	Anti-Catholic Riots in Edinburgh and Glasgow ...	,,
1780.	June. The Gordon Riots in London	,,
1782.	The Committee of Five, Charles Butler secretary ...	Lord Rockingham.
1783.	May 4. Letter of the Committee of Five to the vicars apostolic	,,
1787.	Letter of the Committee of Five to the Catholics of England	William Pitt.
,,	The Committee of Ten, all laymen	,,
1788.	April 19. Butler ordered to prepare a Relief Bill ...	,,
,,	May 9. Memorial presented to William Pitt ...	,,
,,	May 15. Three ecclesiastics added to Committee of Ten	,,
,,	Questions suggested by Pitt sent to the foreign universities	,,
,,	December. The Protestation adopted	,,
1789.	June 16. The new oath framed by the committee first published	,,
,,	October 19. The new oath formally condemned by the four Vicars Apostolic	,,

Chronology of Events.

DATE.		PRIME MINISTER.
1789.	November 25. Remonstrance of the committee against the condemnation of the oath	William Pitt.
,,	Appeal of the committee to the Catholics of England ...	,,
1790.	January 26. Death of Bishop James Talbot ...	,,
,,	May 19. Death of Bishop Matthew Gibson ...	,,
,,	December 5. Bishop William Gibson consecrated at Lulworth	,,
,,	December 19. Bishop Douglas consecrated at Lulworth	
1791.	January 19. Fresh condemnation of the oath by Bishops Walmesley, Douglas, and Gibson ...	,,
,,	February. Schismatical protest against the fresh condemnation of the oath	,,
,,	February 2. Letter of committee to Bishop Douglas, complaining of the condemnation	,,
,,	February. The Rev. John Milner attacks the committee	,,
,,	March 1. Relief Bill introduced into the House of Commons	,,
,,	Relief Bill sent up to the Lords	,,
,,	June 7. The committee beaten and the bill passed ...	,,
,,	June 9. Meeting at the Crown and Anchor Tavern ...	,,
,,	Schism of the "Staffordshire clergy"	,,
1792.	April 12. Formation of the Cisalpine Club ...	,,
,,	The mediation, and publication of the "Buff-book" ...	,,
,,	August 19. Decree of the French Legislative Assembly for the transportation of all priests who refused the revolutionary oath	,,
,,	Arrival of 8000 French priests in England and the Channel Islands, in the autumn	,,
1793.	February 1. France declares war against England ...	,,
,,	Irish Relief Act	,,
,,	Scotch Relief Act	,,
,,	October 10. The National Convention confiscates the property of British subjects in France	,,
,,	Colleges and religious houses of English Catholics in France broken up, their inmates gradually returning to England	,,
1794.	English colleges and religious houses in Belgium broken up, and the flight of their members to England ...	,,
1799.	January 17, 18, and 19. Resolutions of ten Irish bishops	,,
1800.	July 2. Act for the Legislative Union of England and Ireland receives the royal assent	,,
1801.	February. Resignation of William Pitt.	
1803.	Consecration of Rev. John Milner at Winchester ...	Addington.
,,	Supplementary Relief Act	,,
1805.	May. Petitions of the Irish Catholics rejected by large majorities in both Lords and Commons	William Pitt.
,,	May. First public mention of the Veto	,,
1806.	January 23. Death of William Pitt.	

DATE.		PRIME MINISTER.
1806.	Ministry of "All the Talents"	Lord Grenville.
1807.	Lord Howick's Relief Bill	,,
,,	Fall of the Ministry.	
,,	Duke of Portland becomes prime minister	Duke of Portland.
,,	The "No-Popery Ministry"	,,
,,	"No-Popery" cry all over the country	,,
,,	Milner appointed agent to the Irish bishops	,,
1808.	Formation of the Catholic Board	,,
,,	May 21. Milner's interview with Ponsonby	,,
,,	May 21. Debates in both Houses on the "Catholic disabilities"	,,
,,	August 1. Milner's "Letter to a Parish Priest"	,,
,,	September 14. Resolutions of the Irish bishops against the veto	,,
,,	Milner retracts his "Letter to a Parish Priest"	,,
,,	O'Connell makes his first reported speech on Catholic affairs	,,
1809.	Resignation of the Duke of Portland; Perceval Prime Minister.	
1810.	January 31. Interview between the Catholic gentlemen and Lords Grey and Grenville	Perceval.
,,	February 1. The "Fifth Resolution" passed at the meeting at St. Alban's Tavern	,,
,,	May. Debate on the Catholic petition in the House of Commons	,,
,,	June. Debate on the Catholic petition in the House of Lords	,,
,,	Motions in favour of Catholics defeated in both Houses	,,
1812.	May 11. Perceval shot by Bellingham.	
,,	June. Lord Liverpool becomes prime minister.	
,,	June 22. Canning carries his famous resolution in favour of Catholics by a majority of 129	Lord Liverpool.
,,	First meeting of the Vicars Apostolic at Durham, Milner being present	,,
1813.	Meeting of the Catholic Board	,,
,,	February. Meeting at Lord Clifford's house	,,
,,	February. Grattan carries a motion in favour of Catholics by a majority of 40	,,
,,	March. Grattan carries a further motion by a majority of 67	,,
,,	April 30. Grattan introduces his Relief Bill	,,
,,	May 11. Sir J. C. Hippisley's motion ridiculed by Canning, and lost	,,
,,	The "Schismatical Bill" of 1813 passes a second reading	
,,	May 19. Milner arrives in London	,,
,,	May 24. Call of the House to consider the bill in committee	,,

VOL. II.   Z

344   *Chronology of Events.*

DATE.		PRIME MINISTER.
1813.	May 24. Abbot carries his amendment, that Catholics shall not be allowed to sit in either House of Parliament	Lord Liverpool.
,,	May 24. The bill of 1813 abandoned	,,
,,	May 29. Expulsion of Milner from the Select Committee of the Catholic Board	,,
,,	October. Second meeting of the Vicars Apostolic at Durham, Milner not being present	,,
1814	February 17. General meeting at Lord Shrewsbury's house	,,
,,	April 28. Monsignore Quarantotti's rescript arrives in England	,,
,,	May 2. Milner starts for Rome	,,
,,	May 24. Pope Pius enters Rome	,,
,,	Milner's interview with the Pope	,,
,,	June 17. Address of English Catholic Board to the Pope	,,
,,	June 28. British Catholic petition presented to the House of Lords	,,
,,	June 28. British Catholic petition presented to the House of Commons	,,
1815.	April 26. Cardinal Litta's letter to Dr. Poynter ...	,,
,,	June 2. Milner arrives in London on his return from Rome	,,
,,	May 11. Sir Henry Parnell presents the petition of the Irish Catholics	,,
,,	May 19. Lord Donoughmore presents the Irish petition to the House of Lords	,,
,,	May 30. Sir H. Parnell presents the petition of 6000 Catholics of York, Birmingham, Norwich, and other places	,,
,,	Sir H. Parnell's motion lost by a majority of 81 ...	,,
,,	August 23 and 24. Important resolutions of the Irish bishops	,,
,,	August 29. O'Connell attacks Milner	,,
,,	August 29. First remonstrance of the Irish Catholics. Sir Thomas Esmonde, Mr. Owen O'Connor, and the Rev. Richard Hayes, O.S.F., appointed as a deputation to Rome. Esmonde and O'Connor declining to act, Hayes goes alone	,,
1816.	May. O'Connell retracts his charge against Milner ...	,,
,,	February 1. Letter of Pius VII. to the Irish bishops	,,
,,	Canning joins the Ministry of Lord Liverpool, and emancipation becomes practically an open question	,,
,,	May 11. Petition for relief from English Catholics presented to the House of Commons	,,
,,	June 11. Petition from English Catholics presented to the House of Lords	,,

Chronology of Events.

DATE.		PRIME MINISTER.
1816.	Sir H. Parnell presents the petition of the Irish Catholic Board	Lord Liverpool.
,,	Grattan presents the petition of the "Seceders"	,,
,,	Grattan's motion in favour of Catholics rejected	,,
,,	June 11. Petitions of Irish Catholics presented to the House of Lords	,,
,,	Lord Donoughmore's motion in favour of Catholics lost	,,
1817.	Act for the Relief of Catholic Officers in the Army and Navy	,,
,,	Collision between O'Connell and the Vetoists	,,
,,	The "Conciliating Committee"	,,
,,	May 9. Grattan's motion for a committee to consider the laws affecting Catholics lost by a majority of 24	
,,	May 16. Lord Donoughmore's motion in the Lords for a committee to consider the Catholic petitions lost by a majority of 52	,,
,,	July. Second remonstrance of the Irish board sent to Rome	,,
1818.	February. Answer of Pope Pius to the second Irish remonstrance	,,
,,	July. General Thornton's motion for partial relief lost	,,
,,	The other Vicars Apostolic join Milner in denouncing the bill of 1813	,,
,,	Termination of the Blanchardist schism	,,
1819.	Meeting of the Board of British Catholics to decide upon petitions to both Houses	,,
,,	February 11. Large and influential meeting of Protestants in Dublin to petition for Catholic relief	,,
,,	March 1. Great "Aggregate Meeting" in Dublin for the same object	,,
,,	May 3. Grattan presents thirteen petitions in favour of emancipation, eight being from Catholics, and five from Protestants	,,
,,	May 3. Grattan moves for a committee to consider the Catholic question, but is defeated by a majority of two	,,
,,	May 17. Lord Donoughmore presents a number of petitions in the House of Lords in favour of emancipation, and makes a motion similar to that of Grattan in the Commons. He is defeated by a majority of 41	,,
,,	May 25. Lord Grey introduces a bill for partial relief, but is beaten on the second reading by a majority of 59	,,
1820.	January 29. Death of King George III.	,,

REIGN OF GEORGE IV.

DATE.		PRIME MINISTER.
1820.	A loyal address from English Catholics presented to the King	Lord Liverpool.
,,	June 2. Death of Grattan	,,
,,	June 7. The Duke of Norfolk, in the name of British Catholics, presents a petition to the King, begging that his Majesty will recommend their relief to Parliament ...	,,
,,	Milner receives a rebuke from Rome, and is forbidden to write in the *Orthodox Journal*	,,
,,	The Irish Catholic Board rejects emancipation accompanied by securities, but appoints Plunket (a vetoist) to present its petition for relief in 1821 ...	,,

INDEX.

A

Abbot, Mr. Speaker, defeats Relief Bill, ii. 112
Aberdeen, Lord, ii. 228, 246
Acton, Mr. T., i. 22
Acton, Sir R., ii. 326
Acts, Relief, of 1771, 1774, i. 50; of 1778, 91; Irish of 1778, 122; of 1791, 149; first Scotch, i. 274; the Test Act, ii. 253; Act of Indemnity, ii. 255
Adair, Mr. Serjeant, i. 103
Addington, Mr., i. 287; prime minister, 288; ii. 54
Address of English Catholic Board to Pius VII., ii. 156
Aikin, Dr., i. 144, 287; ii. 69, 93
Alison quoted, i. 292
Allen, Cardinal, i. 216
Ambler, Mr., bigoted opinion on penal laws, i. 103
Andrews, W. Eusebius, ii. 234, 301, 309, 327
Argyll, Duke of, offensive speech, i. 140
Arundell, Dorothy and Gertrude, i. 221
Arundell, Lord, i. 80, 97, 205
Associations, Catholic, in Ireland, i. 253, et seq.
Atkinson, Father, O.S.F., death in prison, i. 34

B

Bagnall, Mr., i. 123
Ball, Counsellor, ii. 279
Bankes, Mr., ii. 218
Banks, Mr., ii. 208
Bannister, Right Rev. Dr., i. 167
Barnard, Rev. J., i. 192
Barrière, i. 218
Bathurst, Lord, ii. 248
Bathurst, Mr., ii. 217
Beaconsfield, Lord, i. 183
Beauchamp, Lord, speech on Act of 1788, i. 101-128
Beauvais, i. 218
Bellew, Sir E., ii. 58
Bentinck, Lord George, ii. 68
Bergholt, Benedictine Dames of, their arrival in England, i. 221
Berington, Bishop Charles, i. 161, 162, 167
Berington, Rev. Joseph, his objectionable writings, i. 155, 240
Berkley, Jane, i. 221
Berington, Mr. Joseph, i. 78
Best, Mr. Serjeant, ii. 218
Bigotry, English and Scotch, i. 275
Bill, Army and Navy, ii. 61; of 1813, ii. 87; Lord Grey's, 319
Blanchard, Abbé, ii. 79 (note)
Blount, Mr. Edward, i. 196
Blount, Sir —, i. 205
Blucher, Marshal, ii. 107
Blunt, Sir W., i. 22
Board, formation of the Catholic, ii. 31
Bodenham, Mr., ii. 116, 119
Boringdon, Lord, ii. 228
Bornheim, Dominican college at, i. 220
Bossuet quoted, i. 1
Bramston, Rev. Mr., ii. 79, 81
Bray, Bishop, i. 311
Brougham, Lord, quoted, i. 188; ii. 150, 198, 260
Buccleuch, Duke of, i. 124

Buckingham, Duke of, ii. 5
Buckingham, Marquis of, ii. 4, 6
Buckinghamshire, Lord, i. 57
Burgoyne, General, i. 131
Burke, Edmund, writes address for Irish Catholics, 1774, i. 57; estimate of Irish population, 77, 78; speech at Bristol, 1780, 83; opinion of penal laws, 91, 93; just to Catholics, 115; presents Catholic petition, 125, 128; his life threatened, 131; speech at Bristol, 134; interview with Milner, 173; helps French exiles, 210; champion of Scotch Catholics, 274; opinion of the veto, 307; tribute of gratitude to him, 308; ii. 11; superior to Grattan, 105
Burnet, Bishop, i. 94
Butler, Alban, prospect at death of, i. 32-34; 79, 85, 217
Butler, Mr. Charles, opinion of Act of 1774, i. 63; on the persecution of Catholics, 80-82; on kindness of George III. to Catholics, 87; on benefits of Act of 1778, 108; opinion of W. Sheldon, 120; on Irish Relief Act, 122; on the Committee of Five, 150, 152; secretary to the Committee, 153; his account of Committee of Ten, 161; prepares a Relief Bill, 163; his account of Protestation, 164; frames a new oath, 165; draws up schismatical protest, 170; called to the bar, 184; his errors, 190; on "the mediation", 201; on the Scotch Relief Act, 283; on Irish Bishops and veto, 312; asserts Milner favours veto, 315; his error in doing this, 326-330; disagrees with Irish Bishops, ii. 9; interviews Lord Grey, 27-29; on the "Catholic Board," 31; on the "fifth resolution," 42; working in London, 83; his conduct called in question, 88, 89; present at meeting at Lord Clifford's, 92; his account of debate on Grattan's Relief Bill, 97; on Lord Castlereagh's amendments to it, 104; scene with Milner at Catholic Board, 117; on Monsignor Quarantotti's powers, 143; on Bishop Bathurst's speech favouring emancipation, 249; on the Test Act, 255; on the Annual Indemnity Act, 259; on the Act of 1817, 260; conversation with Fox, 288; on General Thornton's motion, 290; on Croker's speech, 1819, 317; on the Catholic question, 320-323; on petition to George IV., 329; last interview with Grattan, 331
Butt, Mr., ii. 168
Byrne, Mr. John, i. 262
Byron, Lord, votes in favour of Catholics, ii. 73; quoted, 202, 311

C

Cameron, Right Rev. Dr., ii. 129
Campbell, Lord, quoted, i. 184, 288; ii. 60, 63, 65, 73, 74, 230, 249, 268, 325
Canning, Mr., speech on Act of 1774, i. 64; speech, 1813, 194; quoted, 290; in favour of veto, 308; foreign secretary, ii. 63; fights duel, 70; action in favour of Catholics, 72, 82; allied with Mr. C. Butler, 87; his opinion on Grattan's Relief Bill, 96-98; proposes to insert clauses, 101-103, 111; regrets defeat of bill, 1813, 114; joins Lord Liverpool's cabinet, 229; speaks in favour of veto, 239
Canterbury, Archbishop of, i. 177
Caroline, Queen, her kindness, i. 82; her trial, ii. 202, 339
Castlereagh, Lord, i. 309, 312, 313; ii. 18, 62, 70, 82, 98, 111; hateful to Ireland, 218; 236, 278, 281, 290
Catholic, action, principle of, ii. 273
Catholics, their best policy, i. 7; loyalty of, 22; prejudice against, 54; state of, previous to 1778, 76; duty of, towards Ireland, 250; duty of loyal, ii. 14
Caulfield, James, Bishop, i. 311
Challoner, Bishop, i. 33, 79; joint pastoral, 110; and Bishop Hay, 279
Charlemont, Lord, ii. 311
Charles II. and the Declaration of Indulgence, ii. 250
Charlotte, Princess, on justice to Ireland, ii. 75
Chesterfield, Lord, advice of, ii. 283
Chisholm, Right Rev. Dr., ii. 128, 130, 131
Clare, Lord, ii. 324
Claremont, Earl, ii. 310
Clement XIV., Bull of, i. 220

Index. 349

Clergy, "the Staffordshire," i. 238
Clifford, C. T., i. 80
Clifford, Lord, i. 97; one of Committee of Ten, 161, 205; ii. 33; meeting at house of, 92, 326
Clifford, Sir Thomas, ii. 327
Cloncurry, Lord, ii. 311
Club, the Cisalpine, i. 194
Cobden, Mr., M.P., i. 112; compared with O'Connell, 269
Collingridge, Right Rev. Dr., ii. 39, 110, 127, 303
Committee, first English Catholic, i. 95; of Five, 159; of Ten, 161
Communities, English, abroad, i. 216
Concordat, the Church and a, ii. 25
Consalvi, Cardinal, ii. 279, 291-293, 300, 332
Coombes, Dr., quoted, i. 218, 230
Cortes, Donoso, i. 3
Croker, Mr. Wilson, ii. 265, 269, 317
Cruise, John, Bishop, i. 311
Cumberland, Duke of, i. 85, 230
Curran, Mr., ii. 311
Curry, Dr., i. 257

D

Dalton, Count, i. 260
Daly, Mr. James, ii. 209
Darnley, Lord, ii. 284
Debates, in the Commons in 1815, ii. 211; in the Lords, 221
De la Marche, Bishop, i. 214
Delany, Bishop, i. 311
Delvin, Lord, i. 255, 257
Derby, Lord, i. 42; speech against priests, 139; ii. 168
Dermott, Mr., i. 57
D'Esterre, Mr., ii. 205
Dickens, Charles, rumoured conversion of, i. 140
Dictum of Charles James Fox, ii. 289
Dillon, Edward, Bishop, i. 311
Di Pietro, Cardinal, i. 145
Dissenters, conduct of, in 1780, i. 145
Donoughmore, Lord, ii. 44, 70, 204, 220, 221; important speech of, 223-227; 240, 281, 283, 317
Doran's Hotel, dinner at, ii. 35
Dormer, Lord, i. 97
Douay, Benedictine priory at, i. 217

Douay, secular college at, i. 216, 218
Douglas, Right Rev. Bishop, i. 169, 170, 177, 191, 205; ii. 34, 39, 54
Duane, Mr., i. 184
Duigenan, Dr., ii. 99
Dundas, Mr. H., i. 102, 173
Dunning, Mr., M.P., seconds Bill of 1778, i. 99, 100; speech, 114

E

Edgeworth, Rev. Mr., i. 213
Eldon, Lord, i. 184; ii. 56, 60, 62, 73, 74, 96, 230, 246, 317, 325
Elliot, Right Hon. W., ii. 203, 231, 281
Emancipation, effect of, i. 39; an open question, ii. 230
England, Bishop, ii. 52
England, not a purely Protestant State, i. 39
England, Rev. Thomas, i. 51
Englefield, Sir Henry, one of Committee of Ten, i. 161, 163; ii. 326
Esmonde, Sir Thomas, ii. 291
Expulsion of Milner from Committee of the Catholic Board, ii. 114
Eyre, Mr. Francis, i. 197
Eyston, Mr. George, ii. 168

F

Faber, Rev. Father, i. 47; ii. 24, 13
Fagan, Mr., i. 32, 63
Fauconberg, Earl, i. 177
Fermor, Mr., one of Committee of Ten, i. 161, 163
Fingall, Lord, i. 57, 257, 320, 324; ii. 27, 58, 205, 312
Fisher, Cardinal, i. 212; ii. 87
Fitzgerald, Major-General, ii. 252
Fitzgerald, Mr., i. 322; ii. 216
Fitzherbert, Mrs., i. 234, 236
Flanagan, Canon, quoted, ii. 79, 142, 147
Fleetwood, Sir H., i. 205
Fontana, Cardinal, ii. 329
Foster, Mr. Leslie, ii. 317
Fox, C. J., i. 71; just towards Catholics, 115, 128; sees Milner, 173; speaks for Scotch Catholics, 274; presents petition of Irish Catholics, 317; ii. 11; on the Catholic question, 57-59;

350 *Index.*

becomes leader of House of Commons, 61 ; death, 61 ; gratitude of Catholics due to, 66 ; a dictum of, 288
French clergy, reception of in England, i. 207
French, Edmund, Bishop, i. 311

G

Gentili, Father, i. 47
George III., i. 87 ; liberal to Catholics, 127 ; personal courage, 133 ; favourable to religious orders, 183 ; opposed to emancipation, 230 ; cause of illness, 289 ; ii. 9, 50, 52, 55, 71-194 ; death, 324
George IV., i. 230; his kindness to French nuns, 236; ii. 71, 234 ; kindness to Captain Whyte, 265 ; becomes King, 325 ; his character, 326
Gibbon quoted, i. 132
Gibson, Right Rev. M., i. 164 ; death, 168
Gibson, Right Rev. W., i. 169 ; ii. 40, 54, 81, 127, 132
Gillow, Rev. Mr., ii. 81
Gladstone, Right Hon. W. E., his pamphlet on Vaticanism, i. 13 ; ii. 226
Godden, ii. 257
Gordon, Lord George, opposed to Catholic petitions, i. 128-130 ; president of Protestant Association, 146
Gormanston, Viscount, ii. 58
Grafton, Mr., i. 232
Grattan, Henry, i. 68, 308 ; introduces question of veto, 322 ; ii. 26, 44 ; presents Irish petition, 69-82 ; carries resolution in favour of emancipation, 94 ; brings in Relief Bill, 95, 105, 111 ; declines to help further, 204 ; speech on Parnell's motion, 220 ; and the seceders, 232 ; moves resolution, 235, 281, 313 ; death, 330
Gregory the Great, St., ii. 136
Gregory XVI. and Lord Melbourne, i. 300 ; ii. 168
Grenville, Lord, i. 177, 317, 325 ; ii. 5, 7, 10, 11, 13, 14, 27, 46, 58, 61, 66, 200, 248, 284
Greville, Mr., his memoirs quoted, i. 299
Grey, Lord, i. 55 ; ii. 13, 27, 41, 46, 200, 232, 284, 317-319

Griffiths, Bishop, ii. 33, 168
Guildford, Lord, i. 177

H

Haggerston, Sir C., i. 205   ii. 326
Hales, Sir E., ii. 257
Harcourt, Lord, i. 53
Harrowby, Lord, ii. 284
Hawkesbury, Lord, ii. 58
Hay, Bishop, opens chapel in Edinburgh, i. 124 ; draws up memorial, 129, 274 ; short biography of, 279
Hayes, Rev. Mr., ii. 185, 187, 188, 278 ; his mission to Rome, 291-302
Henry II., ii. 13
Henry VIII., ii. 13
Herbert, Chief Justice of Chester, ii. 257
Hill, Mr. Serjeant, ii. 259
Hinchcliffe, Bishop, i. 104
Hippesley, Sir J. C., i. 194 ; first to speak of the veto, 317-319 ; ii. 95 ; opposes Grattan's Relief Bill, 97 ; opposes Parnell, 214 ; absurd motion of, 238, 281
Hobart, Mr., letter of, ii. 4
Hobhouse, Mr., i. 228
Hoghton, Sir H., on Relief Bill for Dissenters, i. 144
Hope Scott, Mr., Ornsby's Life of quoted, ii. 195
Hornyold, Mr., i. 22 ; one of Committee of Five, 150 ; of Committee of Ten, 161
Hornyold, Right Rev. Dr., signs joint pastoral, 1778, 110
Horsley, Dr., i. 166
Howard, Father John, S.J., i. 220
Howard of Effingham, Lord, i. 29
Howick, Lord, ii. 61, 64, 66
Howse, Sister Frances, i. 232
Humphries, Mr. W., ii. 311
Husenbeth's " Life of Milner " quoted, i. 150, 154, 170, 192 ; unpublished manuscript quoted, 241 ; Life of Milner quoted, ii. 41, 55, 92, 110, 116, 118, 129, 142, 146, 152, 179, 180, 191, 333, 335
Huskisson, Mr., ii. 219
Hussey, Dr., i. 307
Hutton, Sister Mary Austin, i. 232

Index. 351

I

Ignatius of Loyola, St., his orthodox mind, ii. 136 (note)
Ireland, power and influence of, i. 66, 246
Irving, Washington, quoted, ii. 38

J

Jackson, Dr. Cyril, ii. 113
James II. and his dispensing power, ii. 256
Jerningham, Mr. Edward, ii. 31, 309, 327
Jerningham, Sir W., one of Committee of Ten, i. 161, 205

K

Kennett, Lord Mayor, weak conduct of, i. 131
Kent, Duke of, i. 230
Kenyon, Lord, Life of, quoted, ii. 23 (note)
Keogh, John, leader of Irish Catholics, 1792, i. 258–259
Kernan, Bishop, ii. 277
Knox, John, allusions to, i. 123, 276
Knox, Mr., ii. 216

L

Lander, Mr. George, i. 279
Langdale, Charles, i. 2, 28, 248 ; ii. 33, 48
Langdale, Mr., distillery burned, i. 132
Lawson, Sir John, one of Committee of Ten, i. 161
Leeds, Duke of, i. 177
Leigh, Mr., i. 220
Leinster, Duke of, ii. 310
Leo XII., ii. 294
Letter of Cardinal Litta to Dr. Poynter, ii. 160 ; of Dr. Moylan to Milner, 177 ; of Rev. Mr. Hayes from Rome, 187 ; of Pope Pius VII. to the Irish Bishops, 193
Liège, Prince of, i. 220
Lincoln, Bishop of, ii. 53
Lindow, Rev. Mr., i. 160
Lingard, Dr., quoted, i. 254 ; ii. 238, 257
Linton, Lord, i. 97

Litta, Cardinal, ii. 147, 152, 153, 161, 279, 299
Liverpool, Lord, Premier, ii. 70 ; Protestant speech of, 227 ; 284, 317
Loughborough, Lord, ii. 324
Louis XIV. of France, ii. 251
Louis XVI. of France, i. 213
Louis XVIII. of France, ii. 151
Loyalty of Catholics, i. 22
Lucas, Frederick, i. 2
Lyndhurst, Lord, i. 69
Lythgoe, Rev. R., S.J., ii. 168

M

Macaulay, Lord, quoted, ii. 91
MacCarthy, Rev. Dr., ii. 80, 84
MacDonald, Rev. Mr., afterwards Bishop, i. 318
MacDonald, Sir Archibald, i. 174
MacDonnell, Mr. Eneas, ii. 179, 185
MacHale, Archbishop, disliked by England, i. 300 ; his loyalty, 302 ; ii. 174
M'Kenny, Right Hon. T., ii. 313
Macleod, Colonel, i. 283
Macpherson, Rev. P., ii. 146, 158, 178
Malony, Rev. M., imprisoned for saying Mass, i. 83, 106
Mansfield, Lord, lenient to Catholics, i. 84, 87, 88, 131–133
Mansfield, Sir James, ii. 259
Meath, Earl of, ii. 310
Meeting at the Crown and Anchor in 1791, i. 193 ; the "Roman Catholic," 205 ; first, of the Bishops at Durham, ii. 79 ; second ditto, 132
Melbourne, Lord, on appointment of Dr. MacHale, i. 300 ; ii. 174
Melville, Lord, ii. 228, 261–264
Mendoza, a prize-fighter, ii. 304
Mildmay, Sir Henry, i. 228 ; ii. 51
Milner, Right Rev. Dr., a great hero, i. 6, 7 ; his education, 79 ; opinion of Act of 1778, 115 ; praises Mr. Sheldon, 120 ; on origin of Protestant Association, 145 ; vigilance, 1782, 149; opinion of Committee of Five, 150–152 ; on the committee and the Bishops, 153 ; on the committee and the Catholics of England, 155–160 ; his account of protestation, 164, 165 ; present at Bishops' meeting,

167, 168, 170; he fights the Committee of Ten, 172-178; on the oath and protestation, 190; on Cisalpine Club, 194; on "the mediation," 198, 199; on French clergy, 216; on the Cisalpines, 226; on Mr. Wilkes's suspension, 240; on the veto, 305; on the Irish Bishops and the veto, 316; interview with Mr. Ponsonby, 320; protests against Ponsonby's action, 323-325; his "Letter to a Parish Priest," 327; sense in which he favoured veto, 329; his conduct approved by Irish Bishops, ii. 1; he retracts "Letter to a Parish Priest," 3; conversation with Lord Grenville, 15; comments on Milner's conduct, 20-24; and the "Catholic Board," 31; at dinner at Doran's Hotel, 34-38; at meeting at St. Alban's Tavern, 39; on the fifth resolution, 42; consecration as Bishop, 54; differs with Dr. Poynter, 79; meets Bishop Moylan, 81; on Bishops' meeting at Durham, 85, 86; on Mr. Butler's alliance with Canning, 87; present at meeting at Lord Clifford's, 92; his opinion of Sir J. Hippesley's conduct, 98; action on Bill of 1813, 105; his opinion of bill, 108; left alone in opposition, 111; his expulsion from Catholic Board, 116-120; his conduct praised by Irish Bishops, 121; attacked by vicars apostolic at Durham, 124-134; his character, 134-140; on Monsignor Quarantotti, 142; starts for Rome, 150; interview with Pius VII., 152; and with Cardinal Litta, 153; attacked by O'Connell, 181-185; his opinion of Pius VII.'s letter to Irish Bishops, 193; victory virtually won by, 197; his account of debate on Grattan's motion, 1817, 281; his favourable opinion of Parnell, 283; his "End of Religious Controversy," 303; challenged to fight, 304; on end of Blanchardist schism, 306; refuses to sign petition to King, 328; receives rebuke from Rome, 535; his writings in *Orthodox Journal*, 337

Mirabeau, i. 155; quoted, 212
Mitchell's "History of Ireland" quoted, i. 254, 256
Molesworth, Sir W., i. 9

"Monastic Institutions," attack on, ii. 51
Montagu, Mr. E., i. 144
Montalembert, i. 3, 12, 16
Moore, Thomas, on Act of 1774, i. 62
More, Sir Thomas, ii. 13, 87
Mostyn, Mr. Browne, quoted, i. 211
Moylan, P., Bishop, i. 311; ii. 79-84, 176
Mulgrave, Lord, ii. 228
Murat, King of Naples, ii. 161
Murphy, Right Rev. Dr., Bishop of Cork, ii. 181, 184, 192
Murray, Right Rev. Dr., reproves Lord J. Russell, i. 139; ii. 176, 192

N

Napoleon I., ii. 13, 61, 143, 151 (note), 161, 225
Newburgh, Lord, i. 205
Newman, Cardinal, quoted, i. 43, 195
Newport, Sir J., i. 322; ii. 216
"No-Popery" cry of 1807, ii. 63
Norfolk, Duke of, i. 85; signed address to King, i. 97; ii. 228, 308, 326
Normanby, Lord, ii. 317
North, Lord, i. 53, 67; sympathy with Catholics, 126, 128; house attacked, 131
Norwich, Bishop of, Bathurst, ii. 247, 284, 317
Nugent, Lord, ii. 308
Nuns, the Princethorpe, and the Prince Regent, i. 233; the Taunton, and George III., i. 232

O

O'Connell, Daniel, i. 6; his power, 68, 69; 150, 157; opposes John Keogh, 260; founds Catholic organization, 263; repeal, 264-266; ii. 9, 46, 64; proposes vote of thanks to Milner, 121; attacks Milner, 181; apologizes, 185; on Grattan, 204; speech on disunion, 206; and Protestant co-operation, 271; collision with the vetoists, 275; speech, 1817, 278; dinner at Tralee, 285; speech in Dublin, 1819, 312; his anxiety, 332; his high position and authority, 340

Index. 353

O'Connell, John, quoted, i. 261; ii. 207, 232, 274, 286
O'Connor, Charles, of Belanagare, i. 257, 260
O'Connor, Mr. Owen, ii. 291
O'Leary, Father, i. 77; ii. 51
Oliver, Dr., quoted, i. 85, 201, 220
O'Loghlen, Mr., first Catholic judge, i. 47
Ompteida, Baron, ii. 295
Orleans, Bishop of, i. 212
O'Reilly, Bishop, i. 311
O'Rourke, Rev. John, quoted, i. 261; ii. 205
Orthodox Journal, Milner's writings in, ii. 337
O'Toole, case of the girl, i. 256

P

Parker, Captain W., ii. 265
Parnell, Sir H., i. 57, 70; presents Catholic petitions, ii. 207-209; moves relief resolution, 212, 213, 232; presents another petition, 234; seconds Grattan's emancipation resolution, 235, 278; praised by Milner, 251
Paulet, Lord Henry, ii. 262
Payne, an informer, i. 83, 87
Peach, Rev. E., ii. 304
Peel, Sir Robert, glad to send message of peace to Ireland, i. 52; his motto, " Register, register," 75, 112, 136; in favour of emancipation, 230; what made him a statesman, 268; gratitude due to, ii. 68; speech on question of veto, 196, 197; on O'Connell's position, 211; attack on Catholic associations in Ireland, 216; opposes Grattan's resolution, 236
Penderells, the, i. 12
Perceval, Spencer, ii. 62, 64; premier, 70; death, 70
Persons, Father, S.J., i. 216
Peterborough, Bishop of, ii. 317
Petre, Mr., quoted, i. 210
Petre, Lord, i. 95, 97; one of Committee of Five, 150, 158; of Committee of Ten, 161-164; 1796, ii. 259
Piercy, Mary, i. 221
Piggott, Mr. Nathaniel, i. 184
Pilling, Rev. W., i. 168
Pitt, Mr., i. 40, 71, 114; receives deputation of Catholics, 163; speaks on Relief Bill, 174; on religious orders, 183; on the Act of 1791, 186; grant for French exiles, 210; his resignation, 1801, 287; resignation discussed, 288-296; ii. 9, 19, 50; his second ministry, 55; opposes emancipation, 59; death, 61; gratitude due to, 66; often deceived, 283
Pius VI., ii. 19
Pius VII., concordat, i. 213; ii. 13, 143, 152, 158, 161, 166; letter to Irish Bishops, 192; receives Irish remonstrance, 296
Pius IX., on persecution, i. 41; re-establishing hierarchy, 136; ii. 13; on national customs, 273
Plowden, Father, S.J., 168, 176, 197, 201
Plowden, Mr., i. 64, 262, 316
Plowden, Mr. Francis, ii. 147
Plunket, Mr., ii. 200, 331, 339
Plunkett, Bishop P. J., i. 311
Plunkett, Oliver, Archbishop of Armagh, ii. 263
Pole, Mr. Wellesley, ii. 219
Ponsonby, Mr., i. 321, 323; ii. 5, 20, 104
" Popery," the bugbear of, ii. 243
Portland, Duke of, ii. 8; premier, 62; death, 70
Poynter, Bishop, i. 320; ii. 34, 39, 79, 88, 106, 129, 132, 145, 162
Preston, Mr., i. 57
Proctor, Father, O.P., i. 220
Progress of the Church in England, causes of, i. 45, *et seq.*
Protest, the " schismatical," i. 170
Protestants, great meeting of, in favour of emancipation, ii. 311
Protestation, the, i. 164
Pugin, his crusade for Gothic architecture, i. 3

Q

Quarantotti, Monsignor, ii. 37, 126, 141-152

R

Radcliffe, Mr., an artist, ii. 304
Ravignan, Father, S.J., ii. 274
Rawdon, Lord, i. 176, 177

Redesdale, Lord, i. 172; ii. 246
Registration, duty of, i. 45
Relief, fear the great motive of, i. 68
Religious orders under Act of 1791 and 1829, i. 181, *et seq.*
Rescript, the Quarantotti, ii. 141
Resolutions of Irish Bishops in 1799, i. 309; ii. 18; in 1808, 2; the celebrated "fifth," 30
Ripon, Lord, appointment of, to India noticed, i. 251
Robertson, Dr., the historian, persecuted, ii. 124
Rockingham, Marquis of, i. 105
Rome, Milner's journey to, ii. 151
Rose, Mr., i. 290; ii. 53
Russell, Lord John, i. 8, 99; offensive letter, 139, 293, ii. 13; on the "No-Popery" cry of 1807, 64; his action in 1828, 320
Ryan, Mr., ii. 58

S

St. Alban's Tavern, celebrated meeting at, ii. 39
St. David's, Bishop of, i. 177
St. Omer's, College of, i. 216-218
Sales, St. Francis of, ii. 81
Salisbury, Bishop of, i. 177
Saul, Mr., i. 256
Savile, Sir George, introduces Relief Bill, 1778, i. 99; house pillaged, 131
Seaton, Sir Alexander, S.J., i. 279
Scott, Sir Walter, quoted, ii. 182
Scully, Mr. Denis, i. 259; ii. 58
"Seceders," the, ii. 233
Sharrock, Right Rev. Dr., i. 167; ii. 54
Shee, Mr. Serjeant, i. 251
Sheil, Mr., quoted, i. 50, 253, 255, 257; ii. 205
Shelburne, Lord, i. 106
Sheldon, Mr. R., i. 22, 25
Sheldon, Mr. W., secretary to Catholic Committee, 1778, 95; straightforward conduct of, 115; 120, 198; ii. 48
Sheridan, R., i. 78, 228, 322
Shrewsbury, Earl of, i. 97; ii. 58, 203, 326
Sidmouth, Lord, ii. 58, 277
Smith, Dr., ii. 81
Smith, Mr. W., i. 173; ii. 289

Smith, Right Rev. Dr., ii. 129
Southwell, Lord, ii. 58, 275
Spencer, Father Ignatius, i. 2
"Staffordshire clergy," fifteen, list of, i. 242, 243
Stahremberg, Count, ii. 57
Stanhope, Lord, framer of protestation, 1789, i. 164, 200; ii. 221, 246
Stanhope, Lord, quoted, i. 130, 132, 145, 289, 291, 294; ii. 50, 52, 57
Stapleton, Bishop, i. 242; ii. 55
Stapleton, Mr. Thomas, one of Committee of Five, i. 150
Stone, Rev. Father, S.J., i. 203, 220
Stourton, Lord, i. 97; one of Committee of Five, 150, 158; of Committee of Ten, 161, 205
Strickland, Father, S.J., i. 220
Strickland, Rev. Dr., i. 168
Stuart, Prince Charles Edward, i. 76
Surrey, Earl, i. 97
Sussex, Duke of, i. 230; ii. 221, 228, 247
Swire, Dr., ii. 325

T

Taaffe, Lord, i. 257
Talbot, Bishop, i. 84; signs joint pastoral, 1778, 110; and Committee of Five, 159-161, 164; condemns oath, 167; death, 168
Talbot, Bishop T., i. 88; signs joint pastoral, 110; 160, 167, 170
Talbot, Lord, ii. 312
Talleyrand, i. 212
Teynham, Lord, i. 97
Therry, Mr., quoted on Pitt's resignation, i. 292; on Pitt's second ministry, ii. 55; on Canning's conduct, 71
Thomas of Canterbury, St., ii. 13
Thornton, General, ii. 288
Throckmorton, Sir J., i. 95; one of Committee of Five, 150; writes schismatical pamphlet, 154, 158; of Committee of Ten, 161, 168; ii. 163
Thurlow, Attorney-General, i. 101
Tone, Theobald Wolfe, i. 257
Torrens, Mr. M'Cullagh, quoted, i. 293; ii. 57, 71
Towneley, Mr., one of Committee of Ten, i. 161
Trévaux, Abbé, ii. 79

Index.

Trimleston, Lord, ii. 58
Troy, Bishop, i. 311 ; ii. 176, 179
Turner, Mr., i. 104
Turvile, Mr. Charles, i. 196

V

Veto, nature of, i. 297, *et seq.*; Edmund Burke on the, 306; earliest mention of, 306; first public mention of, 317; Lord Grenville and the, ii. 15; Sir Robert Peel on the, 197

W

Wales, Prince of, i. 234, 235. *See* George IV.
Walmesley, Right Rev. Dr., O.S.B., his pastoral, 1778, i. 110, 164-171, 197, 239
Walpole, Mr., maxim of, ii. 283
Walsh, Bishop, ii. 38
Walsh's "History of Scotland" quoted, i. 279
Walton, Right Rev. Dr., signs joint pastoral, 1778, i. 110
Webb, Rev. J., tried for saying Mass, i. 84, 88
Wedderburn, Mr., i. 133
Weedall, Rev. Dr., ii. 86 (note), 138, 337
Weld, of Lulworth, Mr., i. 176, 232; ii. 119
Weld, Sister F. Sales, i. 231
Wellesley, Marquis of, ii. 73
Wellington, Duke of, his reason for emancipation, i. 71, 230, 295; Secretary for Ireland, ii. 62 ; a comparison with, 107
Wesley, John, inflammatory writings, i. 146, 147
Westmoreland, Lord, ii. 5
Weston, Mr. John W., i. 197
Whitbread, Mr., ii. 218
White, Rev. Thomas, ii. 105
Whitgreave, Mr., loyal to Charles II., i. 22
Whyte, Captain E., R.N., case of, ii. 260-269
Wilberforce, Mr. W., i. 173; ii. 238
Wilkes, Mr., speech of, i. 125
Wilks, Rev. Joseph, O.S.B., i. 161, 162, 170, 197; and "the Staffordshire clergy," 238
Willis, Dr., i. 287
Windham, Mr., i. 173, 228; ii. 64
Wiseman, Cardinal, his large-heartedness, i. 2 ; his influence, 36 ; ii. 13, 33, 198 ; on Cardinal Consalvi's visit to London, 294
Worcester, Bishop of, ii., 317
Wyse, of Waterford, Mr., i. 257; ii. 149, 181, 233, 279

X

Xavier, St. Francis, ii. 136 (note), 337

Y

York, Cardinal, ii. 52
York, Duke of, i. 230, 231
Yorke, Mr., i. 324; ii. 215

www.ingramcontent.com/pod-product-compliance
Lightning Source LLC
Chambersburg PA
CBHW020236240426
43672CB00006B/545